NP
July 2013

D0045826

Life with My Sister Madonna

Life with My Sister Madonna

by Christopher Ciccone

with Wendy Leigh

SIMON SPOTLIGHT ENTERTAINMENT

New York London Toronto Sydney

Simon Spotlight Entertainment
A Division of Simon & Schuster, Inc.
1230 Avenue of the Americas
New York, NY 10020

First Simon Spotlight Entertainment hardcover edition July 2008

For more information about special discounts for bulk purchases, please contact Simon & Schuster Special Sales at 1-800-456-6798 or business@simonandschuster.com.

Designed by Linda Dingler

Manufactured in the United States of America

10 9 8 7 6 5 4 3

Library of Congress Cataloging-in-Publication Data is available.

ISBN-13: 978-1-4165-8762-0
ISBN-10: 1-4165-8762-4

For my father, Silvio, and to Joan,
who has always been a mother to me.

INTRODUCTION

For anyone who came into contact with Madonna, to know her at all you had to know [Christopher]. *The one was incomprehensible without the other. He was her dark side and she was his.*

Rupert Everett, *Red Carpets and Other Banana Skins*

SOME READERS MAY say that my dark side caused me to write this book, others that my sister's did. Some may say that seeing Madonna through my eyes is a way of fully comprehending her; others who believe she walks on water won't.

There are many ways of looking at this story—as a memoir of a shared childhood, as the celebration of an icon who turns fifty this year, as my autobiography . . . and as my answer to the eternal question "What is it really like being Madonna's brother?"

I had originally hoped that this book would also be a way for me to define myself and separate from my sister at last. Instead, it has been a catharsis. After getting some perspective on our story, I finally understand and accept that one aspect of my life will never change: I was born my mother's son, but I will die my sister's brother.

I no longer balk at the truth, because when all is said and done and written, I am truly proud that Madonna is my sister and always will be.

PROLOGUE

His dream must have seemed so close he could hardly fail to grasp it.

F. Scott Fitzgerald, *The Great Gatsby*

THE LANESBOROUGH HOTEL, LONDON, ENGLAND,
8:30 A.M., SEPTEMBER 25, 1993

THE ALARM CLOCK rings in a low-key British way. I get up, peer through a gap in the thick, purple silk drapes, and the sun glimmers back at me. Luckily, the weather's fine. After all, this is the UK, land of rain and fog. *The Girlie Show* tour, which I designed and directed, opens tonight, and we don't want the crowd getting drenched before the show even begins.

We. The royal *we.* Madonna and me. My sister and I, she who is still fast asleep in a mahogany four-poster bed in her suite adjoining mine. The royal *we,* so fitting for a woman who is sometimes a royal pain in my ass. Although Buckingham Palace, the queen of England's residence, is just across the road, in my estimation and that of millions of fans, she is the real queen of the universe—Madonna Louise Veronica Ciccone, my elder sister by twenty-seven months, who, just eleven years after the release of her first record, is now one of the most famous women in the world.

I eat an orange. No big English breakfast for me, no matter how much I like it. Otherwise, I'll probably throw up when Madonna and I take our scheduled six-mile jog at eleven. Just as we did yesterday, just as we will do tomorrow—and on every other day during the tour.

Schedule, in fact, is my sister's middle name. Up at nine in the morning, in bed by eleven at night, with every hour in between planned by her as rigidly as any military campaign. With her mania for making lists, for running her life according to a timetable, in another incarnation Madonna could easily have run a prison, directed airport traffic, or been a five-star general.

Sadly for her, though, her nights can't be structured or played out according to a strict schedule, because she is an insomniac and rarely sleeps more than three hours each night.

Madonna's insomnia only became apparent to me when we were living together in downtown Manhattan at the start of her career. Whenever I woke up during the night, she would be in the living room, perched on a white futon, which—no matter how many times we washed the floors—was always dirty. She was usually dressed in a white oversize men's T-shirt, baggy, white cowboy-print sweats, sucking Hot Tamales, her favorite cinnamon-flavored candies, and reading poetry—often Anne Sexton, whose lines sometimes inspired her lyrics. Or the diaries of Anaïs Nin, who, along with Joan of Arc, is one of her heroines. Anything to get her through those long, hot, airless Manhattan nights, nights when her mind didn't switch off, when fantastical candy-colored visions of her future sparkled in her brain. Unbridled desire for fame and fortune, you see, is incompatible with sleep.

This morning, though, I am confident that my sister is sleeping, a deep sleep. Her tightly wound high-octane energy has meant that when she is on the road, she sometimes needs a sleep aid. But who can blame her? She's now a superstar, a legend, one of the universe's most famous women, and in just eleven and a half hours seventy-five thousand fans will be screaming for her, throwing themselves at her feet, worshipping her. The pressure to perform, to entertain, to sustain, and to simply remain Madonna is immeasurable, and even I—who am now the closest person on earth to the Queen of the World—can't truly fathom how it feels to walk in her size-seven shoes, stalked by so much expectation, so much adoration, so many who love her, so many who hate her, so many who long for her to fall flat on her famous face.

NINE AND TIME to wake my sister. I unlock the door between our suites. Too late. Loud snorting—not a pretty sound—is coming from her opulent marble bathroom. She's in the midst of her morning routine: swallowing a great gulp of warm salt water, gargling, snorting it up her nose, and then spitting it out. Abrasive in the extreme. But essential, she believes, for maintaining her voice.

I flick through CNN for five minutes. Then I open the adjoining door to Madonna's suite again. My sister, dressed in a white sweatshirt and black Adidas sweatpants, is sprawled on her powder-blue satin-covered bed, drinking black coffee with sugar, nibbling sourdough toast.

I grab a bite and then give her a brief kiss. "You okay, Madonna?"

She nods. "But I still didn't sleep much."

Like our father, a man of few words, neither of us have any use for small talk, as we know each other's glances and gestures by heart and can decode them with unerring accuracy. So that when my sister places her hands on her hips, fishwife style, I know there's trouble. When she starts picking on her nail varnish, usually red, I know she's nervous. And when she tucks her thumb into the palm of her hand and wraps her fingers around it—a childhood habit of mine, but which she may have appropriated because she believes her fingers are too stubby and always tries to hide them—I know she needs reassurance. And for the past ten years, day and night, I've been happy to give it to her.

My job description may not be conventional—although I might sometimes be termed Jeeves to Madonna's Bertie Wooster—my ability to reassure my sister in times of trouble or self-doubt is one of the primary reasons that—unlike a myriad of less fortunate others to whom she has granted admittance to Madonnaland, then summarily exiled—I have survived. I have endured both as her "humble servant"—as I sometimes sign my letters to her when I want to give her a hard time—and as the one person in our family ever to work for her long-term as her assistant/dresser/shoulder-to-cry-on, and as the only family member with whom she still maintains a close relationship at this point.

At eleven sharp, we jog through Hyde Park, dogged by a group of seedy-looking paparazzi, all desperate for a shot of the Material Girl sans makeup. Madonna pulls her baseball cap down to obscure her face. We just keep on jogging.

At one, Madonna in her black, stretch Mercedes limo and I in my chauffeur-driven sedan are ferried to Wembley Stadium, in northwest London, just an hour away. We never ride to and from shows together, as we both want the freedom to arrive and leave whenever we like.

Clusters of fans are already milling around by the stadium gate, some hoping to score a last-minute ticket, others to catch a glimpse of Madonna as we drive in. No chance of that, though. Our windows are blacked out, and when the cars stop at the back entrance, we head straight for her dressing room.

As always, the promoter has lived up to every single one of Madonna's requirements, all listed in a rider to her contract. Her dressing room has been painted all white, because she believes a white background frames her to the best advantage. Consequently, she insists that all her towels and bed linens also be white. Sigmund Freud would probably have a field day analyzing her predilection for the color symbolizing virginity. All her friends, family, and admirers know about her preference for white, and large vases of gardenias, white tuberoses, and white lilies—all her favorite flowers—fill the room. The scent is overwhelming. There are also four boxes of Hot Tamales, and packets of mint and lemon tea. Bottles of Evian—always at room temperature, never cold—are on hand, here and onstage, where I place them strategically, according to where I know she will always need them. Meat products are banned from the dressing room, as is alcohol, so that even if some obsequious promoter sends a few bottles of Cristal to the dressing room, at the end of the night they will be given away, unopened, and so will all the flowers.

Fortunately, the outside temperature is chilly, so for once the dressing room isn't sweltering. Even in hot climates, no matter how steamy the weather, Madonna flatly refuses to use air-conditioning. She claims she is never warm enough, is always too cold, and that air-conditioning is unhealthy for her voice. Even in high summer, in the suffocating heat of Miami, New York, or L.A., her windows remain wide open and the air-conditioning off.

Here and in every other dressing room she ever occupies, she has hung our late mother's crucifix over the vanity mirror. Our mother's photograph, taken a few years before her death, is also always on display. She was only thirty when she died. Yet none of us—not our father, not our brothers and sisters, not me, and certainly not Madonna—ever mention her name to one another, except on rare occasions. That just isn't the Ciccone way. Although we are Italian on our father's side, and French Canadian on our mother's, we were born in Michigan and, when all is said and done, are Midwesterners to the bone.

I go onstage, where I look for any imperfections on the floor so no one—not the dancers or, heaven forbid, Madonna herself—will trip, make sure all the hydraulic lifts are working, all the lights are in the right position for the first number, and all the props are correctly placed.

Madonna spends an hour in her dressing room doing vocal exercises—scales and breathing—and simultaneously stretching, limbering up for the show, rather like a cross between Anna Pavlova and Muhammad Ali in his prime.

NEXT I SUBMIT to a press interview in town with one of the less lurid London papers because my sister refuses to do them anymore and has sent me in her stead. I am polite, friendly, and hope that my interview will favorably impact on tomorrow's reviews, which we will read together over breakfast.

If Madonna does get a negative review, such as on *The Virgin Tour* when one or two critics lambasted her for being overweight, I know she will toss her head, pretend not to care, then rip up the review and fling it into the garbage. But ten minutes later, she will ask, "Christopher, do you really think they were right? Does my midriff really look fat?" I tell her that of course they were wrong, of course it didn't—even though it did—and she is happy.

I'm thankful that I don't have to do any more media during our London stay, as I always prefer to remain in the background. Madonna isn't doing any television either. In one of the most interesting dichotomies within her multidimensional psyche, while she is eminently comfortable simulating sex in front of a stadium audience of thousands during the *Blond Ambition* tour, and in a scene in the documentary *Truth or Dare* blithely demonstrating her oral sex technique on a bottle, anytime she has to appear on television, she becomes a basket case.

In fact, I felt awful for her when I watched her hands shaking in a trembling televised performance of Stephen Sondheim's "Sooner or Later (I Always Get My Man)" from *Dick Tracy* at the 1991 Academy Awards. There were no screaming fans, and she—who always hated not moving while she performed—had to stand still while she sang.

Had she been singing to an audience of fans, she wouldn't have been at all nervous. But this time she was performing in an auditorium full of established actors and actresses, a group of people to which she didn't really belong, who didn't respect her as an actress but whose respect she desperately wanted to win. Hence her fit of nerves.

Her nerves about appearing on TV surfaced again in 1994 when she went on the *Late Show with David Letterman* and ended up saying "fuck" thirteen times because she was so terrified and couldn't think of anything else to say. Yet when I broached the subject, she refused to admit to TV fright and just said, "Because I felt like it," defiant as a four-year-old caught with her hand in the cookie jar. That's her way: downplay any insecurities, cover them up. Take the offensive.

BACK AT WEMBLEY Stadium at three, Madonna and I go onstage for sound check. She sings one and a half minutes of each song, then rehearses some of the show's more intricate dance moves for about an hour. When she finally comes offstage, I see that she's far from tired, the adrenaline already coursing through her veins. Her blue eyes are bright, her skin is luminous, her color high—partly because of the pink Puerto Rican Majal face powder she always sends me to buy for her from a drugstore on Sixth Avenue and Fifteenth Street in Manhattan—partly through sheer excitement.

Then at four we lunch together—carrot soup, veggie burgers, salad—all cooked by her vegetarian chef, who travels with us. During lunch, we dissect the previous day's dress rehearsal: the mood of the band members and the dancers, which one is pissed off, which one needs to be coaxed and cajoled into doing the job properly, and which one has to be stroked—all in the interest of making tonight's show spectacular.

On opening night, and for most of the tour, that's my job, but Madonna has already made it easier. On all the tours—through a combination of charm, flirtation, and some maternal concern—she does her utmost to gain the dancers' trust, loyalty, and friendship. To bring them as close to her as possible, but not too close.

Everyone who works for her inevitably goes through the same stages. Stage One: disillusionment with the cold world outside. Stage Two: luxuriating in the sunlight of Madonna's warmth and attention. Stage Three: moving through the sunlight, toward her. Stage Four: finding themselves in the coldest place of all, the place right up close to her. That, as far as she is concerned, is far too close for her comfort. Get to that stage, and she will feel that you know too much, you are a liability, and the result is a foregone conclusion. Stage Five: no more sunlight, no more closeness, no more Madonna.

Each tour, I would watch the dancers quickly fall under Madonna's spell. Getting closer and closer to their perceived paradise of being anointed her close platonic friend and intimate. Then, at the end of the tour, being hurtled out into the cold world once more, never to see her again, except on TV, in a movie, onstage—but only from the audience's perspective.

One dancer on each tour will, however, spend more time with her, will receive special preference, be more intimate with her—and that person is a heterosexual dancer on the tour. On *The Virgin Tour* the dancer Lyndon B. Johnson filled that role. On the *Who's That Girl?* tour, the dancer Shabadu. On the *Blond Ambition* tour, the dancer Oliver Crumes. And on *The Girlie Show,* dancer Michael Gregory.

The die was always cast during auditions, when Madonna inspected a lineup of dancers, much as Catherine the Great was wont to inspect a lineup of potential lovers. In Michael's case, we held the dance auditions in New York and West Hollywood. We took Polaroids of the final ten candidates and videotaped them dancing. Then Madonna and I went home, examined the Polaroids, and viewed the videos together.

Of all the candidates, I found Michael the weakest dancer, the one with the least personality. Yet Madonna fought me and insisted that we hire him. I decided there was no point in trying to thwart her, so he was hired.

Here in London on *The Girlie Show,* he is now her chosen straight man, the boy to whom she turns whenever she is bored by the many gay men on the tour—me included—and to whom she will be maternal, kind, almost loving. It wasn't a question of whether she and her straight man on tour ever make love, just that he is her insurance against the loneliness of the road.

At four thirty, she has two hours of personal time; her chiropractor gives her a treatment, she has a massage, after which she remains on her massage table, trying to sleep, but fails.

At six thirty, she puts on part of the costume she will be wearing in the show's first number: black, sequined shorts and bra, long black gloves, and the trusty black fishnets she always wears—even under trousers, jeans, or leggings—because she believes they protect her leg muscles. Even though her mind is running a mile a minute, while her hair and makeup are being done, she sits remarkably still, ever the disciplined trouper.

At seven thirty, it's time for her new dresser, Daniel Huber, to finish dressing her. Although Madonna has now elevated me to director, she still tried to persuade me to carry on as her dresser, but I refused. She initially kicked against my refusal, but in the end capitulated. So now she's about to strip naked in front of Daniel Huber. I know she's at her most vulnerable, and that vulnerability will escalate as the show progresses. For although Madonna is notorious for her lack of inhibition, for posing nude for art students, modeling topless for Gaultier—in private, she is far too shy and prudish to allow herself to be seen naked at close quarters by a stranger. Diametrically opposed to her sex-goddess image, I know, but undeniably true.

I've briefed Daniel ahead of time on the requirements for being Madonna's dresser, and strategies for surviving the job without going crazy. So he fully understands that the best policy is to remain silent—no matter what abuse Madonna will inevitably dish out to him—and to talk only when answering the ubiquitous question "How do I look?" to which he is duty-bound to always respond, "Wonderful, Madonna, wonderful."

Thus armed with my advice, he helps her into the rest of her costume—high, lace-up black patent leather boots and eye mask—then hands her the riding crop she will brandish in the first number, "Erotica."

At ten to eight, Madonna, the dancers, the band, and I all join hands and form a circle. Madonna leads the prayer: "Dear God, it's the opening night of the tour in London. Please watch over my dancers and my band. I know everyone is nervous, me included. We've worked really long and hard to get here. Please help us make this a great show. I love you all. Go out there and break a leg. Kick some ass. Amen."

Then it's showtime.

With security leading the way, Madonna and I, and her two backup singers, Niki Harris and Donna De Lory, all hold hands and begin the long walk from the dressing room, down the tunnel, then backstage, singing Stevie Wonder's "For Once in My Life," while Madonna's manager, dapper Freddy DeMann, with his pencil moustache, chews gum ferociously and follows behind.

When we arrive at the back of the stage, Niki and Donna take their positions with the band. Madonna and I continue down a narrow access tunnel that leads under the stage, from where she will make her first entrance.

Madonna and I wait there alone, holding hands. She is not shaking now. She is calm in the extreme, secure in the knowledge that she knows every dance step, every lyric by heart. She is confident, in control, with little self-doubt, aware that once she is on the stage, in front of her audience, she will be where she belongs, doing what she does best.

I kiss her on the cheek and say, "You look amazing. You're going to be great. I can feel it. There's nothing to worry about. Everything is going to be perfect."

She nods wordlessly, her eyes suddenly big and almost childlike. Before she takes her place onstage, out of habit I hold out my palm and she spits her Ricola cough drop straight into it.

Then she gives me an elated, slightly frightened smile that says, "Here we go," takes a deep breath, squares her shoulders, and steels herself to face her audience.

The lights go up, and a burst of screaming hits us. An intense jolt of electricity bolts from the seventy-five-thousand-strong audience onto the stage and crashes over us like shock waves, powerful and exhilarating.

Circus music booms through the stadium. Onstage, in front of a red velvet curtain, dancer Carrie Ann Inaba, naked except for a red G-string, slithers down a forty-foot pole, while a blue satin-clad clown—the leitmotif of the show—watches onstage.

I am now standing in the pit, the five-foot gap between the front-row seats and the stage. As Carrie Ann reaches stage level, then slides below, the curtain goes up to reveal Madonna on a smoke-filled stage, singing "Erotica." Her close-cropped blond hair glitters in the limelight and she cracks the whip.

Her dancing is elegant, fluid, a tribute to the early training we both shared. And her body is a work of art, thanks to the daily two-and-a-half-hour gym regimen she follows when she's not on tour. Her yoga classes, too, are responsible for her perfect tone and muscle definition, her queenly posture, her poise. In a yoga class, of course, all her competitive instincts come to the fore. Whether it is yoga or friendships or Kabbalah, my sister always has to be the best, the greatest—the one woman who can wrap her leg around her body twenty-five times and stand on one finger.

Madonna's competitive spirit, of course, is part of what made her—well, Madonna. That, and her intelligence, her capacity to learn, her superlative memory, her unrivaled charm, and her talent for live performance, which—as I watched her in *The Girlie Show*—takes my breath away. I marvel at her connection with the audience, the vivacity and precision of her performance, the grace of her hand gestures, the artful turn of her head, exactly as we rehearsed them together.

For the next number, "Vogue," Daniel has added a black sequined headdress to her outfit, part Erté, partly Zizi Jeanmaire. The passionate interest Madonna and I both share in the icons of the past has heavily influenced the content and the vibe of *The Girlie Show*, and in particular *The Virgin Tour* scene in which she parodies Marlene Dietrich.

Throughout our time living and hanging out together in downtown Manhattan, and when I lived with Madonna in Los Angeles—initially in the home she shared with her first husband, my then brother-in-law, Sean Penn, and later in the one she sometimes shared with Warren Beatty—we used to stay up until all hours watching old movies together. Dietrich's movies—especially *The Blue Angel* and *Morocco*—were particular favorites, but we also loved Louise Brooks in *Pandora's Box*, Joan Crawford's *Mildred Pierce*, Claudette Colbert in *It Happened One Night*, and Judy Holliday in *Born Yesterday*.

Madonna's hitherto unrealized dream is to become a great movie star. I wish her well, but secretly believe that the only part that she is truly capable of playing is that of herself, Madonna. A part that she has created and curated. And what a part it is: cross Shirley Temple with Bettie Page, Elizabeth I with Lucille Ball, Bette Davis with Doris Day, and you have a flavor of the artist known as Madonna.

THE MOMENT THERE is a brief interlude between songs during *The Girlie Show* and Madonna goes offstage, I run backstage to her dressing room. If she was calm before the performance, during the interval she is always extremely nervous and jumpy. While she retouches her makeup and sprays herself with Annick Goutal's Gardenia Passion, her favorite perfume, I give her a heightened version of my standard pep talk:

"You look fantastic. Your voice is strong. And your moves were terrific."

She stops trembling, takes a gulp of Evian.

And strides back onstage.

Part of what I said to my sister was true, part was slightly bullshit. Her moves are, indeed, terrific. Her voice, however, is another matter. My sister's unwillingness to submit to the drudgery of regular singing lessons is a by-product of the supreme self-confidence with which she was born. That self-confidence has overridden any lack of training. She's a showman—some may have better voices, but she is the living embodiment of the fact that discipline, vision, ambition, determination, drive, and, of course, self-confidence are what make a superstar. Her legendary self-confidence also seems to be a family trait that I've inherited: I relish testing myself and I always embrace a challenge. Although I've been a designer, an artist, and am now a director, I have eschewed any formal training in these disciplines. Moreover, like my sister, I rarely submit to authority and prefer to plunge into a career and learn as I go along.

Until now, our strategy has worked for both of us, but now Madonna is starting to realize that the lack of a strict regimen of vocal training means that her voice is too thin for the demands she now places on it. One of her solutions is to hire Donna to be one of her backup singers, as her voice mirrors and supports Madonna's. In contrast, Niki is on hand to provide the soul. Most of the time, Donna and Niki compete over who gets to sing which harmony, who is closest to Madonna, and who gets the most attention from her.

Niki has a better voice than Madonna. Her voice is fully trained, and Madonna fights to keep her at bay because Niki is fully capable of drowning her out and often does. When that happens, Madonna sometimes orders Niki's mike to be switched off.

Once or twice, Madonna has even raised the possibility of firing Niki. Not that she would ever do it herself. A remarkable chink in my sister's dominatrix-style armor is that—although she makes a big show of screaming orders to her underlings during rehearsal, on the road, and, in particular, when she is playing to the cameras as in *Truth or Dare*—she is utterly terrified of confrontation, avoids it at all costs, can never bring herself to fire anyone face-to-face, and always delegates that task to one of her minions, usually me.

MADONNA IS SINGING "Holiday" now and, transformed by her blond Afro wig and sequined clothes, is every inch the seventies disco queen, skipping around the stage, joyful, euphoric, completely relaxed and happy. For the first time tonight, I catch her eye and wink. She winks back at me. A few moments later, she throws me a quick, triumphant smile, a tacit acknowledgment that all our work together has paid off, and that *The Girlie Show* is a success. I smile back, elated by our complicity. She ends the show on "Everybody"—her first hit and the first song she ever cowrote—the audience goes wild, and the stadium floor heaves with the dancing crowds.

Madonna exits the stage. After a few minutes, a performer in the blue satin Pierrot costume and sad-clown mask reappears. This time—although the audience won't know it until she removes her mask—Madonna is playing the clown.

As children, we were rarely taken to the circus, but as adults, Madonna and I loved seeing Cirque du Soleil in Battery Park, Manhattan. We both loved the Cirque du Soleil because of the sexy, bizarre, and fresh way in which they approached the concept of the circus. The Cirque went on to become a great inspiration on our future work together and, in particular, on *The Girlie Show*. There is, however, something of an irony in my sister dressing as a clown, because she is the world's worst joke teller. I cringe whenever she attempts to tell a joke, either in private or in public, because she always botches the punch line.

I understand that her basic inability to be truly funny stems from the childhood loss of our mother. For even in the midst of the upbeat *Girlie Show*, amid the worship of the crowd, the intoxication of the night, the sad clown eyes betray a profound truth about my sister. Like me, somewhere deep inside—because we lost our mother when we were so young—no matter how far Madonna climbs, how famous she becomes, how wealthy, and how loved, her soul will always be pervaded by a secret sadness. Just listen to some of the lyrics she has written during her twenty-five-year career, for such songs as "Oh Father" and "Live to Tell," to name a few.

THE CLOWN SCENE is over now; Madonna removes her mask with a flourish, bows low, and leaves the stage. As I wait for her in the wings, I do my utmost to blot out the deafening applause. She runs up to me, I throw a large white towel over her, put my arms around her, and hurry her out the stage door. She's dripping with sweat and breathing heavily. I can tell by the look on her face that she knows the show has gone well. Within seconds, she's in the limo with her assistant, Liz, her publicist, and her manager, Freddy, rehashing the show, while inside the stadium "Be a Clown" booms through the sound system, and the audience screams for more Madonna.

Back at the hotel, Madonna's suite is filled with yet more white flowers. She removes her makeup, takes a shower, then we go downstairs and join the cast and crew for a private champagne party in the Library Bar.

On opening night here in London, she could easily have celebrated her success with England's glitterati, who would all willingly have flocked to pay tribute to her. But that has rarely been her way. Apart from when we play Detroit or L.A., she always leaves the stadium straight after the second encore, then spends the rest of the evening hanging out with her team, the dancers and musicians from the show, whom she concedes are partly responsible for her success.

While one of Madonna's favorite phrases is "This isn't a democracy," and she is utterly unable to laugh at herself, I am impressed at how egalitarian she is to party with her team on opening night rather than with other celebrities. At the same time, way at the back of my mind, in a dark place I try not to probe, a voice I've spent a lifetime studiously ignoring tells me that part of the reason my sister doesn't relish hanging out with celebrities is that if she did, she would no longer be the only big fish in a small pond, the queen bee, the star. Moreover, the majority of celebrities—her equals—wouldn't laugh at her unfunny jokes, pander to her moods, or make her the center of their universe, the way her acolytes invariably do.

She doesn't stay long at the party. Instead, less than half an hour after we first arrive, she asks me to take her up to the suite.

In the elevator, I am suddenly overwhelmed by a rush of euphoria. My opinion of my sister as a performer is at an all-time high. On a personal level, as a brother, my love for her is unbounded, and we have never been closer.

"You were great tonight, Madonna," I say, "really great."

We hug each other.

"I love you, Christopher, I really do," she says, "and I'm very proud of you."

"I'm proud of you, too. And thank you for giving me this opportunity. Love you."

I check that she has enough lemon tea in her room and that her humidifier works. Then I go back to my suite.

Tonight, we are on top of the world, my sister and I. And no one and nothing can touch us, not even our own human fallibility. We live for the performance, the show. The love, the closeness, the creativity.

Tonight, I know without a shadow of a doubt that we are in step, in sync, in unison, Judy Garland and Mickey Rooney putting on a show, you and me against the world, together, now and for always. I contemplate our glorious future, both personal and professional, and it shimmers before me, flawless and without end.

My own words echo in my mind: *Thank you for giving me this opportunity. Love you.*

Thank you for giving me this opportunity. Love you.

THEY SAY THAT those whom the gods wish to destroy, they first make mad with pride. They also say that what the gods give, they can also take away. Tonight represents the high point of my life, but in the future both sayings will epitomize not a god, but a goddess—my sister Madonna.

She will become mad with pride, with fame, with the oleaginous pandering of the sycophants, the mindless adoration of the masses. And what she has given me—the joy of creating with her, of being with her, of loving her and being loved by her—she will ultimately take away.

ONE

The great advantage of living in a large family is that early lesson of life's essential unfairness.

Nancy Mitford

I AM ELEVEN years old and just another of the eight Ciccone kids about to have dinner with our father and stepmother, Joan, in the harvest-yellow kitchen of our home on Oklahoma Avenue, Rochester, Michigan. We are squashed around the dark oak table—just recently stripped and restored by Joan, and still stinking of varnish—and we are happy because we know we are getting chicken tonight.

My four sisters are all wearing variations of maroon velvet dresses with white lace collars, all made by Joan from the same Butterick pattern. Madonna hates hers, but Joan has told her to "shut up and put it on" and has made her wear it anyway. Another night, Madonna might have run to our dad, and he'd probably have given in and let her wear something else, but tonight he was at a Knights of Columbus meeting and arrived home just in time for dinner.

As always—not because we are poor, but because Joan is frugal—she has only made two chickens to divide between the ten of us. I feel as if I've spent half my life fighting to get the breast, which I love, but failing, simply because I'm too slow off the mark and everyone else beats me to it. Tonight, though, I've made up my mind that I'll get the breast at last.

But before I can swing into action, it's my turn to say grace.

We all stand up and hold hands.

I take a deep breath. "Dear Lord, thank you for this beautiful day. Thank you for all my brothers and sisters."

My elder brother Marty, who has just been caught smoking in the basement and has been disciplined by my father, snickers.

My younger sister Melanie—born with a silver streak on the left side of her hair, across her left eyebrow and left eyelash—assumes I'm sincere and flashes me a tender, beatific smile.

My elder brother Anthony, who is coming down from a bad peyote trip and is still clutching Carlos Castaneda's *Separate Reality*, closes his eyes tightly.

My sister Paula, always the underdog, makes a face.

My baby half sister, Jennifer, gurgles.

My baby half brother, Mario, in his high chair, plays with his rattle.

My father and my stepmother exchange a quick approving glance.

My older sister Madonna lets out a loud, prolonged yawn.

I glare at her and go on.

"Thank you for Grandma Elsie and Grandma Michelina. Thank you for our father and for Joan. Thank you, dear Lord, for the food we are about to receive, and could I please have a chicken breast tonight?"

Everyone cracks up, even Madonna.

I strike out. I don't get the chicken breast. Not quick enough off the mark because I am still heartily laughing at my own witticism. Poetic justice, I suppose. But at least I don't go hungry—because no matter how often my sister Madonna has portrayed herself as the quintessential Cinderella and insinuated that Joan was our wicked stepmother, Joan has never starved or mistreated us.

On the other hand, she doesn't believe in lavishing expensive food on us either. She always reserves any delicacies—Greek olives, Italian salami, expensive cookies—for her guests, whereas the kids' biggest treat is granola. Whenever Joan isn't around, no matter how much else we've eaten that day, just for the hell of it we sneak into the kitchen and pilfer a gourmet cookie earmarked for the guests.

One Saturday morning, when I am fifteen, she summons us all to what she terms "the Formal Dining Room." She has spent the last few months redecorating it, during which time we have been banned from going in there. I assume she is about to unveil her latest decorating feat to us. While my siblings aren't exactly clamoring to view the new and upgraded dining room, I, at least, am slightly curious about the results. I just hope that Joan doesn't expect me to applaud her efforts, because insincere applause isn't yet part of my repertoire. That will come later, on the many occasions when I sit through one of my sister's movie performances and don't want to hurt her feelings.

Consequently, I find it difficult to mask my reaction when we file into the Formal Dining Room. Moss-green shag carpet, strips of stained wood on the walls, tiles in between them that Joan describes as "antiqued," one of her favorite words. I know it's the seventies, but nonetheless, my design instincts have already begun to form and I am far from overwhelmed.

But Joan hasn't summoned us to the Formal Dining Room so we can admire her decorating prowess, but because one of us kids is in deep trouble. In Judge Dredd mode, she announces that the angel food cake she's only lately bought for coffee with her friends is missing, and she wants the culprit to come clean.

"You'll sit here all day, until someone confesses," she decrees.

None of us says a word. She puts an Andy Williams album on the turntable. I think to myself, *Torture by music?* I fix my eyes on the Asian landscape—a fall scene of junks sailing along a river—that our father has brought back from his recent L.A. trip and mentally repaint it myself.

After an hour, Joan leaves the room. We sit around the table in silence, examining one another's sheepish faces, each of us secretly trying to guess the identity of the culprit. Although I don't openly accuse her, I mentally finger Madonna for the crime, simply because I know that although angel food cake tastes too bland for her, she may like the name. Besides, filching it would be another notch in the gun that—figuratively speaking—she has continually pointed in Joan's direction. Half an hour later, Joan returns and announces that a neighbor has come forward and says he witnessed the theft through our kitchen window. Moreover, he has identified the thief: me.

I am innocent, but have no way of proving it. Besides, my friends are waiting for me in our tree house. They've just received the latest *Playboy* in the mail, and I am dying to get out of the house and sneak a peek at it. So I confess to having stolen the angel food cake. I am duly punished for my transgression: grounded for a week, without any TV. Many years later, the true culprit is unmasked when Paula confesses that she took the angel food cake, but by then it was far too late, as I had long since been punished. My own fault, of course, for having confessed to something that I didn't do. The birth of a behavior pattern, I suppose, and a harbinger of things to come.

Since Joan married our father, one of the pleasanter rituals she's established is that each of us can select our own birthday cake. Madonna always picks strawberry shortcake. My choice is always pink-lemonade ice cream cake.

Soon after the angel food cake debacle, I am on tenterhooks as to whether Joan will still make me my favorite cake. To my relief, now that I have been punished for supposedly stealing and have paid the price for my crime, Joan has forgiven me. And I get my pink-lemonade ice cream birthday cake after all.

Making cakes is Joan's greatest culinary accomplishment. But in general, she was an abysmal cook back then. She makes Spanish rice, but forgets to put in the rice and often serves us a massive bowl of stew from the freezer and, with a self-satisfied smile, says, "I just cooked this fresh."

"Freezer fresh!" we all chant under our breaths, careful that our father doesn't hear us because we don't want to make him mad. He demands that we treat Joan with the highest respect and insists we call her Mom. All of us struggle with the respect mandate and, for many years, practically gag when we obey our father and address Joan as Mom.

My natural mother, who was named Madonna, died when I was just three years old. I have only one clear memory of her. I am running around the green-grass backyard of our small, single-level home on the wrong side of the railroad tracks and step on a bee. As I cry my eyes out, my mother gently places me on her knee and soothes the sting with ice. I feel safe, protected, and loved. For the rest of my life, I will yearn to recapture that same feeling, but will always fail.

The sad truth is that I was too young when my mother died to ever really know her. For me as a child, the only way in which she existed was through pictures. One of the many I loved was taken of her sitting astride a buffalo—she is so vibrant, so charismatic, so alive, such a star. Looking at her then, I couldn't believe she was dead, that I would never see her again. Nor could I reconcile her joie de vivre with her extreme piety.

I only learned about my mother's intense religious devotion twenty years ago, when my father sent all of us a bundle of her love letters to him. She wrote those letters when my father was away in the air force, and he and my mother were courting.

I read just one of these romantic missives written by my mother. After reading it, I couldn't bring myself to read any more as I am not a very religious man, and the extremism of my mother's religious sentiments is difficult for me to grasp. Although her letter is loving and sweet, to me it seems a bit fanatical. All about how God is keeping her love for my father alive, God this and God that. I am unable to read any more because I have quite a different picture of my mother in my head and don't want to distort it.

My father sends Madonna copies of those same letters, and I imagine that she also reads them. Nonetheless, we never talk about the letters, or about our mother. We avoid even mentioning her name.

We Ciccones may be afraid to confront our emotions, but little else fazes us. After all, we have pioneer blood in our veins and are proud of it. In 1690, my maternal ancestors, the Fortins, fled France and sailed to Quebec, then a complete wilderness, and settled there. Quintessential pioneers, they wrested a life for themselves and their families out of that wilderness.

More than two hundred thirty-five years later, my grandmother Elsie Fortin, and my grandfather Willard Fortin, marry and honeymoon in splendor at the Waldorf-Astoria in Manhattan. Although Elsie will spend a lifetime denying it, the family tree confirms that she and Willard are, in fact, distant cousins. Maybe that explains why Madonna and I, along with our brothers and sisters, are such intense human beings, our personalities and characteristics, our strengths and weaknesses, so magnified.

Our Ciccone ancestors, too, are unconventional and enterprising. At the end of World War One, my paternal grandfather—Gaetano Ciccone, then just eighteen—was forced to dig ditches high up in the Italian Alps and nearly froze to death. Convinced that the Fascists, whom he hated, were about to take power in Italy, he quit the army and returned to his home in Pacentro, a quaint medieval village in Abruzzi about 170 kilometers east of Rome.

There, a match was made between him and one of the village girls, Michelina, whose father paid him a $300 dowry to marry her. With that money, in 1918, he bought a ticket to America, got a job in the steel mills in Aliquippa, Pennsylvania, then sent for Michelina.

My grandparents had five sons, which is surprising, given that as far back as I can remember, my grandmother and grandfather don't sleep in the same room together. Even in old age, each and every night, my grandmother assiduously bolts all seven locks on her bedroom door.

My grandparents live in an old, two-story yellow-brick house with creaking floorboards, a dank basement, and a dark, gloomy attic where bats sometimes fly around. Grandmother Michelina's taste in furnishings is austere in the extreme. The large, imposing burgundy mohair living room set is uncomfortable, and I don't like sitting on it. All in all, the house is dark and brooding, much like my grandparents.

My grandmother spends most of her time in the kitchen, cooking Italian specialties such as gnocchi. When she isn't cooking, she is constantly in her pale yellow bedroom whose wood floors are all worn away from her continual pacing. Rosaries hang all over the room, faded Palm Sunday fronds are affixed to the wall, candles constantly burn, and pictures of Jesus are on every surface. If ever I go into the room, I find my grandmother on her knees, praying to the Virgin Mary, probably that my grandfather will quickly die and quit bugging her at last.

All I remember of my grandfather is a heavyset, hunched-up old man who drinks too much and only lightens up when he shows us how he can peel an orange in one try. After he dies, my grandmother continually moans that he is haunting her.

Generally, we don't like visiting our father's parents. Luckily for us, we only spend part of the summer with them. We do like our Ciccone uncles, though, in particular Uncle Rocco, after whom Madonna named her son.

As children, we favor our Fortin family, in particular our mother's mother, Grandma Elsie Mae, whom we call Nanoo. She always tells me that I was my mother's favorite and that she used to call me the "Show Me!" kid, because I always used to point at things and demand, "Show me!"

In many ways, Nanoo is a second mother to all of us. She was widowed a year before my birth, has soft, curled brown hair, arranged in the style of the fifties, kind brown eyes, generally wears pastel-colored dresses, very classic, never flashy, and always smells of L'Air du Temps, her favorite perfume. She is a lady in every sense of the word.

Nanoo's husband, our late grandfather Willard, a timber merchant, was relatively wealthy. Pink is Nanoo's favorite color, so one birthday he gave her an all-pink kitchen: a pink stove, pink refrigerator, pink dishwasher.

Nanoo's home is elegant, just like Nanoo herself, and is furnished with all things comfortable—such as the burnished yellow leather davenport on which I always love playing. In her basement, there is a wood-paneled barroom, shuffleboard, and an incinerator—which fascinates me.

Nanoo is quite liberal. Her sons smoke pot in the basement. She calls me Little Chris. I love going to her home because she loves us unconditionally and gives us all equal amounts of attention. When she finds out that my favorite candies are Circus Peanuts, orange marshmallows in the shape of peanuts, she starts keeping them for me in a chicken-shaped ceramic dish on her kitchen counter.

She lets us eat as many desserts as we want and cooks us our favorite foods: savory meat pie and chicken soup with thick noodles, a special recipe from northern France. To this day, I still make both recipes and always think of her. In fact, two months ago I spent a few days with her in Bay City.

Nanoo is ninety-eight in 2008, and the second part of her life has been sad: Her husband died before his time, and she lost four of her eight children when they were young adults. She also had to stand by and watch as many of her remaining children struggled with alcoholism—an ongoing problem with many of my aunts and uncles, one that continues to haunt our family—but she has always been incredibly stoic. A few years ago, she was hit by a car and needed two knee replacements. Now she is almost blind and living in reduced circumstances, and fifteen years ago she was forced to move into a smaller house.

Nanoo's home was a haven for us Ciccone children, a place

where we were all equal and Madonna wasn't the star, the way she was at home. Nanoo's refusal to deify Madonna may, in part, be an explanation for the following scenario: When Madonna first became wealthy, I suggested she pay off Nanoo's house, buy her a car, and engage a full-time driver and cook for her, anything to make her life easier. After all, aren't rock stars who hit it big supposed to take care of their families? But my sister—who in 2008 is worth in excess of $600 million and who has reportedly donated an estimated $18 million to Kabbalah—opted at the time to send our grandmother just $500 a month and to pay her monthly household bills, for Madonna, a drop in the ocean. When I think of Madonna's wealth, I can't help but think she's being stingy with the grandmother who helped raise us.

Nanoo, however, doesn't think that way and is grateful to Madonna for helping her and would never for a moment expect or ask for anything more.

DURING THE KOREAN War, my father, Silvio—"Tony"—is stationed in Alaska. There, he serves with my mother's brother Dale, and they become fast friends. Soon after, my father is best man at Dale's wedding, where he meets my mother. They fall in love and on July 1, 1955, are married in Bay City, Michigan.

My parents move to Thors Street in Pontiac, a satellite city to Detroit. The neighborhood is opposite a large, empty field that will later become the site of the Pontiac Silverdome. Subsequently, Tony, Marty, Madonna, Paula, me, and Melanie are born in that order. Our parents have chosen to live on Thors Street because it is in a planned community that is one-third Mexican, one-third black, one-third Caucasian, and they hope that living in such a multi-racial community will foster racial tolerance in all of us children. Madonna's "Like a Prayer" video, featuring her kissing a black saint—which she conceived to highlight her belief in racial equality—is one of the many proofs that they succeeded.

Our backyard is right next to the train tracks, beside a big chain-link fence. Right near our house is also a massive electrical tower, which continually emits a buzzing noise that drives us crazy. Behind the tracks, a slope drops fifteen feet down into the sewers. When we are old enough, we climb down the manhole next to the tracks and follow the sewers wherever they go. This is our version of playtime.

Although our father isn't really allowed to tell us because his job is so top secret, he works in the defense industry, designing firing systems and laser optics, first at Chrysler Defense and then at General Dynamics. One day, when I am in high school, he comes home with a revolutionary night-vision telescope, plus a photograph of a tank. After he shows them to us, he warns us never to talk about it. We all promise not to. But now I know what my father does for a living, and I think his profession is cool.

He feels he can trust us to keep our word because, from the time that we were small, he has drilled us in the importance of honesty and ethics. The early loss of our mother may have put a combination of sorrow and iron into Madonna's soul—as it did in mine—and may well have contributed to her insatiable craving to be loved and admired by the entire world. That craving helped catapult her to stardom. But if the untimely loss of our mother indirectly drove Madonna to become a star, it is our father who instilled in her the tools that maintained her stardom: self-discipline, reliability, honor, and a certain stoicism.

Our father's stoicism comes to the fore when, on December 1, 1963, our mother dies at the age of only thirty. Madonna is old enough to remember our mother's death and has spoken to the media many times about the days before she died, her death, and the aftermath. "I knew she was sick for a long time with breast cancer, so she was very weak, but she would continue to go on and do the things she had to do. I knew she was very fragile and kept getting more fragile. I knew that, because she would stop during the day and just sit down on the couch. I wanted her to get up and play with me and do the things she did before," Madonna remembered.

"I know she tried to keep her feelings inside, her fear inside, and not let us know. She never complained. I remember she was really sick and was sitting on the couch. I went up to her and I remember climbing on her back and saying, 'Play with me, play with me,' and she wouldn't. She couldn't and she started crying."

Our mother spent a year in the hospital, but, according to Madonna, strove to put a brave face on her suffering and never betrayed it to her children.

"I remember my mother was always cracking up and making jokes. She was really funny so it wasn't so awful to go and visit her there. I remember that right before she died she asked for a hamburger. She wanted to eat a hamburger because she couldn't eat anything for so long, and I thought that was very funny. I didn't actually watch her die. I left and then she died."

Although I was only three when my mother was on her deathbed, I remember nestling in her warm and comforting arms. We are in a strange white room with hardly any furniture. My mother is lying in an iron bed, and my father and all my brothers and sisters are standing around the bed in front of us. They start to leave the room. I snuggle closer to my mother. My father lifts me gently out of her arms. I struggle against his strong grip. I don't want to leave my mother. I start wailing pitifully. The next thing I remember, we are in the car and I cry all the way home. I never see my mother again. Nor am I taken to her funeral.

I have few memories of my life in the first few years after my mother's death. All I remember is that afterward, a series of women look after us, and that Joan is one of our nannies.

Joan, our "wicked" stepmother—is the woman whom I now, of my own volition, call Mom. She's certainly earned the title. With the passing of time, I've grown to love her and, in retrospect, believe that only a slightly crazy woman, or an extremely romantic and brave one, would marry a man with six children.

But when she first comes into our lives, we all simply despise her. The seeds are sown by the Fortin side of our family, who—after our mother's untimely death—dream of our father marrying one of her close friends. He dates her for a while and then decides not to.

When our father marries our nanny Joan instead, the Fortins are incensed and forever after refer to her as the Maid. I prefer to think of Joan as the Sergeant Major, because as soon as she marries our father, she sets about organizing his unruly children according to a timetable, rules, and regulations. Rather like a five-star general. Ironically, although Madonna won't like the comparison, as she has grown older, the one person in our family whom she most resembles is Joan. Much as hearing this will drive her crazy, in recent years she has become more and more like Joan, insisting that everything has to be done her way, according to her timetable, and that life must be lived by her rules.

Whenever Madonna and I live together for any period of time, I am automatically subject to her stringent set of rules, which include banning me from smoking in the house, and her insistence on maintaining perfect tidiness. Sometimes, her decree that I stick to her rules leads to a battle of wills between us. The truth is that I sometimes feel the need to assert myself and rebel against the hold she has over me. Moreover, I am not fond of rules, and often tire of obeying the ones Madonna sets so stringently. I know that I'm being the little brother, kicking against my big sister's rules and regulations, but I cant't help it.

An example; I get up early for breakfast, make myself some sourdough toast, and leave the dishes in the sink because I intend to do them when I get home later in the day. I go upstairs, only to hear Madonna screeching, "Christopher, you didn't put the damn dishes in the dishwasher again."

I am suddenly overcome with the sense that I am back home again and that Joan will rush out at any moment and chastise me.

"I'll do it when I get home," I yell back.

"Do it *now*!" she screams.

I don't. She does, with a great deal of clattering and complaining. She's irritated and I guess I don't blame her. I also understand why her behavior is sometimes a carbon copy of Joan's. For just as Dietrich was one of the major cinematic influences on Madonna, her family—Joan and my father—also played a big part in making my sister the legend she has become, as I, too, would down the line.

Thinking back to my childhood, I suppose Joan had little alternative than to rule us with a rod of iron. We were so wild, so willful, so set on undermining her at every turn. And I am sure that when she first married my father, she wasn't fully prepared for us pint-size saboteurs determined to make her life miserable.

Small, blond, Nordic, born in Taylor, Michigan, Joan, always in her green capri pants, with her love of antiques, "antiquing," and freezer food, may well have started out in life as an archromantic. After all, she married our father the same year *The Sound of Music*—the tale of Maria, a governess to Captain Von Trapp's seven children, who ultimately married him, whereupon the whole family all lived blissfully ever after—was first released and probably thought we'd become a Midwestern version of the Von Trapps and she'd be Maria, warbling "Climb Every Mountain" while we all clung to her adoringly.

Instead, Marty and Anthony—probably deeply disturbed by the death of our mother—turn out to be the wildest kids in the neighborhood and sometimes make her life hell. Mostly, though, they take out their ire on us, their siblings. One time when Madonna isn't looking, they pour pine sap into her hair, and she can't remove it, so great chunks of her hair have to be chopped off, while she screams "My hair! My hair!" Then—when she sees her shorn image in the mirror—she bursts into tears. My brothers, however, remain unrepentant and continue to vent most of their aggression on her, and not on the rest of us, perhaps because she has always hogged our father's attention and they sense that he may love her best.

By now, the Ciccone family has moved away from Pontiac and settled down on Oklahoma Avenue in Rochester instead. Our new home is a two-story, redbrick colonial, with green aluminum siding and a wagon wheel embedded on the front lawn.

The move to Oklahoma Avenue is exciting. There is a little creek at the back of our house, and a massive old oak tree in the backyard that I love to climb, until I fall out of it and almost break my back.

The most glaring difference between Pontiac and Rochester is the alarming lack of people of color living in the neighborhood. Everyone is white, and I often wonder what happened to our multiracial little world.

On the other hand, life chez Ciccone is never dull or uneventful. One morning during the summer, Madonna and I are in the kitchen having breakfast when we hear Anthony and Marty yelling our names.

"Get out here, Madonna and Chris, we wanna see you right now!"

Just yesterday, our father—much against his better judgment, and only because they have promised him they will rid the yard of the scourge of squirrels currently swarming everywhere—bought Anthony and Marty BB guns.

Madonna and I exchange glances, then sneak out the side door and into the garden. Petrified that Marty, stocky and terrifying even without the BB gun, and Anthony, tall and intimidating, will start firing at us, we run as fast as we can.

We get to the slimy green swamp behind our house and start wading, not caring that we both end up looking like understudies for Elphaba in *Wicked*. Fortunately for us, Anthony and Martin turn out not to be so intrepid. They prowl the edge of the swamp, fire the guns at us, and cast around for a way of catching us without getting all slimed up as well. Meanwhile, Madonna and I are halfway to Hitchman's Haven—an old, boarded-up Victorian mansion, set on sixty acres with a large pond, surrounded by massive weeping willows and ancient oak trees—where we hide out for the rest of the morning until we know Marty and Anthony are safely inside the house scoffing their lunch.

According to local lore, Hitchman's is a former asylum where Judy Garland was once an inmate. Unlike ex-child-star Judy, Madonna neither sings nor dances as a child. But when it comes to cozying up to our father and grabbing all his attention, she definitely upstages the rest of us—not because she is in training for a future career as an actress, but because she is clearly suffering from some type of Electra complex—the female version of the Oedipus complex.

All of us kids are competing for our father's love and attention, but ever the competitor, Madonna usually wins and gets it. No matter that she is too old to sit on our father's knee, she clambers up and stays there. At Easter, she demands that out of all the dyes we use for coloring Easter eggs the blue dye be reserved just for her, and he makes sure it is. At her confirmation, she demands a special dress and gets it from him. And whenever possible, she snuggles close to our father and pushes the rest of us away.

None of us can quite work out why our father is so in Madonna's thrall. In retrospect, after looking at a picture of her without makeup, the reason becomes dramatically clear: she is the mirror image of our mother. The uncanny resemblance must simultaneously have broken our father's heart and exercised a haunting power over him. Moreover, my sister's very name, Madonna, must vastly have strengthened her emotional hold over him.

I think of my mother with a mixture of love, loss, and longing, and irrational as it may have been, for as far back as I can remember, I believe I unconsciously transferred a degree of those tremulous emotions onto my sister Madonna. And I'm sure my father did as well, which afforded her a certain power over all of us and instilled in her the confidence that she could be and do pretty much what she wanted. A partial explanation, I think, of how our adult relationship would subsequently unfold.

No matter that Madonna generally wins the battle for our father's love and attention, the rest of us keep trying for the leftovers. Consequently, there's always an undertone of animosity among us all, which makes it impossible for us to get to know one another, or to genuinely care about one another. As we grow older, we each sort of break off from the family and do our own things.

Madonna divides her time between studying, cheerleading, and luxuriating in her unchallenged role of daddy's girl; Anthony and Marty are the "bad boys" who become authentic macho men, the kind both Madonna's husbands aspired to be; Paula is always left out; and I am generally lumped together with Melanie and our half-siblings, Mario and Jennifer, and deeply resent it.

Usually, Melanie and I are forced to babysit for Mario and Jennifer, and—to our shame—vent our dislike of Joan upon them, while simultaneously reenacting our older brothers' bullying behavior without realizing that we are robotically repeating their pattern. One time, Melanie and I are alone in the house babysitting Mario and Jennifer. We gravely explain that something terrifying has just happened. There's been a news flash on the TV: a serial killer has escaped and just been spotted prowling around our neighborhood. We whisper that we have to turn off the lights so he won't know we are home, otherwise he might break in and slaughter us all.

Mario and Jennifer huddle together behind the couch, petrified. Meanwhile, Melanie and I sneak into the kitchen, grab butcher knives out of the kitchen drawer, and creep out of the house and into the street. About five minutes later, we burst through the front door, brandishing the knives, and chase Mario and Jennifer around the house in the dark. They scream and cry so much that, in the end, we get them a cup of granola and say we are sorry. When Joan discovers what we have done, Melanie and I are grounded for a week and forced to do double chores.

In the best of times, even if we are all being close to angelic, chores remain a fact of life for us. First thing every morning, we all check the chore list Joan has posted on the refrigerator. An example from my late teens: "Christopher to do the dishes and clean the yard. Paula to do the laundry. Marty to take out the garbage. Melanie to polish the cutlery. Mario to match the socks. Anthony to cut the grass. Jennifer to mend the clothes."

Generally, my older brothers never have to do dishes or the laundry. And my sisters are never enlisted to cut the grass or take out the garbage, but I always have to do both the girls' chores and the boys'. I never understand why. I don't mind doing the laundry, though, because that way I can get a march on my brothers and sisters by grabbing the only 100 percent cotton sheets we possess, a floral print. When I do, I feel as if I am sleeping on silk. To this day, I retain an addiction to 100 percent cotton sheets.

Joan rarely allocates any tasks to Madonna, in tacit recognition, I think, of her special place in our father's heart. Besides, I believe Joan is a little afraid of her.

I don't recall my father ever scolding Madonna or disciplining her, except once. Madonna comes home late one night, Joan slaps her, and she slaps Joan back. Madonna is grounded for a week and banned from driving her car—a 1968 red Mustang that we all wish we had.

Another time, Madonna and some friends drive over to the local gravel pit, about twenty miles north of Rochester, where we always go swimming. She and Paula much prefer swimming when they aren't with our father and Joan because our father has banned them from wearing bikinis, which Madonna resents.

During the summer, though, because Madonna wants to protect her fair skin, she never sunbathes like the rest of us. But she's always been a good swimmer and enjoys swimming at the pit. On this particular day, however, we aren't with her.

Late that night, she arrives home with a black eye and a bloody nose. Joan is really upset because she does care about Madonna, and all of us, and asks her what happened.

It turns out that a group of bikers drove up to the pit and started playing loud music. Everyone else was really annoyed, but only Madonna had the guts to go up and say something. So one of the biker chicks beat her up. Madonna shrugged the whole thing off, her confidence and bravery intact.

Apart from the odd excitement, such as Madonna and the biker chicks, our lives fall into a certain rhythm.

School days invariably begin with us all rushing to get ready, always late, flinging our clothes everywhere, making Joan so mad that she invariably comes out with her favorite phrases: "Your room looks like the wreck of the *Hesperus*" or "Your room looks like the Russian army went through it." We, of course, have no idea what she is talking about.

She sighs, then makes us her school lunch standby: cracker sandwiches—two saltine crackers with mayonnaise between them, which we hate. Then we all run for the bus stop, just two houses away, slipping and sliding along the key road, trying to catch up with the yellow school bus, and usually making it—but not always. Which means having to walk the three miles between our home and school.

When we ride home from school in the bus, we crane our heads out of the windows to see if Joan's car is in the driveway. Because if it isn't, we know we'll have a great afternoon. No red-faced stepmother, no one to yell at us or chase us around with a wooden spoon or slap our faces if we defy her.

If Joan is a strict disciplinarian, our father isn't exactly a pushover either. He is a man of action, who makes his intentions clear and doesn't deal in ambiguities. He lets us know when we did wrong and lets us know when we did right. A conservative Catholic, he attends church every Sunday and is a church deacon. If we swear or make a smart-ass comment, he drags us into the bathroom and tells us to stick out our tongues. Then he gets out a bar of soap and scrubs our tongues with it. When he's worked up quite a lather in our mouths, he finally lets us rinse our mouths and spit. It's a long time before any of us make the same mistake again.

If our father and Joan decide we have been well behaved, in the evening we are allowed to watch TV with them in the family room. Our favorite programs are *My Favorite Martian, Mister Ed, The Three Stooges,* and *I Dream of Jeannie.*

We aren't allowed to watch television often, but it isn't banned. Madonna, however, doesn't allow Lola or Rocco to watch any TV whatsoever. But when I last visit Madonna's Sunset Boulevard home, I find it puzzling that there are TVs all over the house.

AS THE YEARS go by, our father and Joan develop a benign, loving companionship. They are not touchy-feely—but then neither am I, nor Madonna, not even when she was married to Sean Penn, or when she was dating Warren Beatty.

Although we are a Catholic family and always celebrate Christmas and Easter, our father belongs to the Christian Family Movement, which fosters tolerance between Christians and Jews. So every year, we celebrate Passover together. I often wonder whether Madonna's early familiarity with this sacred Jewish holiday—and with Judaism in general—was not only the genesis of her attraction to Kabbalah, but what also helped her bond with the powerful Jewish music moguls whom she charmed at the start of her career. As for me, as a child, I assume that our Passover celebrations are part of Easter and, until I become an adult, never quite grasp that there is a difference.

At Christmas, we always attend midnight mass at St. Frederick's or St. Andrew's, which is intensely dramatic and our first introduction to theater. During Lent, our father makes us go to church every morning before school. We are such a large family that we each can't afford to buy nine gifts every Christmas. Instead, about two weeks before Christmas, our father puts a big paper lunch bag on the kitchen table. We each write our names on a separate piece of paper, then put them in the bag. Our father shakes the bag, and we each pull out a name. Then we buy a Christmas gift for the named person, and no one else.

One Christmas, when I am fourteen, I draw Madonna's name, but don't have any money to pay for her gift. My father goes to Kmart for an auto part. Marty and I go with him. The place is abuzz with Christmas shoppers, loud Muzak, and glowing fluorescent lights. I wander the aisles worrying how I am going to get a gift for Madonna. When my father and Marty aren't looking, I steal a small bottle of Zen perfume for her, stick it in my overcoat pocket, and skulk out of the store. Suddenly, I'm grabbed from behind, marched into the manager's office, ordered to empty my pockets, and the Zen falls out. I am caught and fear my father's wrath more than anything else.

Next thing I know, I can hear over the PA system, "Is there a Mr. Ciccone in the store?" Within a moment, my father is in the manager's office. He looks at me, says, "You stupid little shit!" and yanks me out of the store.

In the car, he doesn't say a single word to me, but I know I am in big-time trouble. I am shocked when he does nothing. I suppose he knows that I haven't stolen for myself, but because I wanted Madonna to have her Christmas present.

I realize that it would be heartwarming if I claimed to have stolen the perfume for my sister because I loved her so much, but that isn't true. I didn't then really love her at all. In fact, I hardly knew her. I felt alienated from her, alienated from my whole family. I was not a bad child, not a good child, just quiet, and watching, always observing.

IN 1972, THE whole family takes a road trip across America in our dark green van. True to form, Madonna makes sure always to squeeze herself into the front bench seat, between our father and Joan, practically pushing Joan out of her seat.

Each of us is allowed to bring as many things as we can that will fit in a cardboard Rolling Rock case—Rolling Rock was my paternal grandfather's favorite beer—with our name on it. The girls paint flowers on their boxes; I paint mine with red, white, and blue stripes.

At night, my father and Joan sleep in the van, and we kids all sleep in a dark green army tent that reeks of mold and mildew. We drive for hours and hours, and the whole trip is a free-for-all. We visit the Grand Canyon, Mount Rushmore, the Black Hills of South Dakota, the Hoover Dam, and Yellowstone National Park. When we get to California, Joan suggests driving along Santa Monica beach, but the van gets stuck in the sand. We are all tired and irritable.

Luckily for us, nearby surfers come to our aid and explain to my father that by letting air out of the tires we will widen their surface contact with the sand and the van can be dislodged. We do and it works.

LOOKING BACK, I suppose our grand road trip across America is another example of my father's educational ideals, which include exposing his children to their country. He also believes in the virtue of hard work. When I'm twelve, one morning during summer vacation, he opens the front door, pushes me out, and says, "Don't come back without a job."

I wander around Rochester for hours until I come across a sign at a local country club looking for caddies. I get the job, train for a week, and on my first day at work, I walk out because my employer treats me so badly.

My father, too, has more lofty ambitions for me. In fact, his dearest wish is that all his children become attorneys, engineers, or doctors. Fortunately for Madonna and me, he isn't opposed to the arts either. Thanks to him, all us Ciccone kids have piano lessons. And when any of us admit that we have artistic ambitions—albeit slightly reluctantly—he encourages us to live out our creativity. I'm surprised by his somewhat laissez-faire attitude toward our career choices. Then I learn from my father's mother that my father's brother Guido, a talented painter, was forced by his wife to jettison his ambition to become an artist and work in the steel mills instead. Consequently, he was deeply unhappy for most of his life. Clearly, my father witnessed Guido's unhappiness and vowed that none of his children would suffer in the same way.

Naturally, my father, a deeply private yet even-natured man, never discusses Guido's sad fate. On the surface at least, he is repressed and not in the least bit comfortable with emotions, and will never delve into them—his own, or anyone else's. However, as time goes by, he will relax more, and much to my surprise we will become good friends.

For as far back as I can remember, my father's greatest passion has been wine making. In this, he is following in the footsteps of his own father, who used to grow grapes and make wine in Pennsylvania. He spends much of his free time making wine in the basement. As a result, the house always smells of wine and of vinegar. My father is proud of his wine. Years after I become an adult and leave home, I come back for a family gathering and crack an awful joke, comparing the taste of his latest vintage to salad dressing. He says nothing, but his hurt is palpable, and I feel dreadful and realize how dear his wine making is to him.

Every few weeks, our father tells us to go down to the laundry room in the basement, where he cuts our hair with barber's clippers, which I hate because all my brothers and I have the identical haircut.

On one memorable occasion, he sits me down and says, "Christopher, you need to learn about sex, about relationships between men and women."

I flush scarlet, sink into my chair, and say, "Dad, please, let's cut my hair so I can get out of here. I know how babies are made."

Although my own sexual nature is still a mystery to me, Madonna's precocious sense of her sexuality, as well as her star quality, came to the fore during her first talent show. Her biographers all claim that the talent show took place when she was at St. Andrew's, but I remember it as being at West Junior High School.

I am twelve, and Madonna is fourteen. The whole family goes along to see her perform in the nondescript school auditorium. None of us have any idea what Madonna's act is going to be, but we are excited and want to support her.

We sit in the second row fidgeting as we watch all the other kids' usual run-of-the-mill talent-show turns—one tap dances, another plays the harmonica, another recites a poem—and wait for Madonna to come on.

Then, in a scene straight out of the movie *Little Miss Sunshine*, Madonna suddenly twirls onstage, covered from head to foot in green and fluorescent pink paint, which creates the illusion that she is stark naked. She's wearing shorts and a top that are also covered in paint, but as far as my father is concerned, she might as well be naked. According to his strict moral code, her appearance is utterly X-rated, and he puts down his camera in horror.

Madonna starts dancing—or perhaps *writhing* is a better word. Although Carol Belanger, my sister's school friend, is also onstage dressed exactly the same way, and writhing about just as much, next to Madonna, she fades into the scenery. None can take their eyes off Madonna. Moreover, her performance is the most scandalous one that anyone has ever seen in that conservative community.

Madonna and Carol's act takes about three minutes. When the lights go up, there is little applause. Everyone in the audience is dumbstruck. People exit with a great deal of barely suppressed muttering.

Afterward in the car going home, none of us say a word, and my father keeps his eyes resolutely on the road. We all know that Madonna is in deep trouble. When we arrive home, he calls her into "the Formal" and shuts the door behind them. When she finally emerges, her face is tearstained. Her performance is never again mentioned.

For the next month, her teenage talent-show performance becomes the talk of Rochester. At school, kids sidle up to me and whisper, "Your sister Madonna is a slut." I have already been bullied and called a fag—a word I don't understand—that my sister's being called a slut doesn't bother me at all. But I can imagine that my father is utterly mortified in front of his friends and at work. Little does he know that this is only the beginning . . .

As for me, the night of the talent show marks the birth of my fascination with my sister Madonna. For on that night, I understand she isn't like everyone else; she is profoundly different. It isn't until later that I discover so am I.

TWO

Come away, O human child!
To the waters and the wild
W. B. Yeats

In junior high school, I am as much of a loner as I am at home, and the fag-calling gets worse when, at thirteen, I take up the violin. Luckily for me, after one of the bigger guys at school, Jay Hill—for reasons I never quite manage to fathom—comes to my rescue, the other kids stop bullying me.

Into high school, I decide that my best bet is to ignore the bullies and let them fear me instead. So I grow my hair long, buy a dark green army coat that goes down to my knees, grow a mustache, and lurk around the school silent, brooding, and impassive. After a while, even my teachers grow afraid of me, primarily because in class, my violin case always in hand, I wordlessly stare at them. I have no real friends, but plenty of curious onlookers.

Away from school, I discover science fiction, and in particular Frank Herbert's *Dune,* which evokes the possibility of worlds other than the one in which I live, makes a great impression on me, and becomes my only escape from everyday reality.

Practically daily, I stand on the sidewalk outside my parents' house, smoking a cigarette and watching a plane high above me, and think, *I wish I were on that plane. I've got to get out of here.* Trouble is, I haven't the remotest idea when or how.

During my sophomore year of high school, Madonna starts going out every Thursday night and coming home looking tired but happy. We aren't close enough for me to ask why, but I know something has changed for her. Soon after, she gives up cheerleading, loses weight, and starts wearing black sweats instead of her usual brown-and-gold-plaid skirts and sweaters. I observe the change in her, intrigued.

One rare evening when Madonna and I are at home alone, she finds me reading in my bedroom and tells me that every Thursday night she has been attending Christopher Flynn's Christopher's Ballet School in Rochester. I am taking art classes and violin lessons, so the idea of ballet classes doesn't seem so foreign to me. Consequently, when Madonna asks if I'd like to come and watch one of her ballet classes, I jump at the opportunity. I suppose I am flattered. My big sister has noticed me at last. And I am curious if not a little wary, because I instinctively know that my father won't like my becoming involved in such a female pursuit. But Madonna wants me to come with her, and that is enough for me.

On a cool Thursday evening in the fall, Madonna and I stealthily slip out of the house together. I am wearing blue jeans and a sweatshirt, Madonna is in pink-and-black sweats, and she drives us into downtown Rochester.

In the car, I clam up because I am so apprehensive. Madonna doesn't talk either. I feel as if we are embarking on a great but dangerous adventure together. Then we arrive at a stone building on the corner of East Fourth and Main, just across from Mitzelfield's department store, where Joan would sometimes buy us clothes, if we were lucky and she didn't feel like making them.

Before we walk into the building, Madonna says, "Christopher Flynn is a great guy," so before I meet him, I already know he must be.

We go upstairs to the second-floor studio, and she introduces me to Christopher. I've never met anyone like him in my life. He is around five foot eight, a lean man with dark brown hair, and dressed in gray jazz pants and a tight leotard with a shirt over it. His voice is high and haughty, and I think he sounds like a girl.

I follow him and Madonna into the dance studio and find a group of fifteen girls, ages twelve and up, all in pink tutus and tights, but no guys. I stick out like a sore thumb, but I'm used to that, so when Christopher tells me to sit on the floor and watch, I do.

I can't believe that Madonna is so meekly taking her place among fifteen other girls, all standing at the barre, and—like them—obeying Christopher's every order without question. When he pokes her with a stick because her plié isn't low enough or her turnout isn't correct, she unflinchingly complies. She has never shown our father so much obedience. I develop instant respect for Christopher.

Moreover, the music is beautiful and the dancers are graceful. I think to myself that ballet is pretty cool, but wonder how I fit in.

Class finishes, and everyone leaves but Madonna, Christopher, and me. He asks me if I want to take a class with him. Before I can answer, Madonna chips in, "I think you should, Chris, I think you'd like it."

I don't know whether I can dance, nor do they. I tell them that I don't think my father will appreciate my taking ballet classes.

"I don't think he'd be happy at all," I say, looking at Madonna for affirmation.

"Just don't tell him," she says. "We can figure it out."

We. Suddenly, my sister and I are *we.* A novel experience. And I like it. I also like the idea of studying ballet with her, of having something in common with her other than just our crazy family.

But I still have one reservation: "It's all girls."

"So?" says Madonna, bridling.

Christopher diverts me from any potential conflict with my sister by chatting to me about ballet, what it represents to him, how he'd danced with the Joffrey Ballet in New York.

I am intrigued and think, *Maybe I really can do this.*

In the end, Christopher talks me into joining the class, primarily by challenging me.

"It isn't going to be easy," he says, "I'm not going to babysit you."

A challenge. A new world. Maybe even a way out of Michigan.

I say I'll think about it, and Madonna and I leave.

The moment we get into the car, she immediately says, "So what do you think? How do you feel? Are you going to do it?"

I tell her I'm afraid of our father's reaction.

She says, "Don't worry. I'll take care of it."

My sister is going to take care of something for me. The emotional impact on me is incalculable. The following Thursday, I attend my first ballet lesson with Christopher Flynn.

UNTIL I JOIN Christopher's Ballet, Madonna and I haven't been friends and haven't socialized together. Now, though, every Thursday, we go to Christopher's together. And no one in our family knows. Not even Paula, to whom Madonna is, at this point, really close. Sometimes I wonder why Madonna invited me, not Paula, to come to class with her, but I was playing the violin, and folk dancing, while Paula wasn't into any of that.

So I go to Christopher's, and my life changes. Not dramatically, but subtly. I discover that Christopher is my sister's mentor, that they are close, and that she is even a little in love with him.

As my self-appointed Pygmalion, Madonna often comes to watch me, although she is in a different class, and is complimentary about my progress. Once, the two of us see a TV program about Fonteyn and Nureyev. I fantasize that maybe one day that could be Madonna and me, dancing together, just like Nureyev and Fonteyn. But that's a long way away and I know it. We aren't even buddies yet—more Pied Piper and follower—but I feel that my sister is starting to care about me, and I like the feeling.

Meeting Christopher Flynn and discovering ballet has introduced Madonna to a new world and opened up a possible escape route from Michigan. I think she looked back at the home and family she was so anxious to leave, sensed that I might be like-minded, recognized something within me, and decided to nurture it.

In retrospect, if my sister hadn't reached back and brought me into her world, I might never have escaped Michigan, and my life would have been different. Taking me with her to Christopher's Ballet School was the greatest gift Madonna has ever given me. A once-in-a-lifetime gift.

But . . .

As I grow older and wiser, I learn that Madonna always has her eye on the main chance. No matter how potent the spell she casts over me, no matter how generous the gifts—there is always a sting in the tail, always a but . . .

In the midst of her almost maternal altruism toward me, she

has her own agenda for prompting me to join her at Christopher Flynn's; he doesn't have any male dancers in his class, and he needs one. The romantic in me would like to have it otherwise, but the truth is that Madonna's motives, as always, for whisking me out of Oklahoma Avenue and into her brave and wondrous new world are not unmixed. She adores and venerates Christopher, considers him her father, her mentor, her lover. He needs a male dancer for his class, so Madonna produces me. Yet no matter what her motives, and the bitterness that will one day arise between us, I will always be in her debt.

Madonna leaves home in the fall of 1977 and goes to the University of Michigan at Ann Arbor to study modern dance. Now that she is out of the house, Paula gets a room by herself at last. But although I am wrapped up in high school, I still miss going to class with Madonna and feel a little lost without her.

I'm a senior in high school, but at least I've got my own car at last, a used green Dodge Dart. I haven't seen much of my sister since she left home, but I've thought of her often. She's the first of us Ciccone kids to go to college, which I think is really cool. I am curious about her life there and eager to find out all about it and am delighted when she invites me and my parents to see her perform in her first ballet at the University of Michigan.

So here I am. Seventeen years old. Long seventies hair styled into an Afro. Fu Manchu mustache. Black Sears pants, brown polyester Sears shirt with big sleeves and a three-button cuff—a present from Joan—and brown Sears platform shoes with a blue-and-red stripe on the toe. Driving myself from Rochester to Ann Arbor, I have no intimation that, thanks to Madonna, over the next six hours my destiny—both sexual and professional—will become set in stone.

• • •

At the campus theater, the Power Center for the Performing Arts, I meet up as arranged with my father and Joan. During the show—"Hat Rack," an experimental ballet—I sit with them. They look utterly bemused by what they see onstage; Madonna is wearing a black bra and shorts, and two male dancers are wearing black shorts. Together, they all roll around the stage. Odd angular movements, not at all the ballet I had studied with Christopher Flynn.

I also find the dancing a trifle bizarre, but I still can't take my eyes off the stage, off Madonna. I can't stop thinking that this is the kind of dance I'd like to do. I've never seen movements like this: leaps, turns, bare skin, dancing in bare feet. I am overcome with the feeling that I could do this, I could be a modern dancer. I decide right then to follow in Madonna's footsteps, give up ballet, and study modern dance at college instead. Of course, I don't say a word to Joan and my father about my new resolution. I'm still in a trance, high on my brilliant prospective career.

We all go backstage to congratulate Madonna. She is all flushed and happy, giddy, excited, and glad that her first college show has gone so well. Joan and my father tell her she was great. Joan asks the questions I secretly wanted to ask: What did the ballet really mean? What was the plot? What was your character?

For once, Madonna is polite to Joan and makes a valiant stab at answering.

Then she asks me what I think.

"Interesting, strange," I say thoughtfully.

She asks me if I want to hang out with her later.

Thrilled, not just because she is my sister, but because she is a dancer, living an enviable lifestyle, I say yes, yes, I do.

She changes into leggings, boots, a coat and hat. I tell my parents I'll drive myself home later.

We eat a quick dinner at a restaurant on the corner of Huron and South First Street, the Oyster Bar and Spaghetti Machine.

During dinner, I ask her questions about "Hat Rack." She tries her best to help me make some sense of it.

Then she asks me if I want to go to the club downstairs with her. I'm a seventeen-year-old high school kid from a hick Michigan town. I've never been to a club before. Entranced, I say that I do. And then I follow my sister into yet another new world.

A door stands with a sign saying THE RUBAIYAT in Arabic cursive. Standing in front of it, a sumo-sized man grunts, "Three dollar. No holler."

Madonna pays for both of us.

Inside it's dark, but I can make out an exposed cable-covered brick wall and red banquettes arranged along the walls. In the middle is a wooden dance floor, lit by strobes and Christmas lights. An arched wooden latticework and a large silver disco ball hang from the ceiling. Years later, Madonna will make her entrance from a similar silver disco ball in her *Confessions Tour.* Even at this early stage in her life, no experience, no visual image, is wasted on her.

"Stayin' Alive" pounds through the club.

And then it hits me. The whole place is filled with guys. Guys dancing close, guys dancing apart, guys dancing together.

I nearly freak out.

I turn to Madonna and, honest to God, ask, "But why aren't there any girls here?"

Madonna looks at me, incredulous. "Well, Christopher," she says in an unusually patient voice, "this is a gay bar. You know, for men."

All of a sudden, a wave of relief sweeps over me. I don't know what, I don't understand why. I just know that everything is as it should be.

The DJ spins "Boogie Nights." Madonna grabs my hand and pulls me onto the dance floor. But I am far too busy avoiding the eyes of the men around me to really enjoy dancing with Madonna. I just look down and struggle not to examine either the men or my emotions.

I realize that this isn't Madonna's first time at the club. Later, she tells me that Christopher Flynn first took her there and that they go often.

I don't want the night to end, but when the club closes, I offer to drive her to her dorm.

Once in the car, Madonna asks, "So, Christopher, what did you think?"

I gaze out the car window and hum a few bars of "Stayin' Alive."

"I mean, what did you *really* think?"

I know she expects me to admit that I'm gay, but I'm just not ready to confront my own sexuality. "What do I think?" Then I retreat back into my comfortable shell. "Well, I think it was fun, the music was great."

After that, we arrive at her dorm, and she gets out of the car. We both know that there has been a radical shift between us. My sister has shown me a reflection of my sexuality and I can no longer hide it—at least, not from myself. She has opened my eyes, and I am scared.

I GRADUATE HIGH school and spend the following summer working at a local gas station. I go to college at Western Michigan, and because of *Dune* and other books I read after that, I decide to major in anthropology. I am a romantic at heart, love movies and secretly see myself as a latter-day Errol Flynn, so I decide to minor in fencing. Later, my ideal will be William Holden, but you get the picture.

I make the belated realization that if I ever really want to learn the lessons being taught in college, I can no longer just sit in class and keep my mouth shut. Almost overnight, I am transformed into an adult version of the Show Me! kid. I challenge every assertion made by my teachers. I question everything. Prove it. I don't believe you. Show me. I learn more in one semester at college than I did all the previous years at school.

After the second semester, I decide that I want to continue dancing and take modern dance class as well. I break the news to my father, and to my relief he doesn't get mad. Instead, he looks disappointed, and I feel awful. My elder brothers never finished school, he hoped I'd study to become a scientist, and now he knows that won't happen. He doesn't try to stop me, though. All he says is, "I don't approve, and if you want to take dance classes, you are going to have to pay for them yourself."

So I support myself by working in the dorm cafeteria, and by giving blood as often as possible, for $50 each time. I also befriend various women in my dorm, and they fulfill my newly acknowledged need for female friends, or stand-ins for my sisters.

One chilly winter morning, I see my roommate—with whom I have nothing in common—coming out of the shower naked and I get a hard-on. I am gay. He doesn't notice my physical reaction, although I am utterly embarrassed. Happily, midsemester he moves out of my room, leaving me to a private room and a great freshman year.

At the end of that year, although my father is paying half of my tuition, I run out of cash, transfer to Oakland University, and move back home again.

Enter Madonna once more, primed to introduce me to yet another new and enlightening experience. This time around, though, I initiate it. I have witnessed her smoking pot with her friends, am curious, and want to do what my big sister is doing. So I ask her about it.

Two days later, she presents me with a joint rolled in pink paper.

"That'll be fifty cents," she says, and holds out her hand for it.

So I pay her.

An accomplished businesswoman, even then!

By now, with Christopher Flynn's encouragement, Madonna has left Ann Arbor without graduating and moved to Manhattan. Later, she will claim of that first trip, "I came here with thirty-five dollars in my pocket. It was the bravest thing I'd ever done."

She was, indeed, brave in not graduating, and in defying our father, who was horrified that the first of his children to get into college was now dropping out. I remember that even I thought that what she was doing was extreme.

But as for arriving in Manhattan with just $35 and ending up in Times Square because she didn't have anywhere else to go—that's pure mythology. First of all, she was a middle-class girl with plenty of contacts in Manhattan—other dancers, other instructors—and far from being this lost, friendless little waif who didn't even have a crust of dry bread to eat, she had money in her pocket and a support system all in place.

She may have spent a night sleeping at the Music Building, but that was likely because she was hoping a producer or musician might come by and discover her. Mythology. The further she got into it, the more mythological the story of her first trip to Manhattan became. Shades of Anaïs Nin—the author who was also mistress of embellishing her own biography.

I know, though, that even with far more than $35 in her pocket, and a group of friends, those first few months after moving to the Big Apple couldn't have been altogether easy for Madonna. First, she studied with choreographer Pearl Lang, made a few bucks from posing nude for art students, and spent a few months in Paris as the protégé of two French music producers who wanted to groom her as the latest sensation *américaine.* Afterward, she tells me that she was sick almost all the time she was in Paris—a throat infection—not unrelated, she confesses, to how much she hated being there.

MEANWHILE, I AM safely, if not unhappily, tucked away in my second year of college in Rochester, Michigan. When one of my college buddies invites me to spend part of the summer at her parents' home in Darien, Connecticut, I call Madonna and ask her if I can visit her in Manhattan. She says yes. Moreover, she will take us out to dinner when we get there.

By the time we get to town, en route to Connecticut, Madonna is living in Corona, Queens, in a synagogue that has been converted into a studio, and playing drums in her boyfriend Dan Gilroy's band, the Breakfast Club.

So my friend and I arrive at the airport, rent a car, and drive out to Fifty-third Avenue in Queens, right by the World's Fair grounds, and end up at the synagogue, a big, wide-open space, still with religious carvings on the walls, but with clothes and instruments thrown all over the place. The whole thing seems a bit sacrilegious to me.

But at least my sister seems pleased to see me.

She immediately tells me how great the band is, how big they are going to get, and orders them to play a song for me. She's at the back of the band, playing the drums, but is still drawing all the attention. I feel compelled to look at her, not at the person fronting the band. That's just the way it always is with Madonna.

At the same time, I can't help wondering what has happened to the serious college student, the dedicated modern dancer who dreamed of one day opening her own dance studio. Although she tells me she still takes an occasional dance class, Madonna the modern dancer has clearly gone the way of Madonna the cheerleader, the all-American girl, and Madonna the nascent prima ballerina and besotted disciple of Christopher Flynn.

Now she's morphed into a female, punk Ringo Starr in ripped jeans, a white T-shirt, black fishnets, and her hair pulled back in a ponytail. It seems to me she is just goofing off, with no direction anymore. I am somewhat bemused and rather disappointed, but yet again admire her breathtakingly stubborn sense of self-confidence.

Later in the evening, a stretch limo pulls up outside the studio. Madonna tells us she's taking us to dinner at Patrissy's, a music-business hangout on Kenmare Street in Little Italy. I think to myself how weird it is that she's living like a starving artist, but has suddenly got a limo at her disposal. I remember thinking, or her telling me, that it belonged to some guy she met in Paris, set on wooing her. I am puzzled, but impressed.

However, I am distracted from the studio, and even my sister when we drive over the Fifty-ninth Street Bridge, which seems to me to be spangled with stars, and for the first time in my life I see the lights of Manhattan glittering in front of me. I am engulfed by a sense of wonder. I'm not yet in love with the city, but I'm definitely in lust.

After a brief weekend in the white wilderness of Darien, Connecticut, I go back to Oakland University. To support myself, I work the entire summer, first as a janitor in a retirement home, then in a local hospital's kitchen, which I enjoy.

At college, I devote myself to dance, and by the second semester of my second year in college I'm the lead male dancer in the college company. I am now twenty, and for the first time ever, my father and Joan are coming to see me dance onstage, in *Rodeo,* an Agnes de Mille ballet.

I have never been onstage performing for an audience before, so I'm naturally nervous. I'm also terrified that my father will make the connection between my dancing and my being gay. Since our night at the Rubaiyat, Madonna and I haven't discussed my sexuality again, nor does anyone else know about it. My nerves take over to such a degree that backstage at the dress rehearsal, my mind on the upcoming opening-night ordeal, I trip and fall. I am rushed to the hospital, where an X-ray establishes that I've broken my big toe in two places, and two other toes as well.

I'm in terrible pain, but the next night, after my toes are taped together, accessing some hitherto recessive trouper gene that Madonna and I have inherited from some far-off, unknown ancestor with theatrical leanings, I vow that the show must go on. With that in mind, I go onstage and, with three broken toes, do twelve jetés, one after the other. Every second is agony, but I get through it with nary a whimper. During the intermission, although my father is far from happy that I'm becoming a dancer, he congratulates me and says that he is amazed that I was able to dance with three broken toes.

As the show carries on, the pain does become unbearable, but I endure it in my stoic way, unaware that my suffering will soon be assuaged, my stoicism rewarded with a dancer named Russell.

I've noticed him before, but nothing has happened between us.

Tonight, though, with my mutilated toes, I'm the hero of the hour. And as Russell and I undress in the locker room, primed to take a shower, he stops suddenly and kisses me.

Initially, I am stunned. Then I relax and linger in the moment. I am about to fall into Russell's arms when the locker room door opens. We quickly step back from each other, undiscovered.

Not long afterward, Russell invites me over to his house one night when his mother is asleep. We start watching TV together. His hand touches mine as he rolls on top of me.

"You want to put what where? Don't even think about it!" I say.

Shaken and dumbfounded, I jump up, put my clothes on again, and go home fervently wishing that I knew more about what to put where and when.

Time passes slowly as I discover my homosexuality and lose my virginity while in the backseat of Russell's gold Datsun. One night, at a drive-in movie, I am with Russell in the car, he presses a latch, the car seat flips down, and so do I.

Coincidentally, Madonna also lost her virginity with a guy named Russell—and in the backseat of a car, as well. Clearly, we don't share merely almost identical genes, but also similar fates. Trust her, though, to best me by having her first time in a Cadillac, not a Datsun.

I finally accept that I am gay and even grow to like the idea. But not so much that I want to broadcast it to anyone, not even to Madonna. So I keep my relationship with Russell a deep secret from everyone, especially my family.

A FEW WEEKS later, my parents are out for dinner. Russell and I go downstairs to my elder brother's old bedroom in the basement, figuring it's safe for us to fool around there. And infinitely more comfortable than the vinyl backseat of my Dodge Dart or Russell's Datsun. We take our clothes off and start making out. We are so foolishly oblivious that neither of us hears footsteps on the stairs.

Within seconds, my sister Melanie is standing there in the doorway, her mouth wide open, her face as white as the streak in her hair.

She runs up the stairs again.

I'm screwed in more ways than one.

Russell and I quickly get dressed. I ask him to stay in the basement.

I head up the stairs and come face-to-face with my brother Marty, the most macho Ciccone of all Ciccones.

He gets right in my face and yells, "What the fuck are you doing down here? Are you a fucking faggot? Are you?"

For a split second, I evaluate my alternatives. I decide to stand my ground, and prepare to take what's coming.

"Yes, I am a faggot, Marty." Then, with as much swagger as I have been able to muster before or since, I add, "So what are you going to do about it? Kick my ass?"

Marty takes a step back from me. "That's what I came down here to do."

There is a pause, during which I silently kiss what I consider to be my good looks good-bye.

"But I'm not going to," he finally says.

He marches back upstairs, and that is that.

Or so I believe.

CUT TO THE Ciccone Vineyard, Traverse City, Michigan. My father's seventy-fifth birthday party, two years ago. Marty approaches me while I am sitting on the veranda and says, "There is something I need to apologize for."

I immediately flash back to that night in our basement. "You don't really need to."

"I really do."

"Please, don't. It's cool, we're cool."

But Marty won't be diverted from his mission. "I'm really sorry for what I said, but I didn't like that you were gay, and I'm sorry for being such an asshole."

And that, as far as Marty is concerned, really is that.

By 1980, I make the radical decision that anthropology can wait. So can professional fencing. I decide to become a dancer instead. My father is not happy. He doesn't give me a hard time, though, because I know despite his protestations, he wants me to be happy.

So I move to downtown Detroit, work part-time in a sandwich bar, and take a job with Mari Windsor's Harbinger dance company.

Over the year I spend dancing with Harbinger, I get a deeper education in dance. I discover Alvin Ailey, Katherine Dunham, and new and inspiring styles of dance.

Madonna, however, is not impressed.

During one of our periodic phone calls she says, "If you really want to be a dancer, Christopher, you have to be in New York."

I know she's right, but don't know if I'm ready yet to take on the Big Apple.

Sensing that I am tempted, my siren of a sister says, "Come to New York, and you can stay with me in my apartment. I'll introduce you to people. I'll take classes with you. I'll get you into a company."

Within days, I pack everything I own into my big green duffel bag, and off I go to Emerald City, where I assume Glinda the Good Witch will be awaiting me with open arms.

As prearranged with Madonna, I fly to JFK and take a cab into the city. The driver drops me a few blocks from the address Madonna gave me, so I have to walk a bit. By now, it's late at night and I arrive at Madonna's apartment, in a prewar building on West Ninety-fourth and Riverside, my back aching from lugging the duffel bag. Nonetheless, overflowing with excitement and great expectations, I ring the bell.

The door opens, whereupon I am confronted by Madonna Part Four (Part One, the cheerleader; Part Two, the serious dancer; Part Three, the punk drummer), whom I hardly recognize. She is dressed in an odd-looking outfit: black crop top, short red plaid skirt, black panty hose, ankle boots, black leather studded bracelets, and a black rag knotted into her matted hair.

She takes a lipstick-stained cigarette out of her mouth.

Before I can exclaim, "But, Madonna, you've never smoked before!" in one breath she announces, "Hi, Christopher, you can't live here after all."

Straight and to the point, with no sugarcoating.

"What do you mean I can't live here? I just gave up my life in Detroit. My apartment, my job, everything."

Madonna shrugs. "Whatever . . ."

Seeing my crestfallen face, she relents slightly. "You can sleep on the floor for a couple of nights, but that's it."

I'm dumbstruck.

She reaches into her jeans and pulls out a tablet. "Here, try this. It'll make you feel better."

Feeling like a hick, I ask her what it is.

"Just take it," she says firmly.

I take it from her and later discover that it's ecstasy—or MDMA as it was called at that time.

I also note that, unlike the joint, at least this time, she hasn't charged me.

She beckons me to follow her into the apartment. With wood floors and crown molding, it's one of those prewar apartments with lots of bedrooms that are prevalent on the Upper West Side of Manhattan.

We enter an open foyer that leads into a large living room filled with broken furniture. To the right of us, a kitchen and another living room; to the left of us, a thirty-foot hallway. I am amazed at the size of the place. Walking through the cavernous apartment, I am surprised that my sister has said there is no space for me, but I don't voice my thoughts.

Madonna's bedroom is the third on the right. I later discover that she is only renting her bedroom from an unidentified landlord, and that the apartment isn't hers at all. The bedroom doesn't have any furniture in it, except a mattress with dirty pale blue sheets on it on the floor in the middle of the room. A sink is in one corner; a naked lightbulb swings from the ceiling. The only other light comes in through a window without shades or drapes, boasting a gloomy view of the brick wall opposite.

Piles of punk-style clothes are all over the floor. The cracked plaster walls are all white. There is no art, except for a tattered Sid Vicious poster taped to one of them.

Madonna gives me a faded old blanket and a pillow, leads me into the living room, then leaves me alone. I throw the blanket on the floor, and to my surprise, it moves. Literally. I pick it up again and realize that my sister's announcement has so dazed me that I haven't noticed that I have company, about 5 million cockroaches crawling all over the floor.

Right now, though, I am far too tired and dispirited to care. I put the blanket down again and try to sleep. Meanwhile, the cockroaches crawl all over me.

If the insects don't keep me awake, the various people arriving and departing throughout the night do. Madonna looks in on me, then promptly disappears. What am I doing here?

I am both shell-shocked and angry. My sister initially seemed to be looking out for me, inviting me to stay with her in Manhattan, but now clearly doesn't want me here at all. I simmer with hurt and rejection: Glinda the Good Witch suddenly seems more like Glinda the Bad.

Early the next morning, I knock on Madonna's bedroom door.

After a few minutes, she opens it, bleary-eyed.

"I can't stay here because of the bugs, Madonna. You gotta help me—I've got nowhere else to go."

She thinks for a second, then makes a call.

"Hi, Janice, my little brother Christopher needs a place to stay. Can he stay with you for a couple of weeks?"

I hold my breath while Madonna waits for an answer.

Then she adds, "No, he can't stay here, Janice. I thought he could, but the guy that owns the apartment found out and says he can't."

Now, at least, I know why she changed her mind.

And while I am still a little irritated that she couldn't be bothered to explain that to me in the first place, I am relieved that at least she isn't just throwing me out on the street. And living with Janice Galloway, a dancer from Michigan who went to college with Madonna, turns out to be fun. And I am happy that her one-bedroom, sixth-floor walk-up on First and Ninth is completely bug-free.

Together, Janice and I subsist on canned tuna and crackers. At night, dressed in our jazz pants and leg warmers, we hang out in the gay bar across the street and, during the day, race from audition to audition, surviving from hope to hope.

I live with Janice for about three months in her two-room apartment. Now and again, I hang out with Madonna, and we see Martha Graham's dance company together. Although Madonna has clearly jettisoned her dance career and is set on becoming a pop star, she still loves to see proper dance performances. I love spending time with her, but I am in survival mode, and landing a paying dancing job is all that matters to me.

Finally, to my relief, I am offered a job dancing with an Ottawa-based dance company, Le Groupe de La Place Royale. I call Madonna and give her the news.

"You really think you should take it?" she says. "I mean, it's not New York. It's not where you need to be if you want to be a dancer."

Imitating her blunt manner, which I'll eventually permanently make my own, I inform her that she has been less than helpful to me, that I don't have any money, and that the company has offered me $300 a week, twice what most New York dancers are earning.

She gives a small sigh, says, "Well, fine," and hangs up the phone.

Brother dismissed.

LIFE IN CANADA is quiet, cold, and regimented. Even being part of a dance company feels like a regular job. We take class and rehearse from nine to five, Monday through Friday. Not quite what I had envisioned, but I learn a lot and become a much better dancer.

When I go home to Michigan for vacations, Madonna isn't there, but the rest of my family seems stunned that I've become a dancer and am actually getting paid to do it.

I go on tour with the company to Europe—to Wales, to England, and to Italy—but however glamorous my life seems, I yearn for something more challenging. Naturally, when I hear the siren's call once more, this time luring me back to the Big Apple, I don't turn a deaf ear.

"Come back to Manhattan," Madonna says. "I've got a manager now. I've written a pop song. I've got a contract. I'm making a record: 'Everybody.' *And* I wrote it. Great, isn't it?"

"Great, Madonna, I know that's what you want and I'm glad for you." I try hard not to sound patronizing, but knowing that I'm probably failing.

"But I need backup dancers to go on track dates with me, so how about it?" she says quickly.

"Track dates?"

"Yeah, in clubs all around the city. Coupla hundred a time. They play my record, I sing to it, and we all—you, me, and another dancer—dance to it."

I hesitate for a fraction of a second, my first abortive trip to New York still fresh in my memory.

"And you can come live with me," she continues, as if she were reading my mind.

"I really can?"

"Definitely. You know you're the best, Chris. You know how great we dance together, how great we look together. And I need you."

My sister needs me.

I'm on the next plane.

THREE

Curiouser and curiouser!

Lewis Carroll, *Alice's Adventures in Wonderland*

MADONNA IS LIVING in a fifth-floor walk-up on East Fourth Street between Avenues A and B. Two small rooms, no furniture except a big white futon and a perpetually hissing radiator.

I'm hardly through the door when she plays me "Everybody."

It doesn't really grab me, but I want to be kind to her. Besides, I'm her new backup dancer.

"I like it," I say. "So when do I start?"

She rams a fistful of popcorn into her mouth.

I wait while she chews it.

She takes a sip of Evian.

"Well, Chris, I don't actually need you anymore."

My sister doesn't need me anymore.

I don't know whether to jump out the window myself or push her out instead.

"Are you fucking kidding me, Madonna?"

"Just filled your spot this morning, but if he doesn't work out . . ."

I feel as if she's kicked me in the stomach.

This time, at least, instead of telling me I can't stay, she says I can move in and live with her permanently.

The first thing I do is paint the rusting bathtub white. For the next five days, the fumes practically asphyxiate us.

I spend my days auditioning for dance companies while Madonna races frantically all over town in pursuit of further fame and fortune. Her efforts pay off. As a result of her recording contract—$15,000 to cut two singles, first "Everybody" and now "Burning Up"—her career is on the upswing and she isn't broke anymore. So after a few weeks, she moves to a loft on Broome Street, leaving me the East Fourth apartment to myself. We haven't had time to hang out much together, but now I have to figure out how I am going to pay the rent on East Fourth all on my own, which I can't afford. Luckily, Mark, an neighbor who lives downstairs and works in the shipping department at a company that manufactures greetings cards for the gay market—all featuring naked men—offers me a room in his apartment.

He rents me a room not much bigger than a bathroom and gets me a job at the greeting card company. But the job isn't in the least bit sexy or glamorous. All I do all day is count the cards: three, six, nine, twelve. Three, six, nine, twelve, and put them in boxes. By lunchtime, I'm dizzy with boredom. When I'm not working, I audition for dance companies but don't seem to get anywhere because the competition for the few spots is ferocious.

Meanwhile, perhaps feeling guilty because she has yet again abandoned me, or perhaps because she is aware that I have always loved art, Madonna invites me to come with her to see Jean-Michel Basquiat. She tells me she's hung out with him a couple of times, then throws me a triumphant look that insinuates she's also slept with him. As she intended, I'm impressed.

Basquiat is exactly a month older than me, and already a legend. He's Haitian, with a blond Mohawk and eyes wild from shooting too much heroin. First a graffiti artist, he started out painting T-shirts and postcards and sold them around the Village. Soon he was drawing violent, cartoonish pictures on lumber and foam rubber and selling them by the dozen for thousands of dollars. These days, he is represented by Mary Boone and has just had a sold-out show at the Fun Gallery that everyone in Manhattan can't stop talking about.

I think to myself how clever of my sister to hook up with Basquiat. He is off-the-wall, but he is hip and hot, and for Madonna that's all it takes. She is "in love" with the idea of this infamous artist. Moreover, he lives on the edge, which is honey to her. And above all, his artistic credibility lends her the street cred she craves.

So we go up to his massive loft on the Lower East Side, with canvases everywhere, clothes all over a dark room. In the dim lighting I can make out a sink filled with dirty dishes. The place smells of part linseed and part paint cleaner. In a second room, with the door open a crack, I can see Basquiat's shadow on the wall, painting.

Madonna yells, "Hey, I'm here."

He kind of mumbles hello, without turning to look at us, and keeps right on painting.

Madonna introduces me to him, he says hello to both of us. He and Madonna don't kiss or hug. He just goes on painting.

Madonna and I sidle back into the dingy kitchen. I can't help noticing a small heap of smack on the counter. I am about to say something, but she shakes her head.

"I never talk when he's working," she says.

That's a first! I think to myself.

After around half an hour of watching her watching Basquiat paint, I leave. Still, it's a step up from counting cards.

From then on, Madonna and I start hanging out more. Unlike many of my friends, she never drinks late into the night. In fact, she doesn't drink at all, except for the odd lemon drop—her favorite drink. And her relationship with Basquiat is short-lived because she loathes his drug habits and its attendant behaviors. Like me, Madonna abhors tardiness or unreliability. To this day, we are both punctual and endeavor always to keep our word.

Her charms must have worked their magic on Basquiat, though, as after their breakup he gives her two paintings, one of which—a small one—she still keeps on a little marble ledge in the bathroom of her New York apartment.

She is deep into the downtown scene, hustling "Everybody" all over town. "Everybody" was cowritten by Steve Bray, one of her boyfriends from Detroit. At Danceteria on Twenty-first Street, I meet Mark Kamins, the DJ who helped her land the record deal for "Everybody." She just marched into the club and gave it to him. And, hey, presto, he played it! That easy? I'm not so sure.

According to current club gossip swirling around the eighties' downtown club scene, the easiest way for an unknown female singer to get her record played is to have sex with the DJ. I have no reason to believe this is how Kamins operated, but I do know that Kamins not only plays Madonna's record; he also introduces her to Michael Rosenblatt, the A and R man at Sire Records. Rosenblatt immediately gives her tape to Sire Records' president, Seymour Stein, who likes it so much that he asks that Madonna be brought to see him at Lenox Hill Hospital, where he is being treated for a heart condition. When she arrives, he is in a hospital gown with a drip feed in his arm, but on the spot makes the decision to sign her.

Madonna flirted with Mark and Michael—the two men who were so instrumental in launching her career—which certainly wouldn't have hurt her prospects. In a similar way, she also flirted outrageously with self-avowed lesbian Camille Barbone, her first manager. I doubt that she and Camille had more than a business relationship, but true to Madonna's pattern, I am certain that she dangled just the right amount of sexy bait necessary to hook Camille. As Madonna herself has once confessed, she is a born flirt and automatically turns her flirtatious charms on anyone who crosses her path, particularly if he or she can help her career—which, of course, anyone with whom she flirts naturally ends up doing.

When Madonna is done with Camille and with Mark—like William T. Sherman blazing through Georgia—she's on to Jellybean Benitez, DJ at the Funhouse, one of Manhattan's first Latin hip-hop clubs and the perfect market for her music. After she sweet-talks Jellybean into playing her record, they begin dating. When I meet him, my first thought is *He's a bit short for you.* Again, not her type, but useful. Not for her mythology, like Basquiat—but because, like Mark, he plays her record regularly.

My sister's persistence pays off in spades. In November 1982 "Everybody" hits number one on the dance charts. I still think it's a silly song, but I'm surprised and happy for her.

That fall and into the spring of 1983, I see guys come and go, in and out of my sister's life. None of them linger. She is calling the shots. She isn't one for long, drawn-out hellos or good-byes. In that, I later learn, we differ.

Now VERY MUCH part of the downtown culture, Madonna inevitably becomes aware of Manhattan's hip S&M scene, as well. Its heterosexual heartbeat is the Hellfire Club, and its gay heartbeat the Mineshaft, which was immortalized in Al Pacino's movie *Cruising*.

One of her best buddies, Martin Burgoyne—a charismatic, tall, blond boy from Florida around my age who bartends at Lucky Strike, a small, dim bar on East Ninth Street—wears leather motorcycle boots, is pierced in a number of places, and displays a red handkerchief in his jeans pocket, indicating that he's into S&M. He openly plays on the dark side and likes it. Not my thing at all.

Perhaps due to her friendship with Marty, S&M becomes one of the leitmotifs of Madonna's career, but I don't believe she is into it personally. Nor do I want to have those kinds of images of my sister in my head, unless she is enacting them for publicity purposes—which I believe she always is. However, away from any sexual connotations or role-playing, in the boardroom, in the movie studio, and in most of her intimate relationships, including with me—even though she is far shorter than most dominatrixes—she milks the image for all it's worth. By assuming a *Venus in Furs* persona, composed of part Margaret Thatcher, part Amazonian warrior, part kitten with a whip, part Lola from *The Blue Angel*, she will in the future achieve her goal of coming out on top in all her business and personal dealings.

Marty introduces Madonna to photographer Edo Berteglio and his girlfriend, French jewelry designer Maripol, who designed those seminal colored rubber bracelets that everyone else in the Village is now wearing as well. However mainstream and oft-imitated her concepts would later become, Maripol's influence on Madonna's image can't be understated, as she is responsible for creating her punk-plus-lace look. She also is indirectly responsible for introducing me to the man who will become the first love of my life.

Maripol is art director at Fiorucci, the hip Italian sportswear retail store on East Fifty-ninth Street. In the early eighties, wearing Fiorucci jeans or T-shirts is the ultimate badge of supercool. The store has a café, a tattoo parlor, and quirky salespeople, such as performance artist Joey Arias, who channels Billie Holiday to perfection. Andy Warhol shops there; so do Basquiat and Keith Haring. Madonna and I and half of downtown Manhattan love hanging out at the Fiorucci cappuccino machine, star-spotting.

I am there when Andy meets Madonna. He is the same with her as he is with anyone about to come under the spotlight. He has his picture taken with her, and that's all.

Afterward, she says to me, "Andy's cool, but he's not much of a conversationalist, is he?"

I nod silently in agreement.

I'm in Manhattan for about two months when Maripol calls and tells me there is a vacancy at Fiorucci. One of the salesmen in corduroys, a guy I'll call Danny (not his real name), is going on vacation, and would I fill in? Anything is better than counting greeting cards, so I'm off to work at Fiorucci.

The day I arrive, Danny is leaving on a monthlong vacation. Before he leaves, I catch a glimpse of him in the manager's office. He's handsome, lean, three years older than me and a classic New Yorker who grew up in Queens, but doesn't drive and has never been out of the city.

The moment Danny arrives back from his vacation, I begin pursuing him with a drive to rival Madonna's in the days when she was determined to get her record played by Kamins and Benitez. After some mild stalking on my part, Danny capitulates and agrees to go on a date with me. We then begin a relationship.

However, it quickly becomes apparent that Danny can't take his hard liquor. He is a mean drunk, with violent tendencies.

A snapshot from the start of our relationship: We go to a Halloween costume party, me as Julius Caesar and Danny as a slave boy. Dire miscasting, or maybe just a tribute to my Italian heritage. Whatever the case, we party at a friend's loft. I start to feel sick. I tell Danny I'm leaving, go home alone, and pass out cold.

The next thing I know, there is an almighty crash and Danny hurtles right through our bedroom window, covered in blood, blind drunk, and yelling profanities. When he finally sobers up, he tells me he was downstairs, buzzing, but I hadn't answered, so he'd climbed up the fire escape, then deliberately smashed through the window.

Other times when he's drunk, he takes a swing at me out of the blue. I put a stop to it all one morning when we are walking through Washington Square Park and, with no provocation, he lifts his umbrella and is about to hit me. In the nick of time, I sidestep. I wrest the umbrella from Danny, then pick him up and throw him over a park bench.

I am bigger than him, and stronger, and I've proved it.

I tell him that he's attacked for the last time, and if he ever hits me again, I will hit him back.

He doesn't.

He gives up hard liquor, and our relationship improves dramatically. Two years after our first meeting, I move into his four-room railroad flat on Morton Street. There, we sleep in a single bed with three Siamese cats, Boy, Girl, and Anisette. Danny has painted all the floors and the walls white. An old oil painting of the Madonna and child hangs on one of them. There is no air-conditioning, and the bath is in the corridor. Some nights, I wake up and hear clattering in the kitchen and wonder why Danny is up so late doing the dishes. I go in to see how he's doing and discover that massive water bugs are marching all over the dishes. But I don't care. I'm happy with Danny and our existence of relative domestic bliss. And the cats quickly dispatch the water bugs.

Our lives fall into a pleasing routine of dinner parties, travel, and holidays with his family—as my family as yet knows nothing about him. I am now twenty-four years old, and for the first time in years I feel safe and secure.

In some ways, Danny is my Christopher Flynn, my mentor as well as my lover. And for the next eight years, we will live together in happiness, harmony, and monogamy.

When I first tell my sister about Danny, she isn't the least bit curious. She doesn't ask to meet him, nor does she want to know anything about him. My personal life is of little interest to her—that is, not unless it impacts her or can serve her career in some way, which, down the line, it will.

Her career is heating up and the world now seems to be revolving around her 24-7. "Burning Up/Physical Attraction" hits number three on the U.S. Hot Dance Music/Club Play Chart, and she releases her debut album, *Madonna.* She is still living on Broome Street, and no matter how much money she may now be making, she never mentions it. All I know is that she is well on her way to the top.

Not long after I first meet Danny, Madonna calls and tells me that the backup dancer who beat me to the job hasn't worked out and she wants me to start dancing with her after all. Without skipping a beat, I say I will.

When Danny finds out, he says I am spineless for jumping at the chance to dance with her given our history. I don't think I am. I know I am going on an adventure, and besides, at last I'm going to be dancing with my sister. Moreover, I owe her, because I love dancing, and if she hadn't taken me with her to Christopher Flynn that night, I would never have become a dancer in the first place. Not only that, she introduced me to modern dance, and, at the Rubaiyat, to myself.

So on most Fridays, Saturdays, and Sundays, we work together on track dates, each of which lasts just twenty-five minutes, and when our time is up, we leave the club as quickly as possible. Madonna earns around $1,000 a night, depending on the club. The other dancer, Erika Bell, and I each make $200 or so. Not bad. So we dance behind Madonna with a mix of jazz, modern, and pop dancing. Simple stuff. Martin Burgoyne is roped in as our road manager and promoter and travels to the shows with us.

Every night is the same. An hour before the show—though to call it a show is a bit of an exaggeration—we arrive at the club and go to the always-shabby dressing room. Sometimes there is no dressing room at all, just the club manager's office.

We wait around while Marty collects the cash. In the meantime, the three of us—Madonna, Erika, and I—go over the choreography of each song: "Holiday," "Burning Up," and "Physical Attraction." During those discussions, Madonna listens to me, listens to Erika, and we all work out the exact details of how we are going to choreograph each song in each venue. Generally, we end up doing the same steps every night. During those discussions, we are all equal. Madonna isn't bossy, though she obviously is the boss.

I've long since accepted that she's no longer Madonna the serious modern dancer. She is a pop star now and is well on her way to becoming rich and famous. I believe in her talent as a performance artist and wish she were still a modern dancer, but am forced to concede that, in contrast to being a dancer, being a pop singer is relatively effortless. After all, a modern dancer has to sweat and train and dance until she drops. Nowadays, on track dates all Madonna has to do is sing to the track and bounce around with Erika and me behind her. Not so much cost to her body or her soul, but the route to mass adoration. Her ambition is in high gear, and her life is clearly now about moving forward, about making another record, about becoming famous.

I don't look at her and think my sister is on the way to becoming a star. I am still a trifle disdainful of her switch from modern dance to pop, and it's difficult to envision stardom when you're all scrambling to change in a club manager's grimy office somewhere in East Flatbush.

Erika and I dance behind Madonna at Studio 54, the Roxy, Area, the Pyramid, Paradise Garage, and Roseland. We go down to Fort Lauderdale and perform at the Copa, where I am a bit embarrassed for my sister because disco diva Sylvester is in the audience and Madonna isn't very good that night. We play Uncle Sam's on Long Island, where the crowd just stands still and stares at us. I find the whole experience extremely curious but it puts Madonna in a bad mood. When we drive back in the dark blue Lincoln Town Car Martin has rented for the night, she starts bitching that it cost too much and he shouldn't waste money on expensive cars. But Martin holds his ground and counters that he would never have driven all that way in a minivan. She shuts up. I turn on the radio and we head back to Manhattan.

Most nights, though, we have a good time. After the show we all usually hang out and dance together. There is only one bad moment, a night at Roseland when Martin offers me some coke. My first line, and I hate it. Afterward, dancing onstage, I feel like a crazy person. I can't remember any of the steps, as I twirl around and around and feel awful for the next few hours. I realize I can't do drugs and dance.

"Holiday" has hit number one on the U.S. Hot Dance Music/ Club Play Chart. By now Madonna, Erika, Martin, and I are the coolest kids on the block, or so it seems to me. We get into all the clubs for free and rarely have to pay for drinks. Sometimes, I have the illusion that the four of us are all equal, but I know that isn't the truth. For as much as we may work out our moves together, the primary reason for our gigs is to propel Madonna's career to the next stage. Our track dates aren't about us all becoming famous together, or Madonna and me becoming closer as brother and sister, but about her and nothing else. It's fun, though, notwithstanding.

In May, when Madonna is performing "Holiday" at Studio 54, with Erika and me dancing behind her, she does finally meet Danny and is polite, but clearly indifferent to him. Through the years, she will treat him in much the same way as she always treats Joan—rarely mentioning his name, rarely addressing him directly, and rarely curious about our relationship. She acts as if he doesn't exist and is merely a figment of my imagination, rather than my life partner.

In July 1983, Madonna meets Freddy DeMann, Michael Jackson's manager, who, at the suggestion of Seymour Stein, the boss of Sire, her record label, signs her as his client. Erika, Marty, and I are on the way out, but we don't yet know it.

"Holiday" enters the Hot 100 U.S. singles chart, Madonna films a cameo appearance as a nightclub singer in the movie *Vision Quest*, and she's even photographed by Francesco Scavullo, who dubs her Baby Dietrich. There is no question that Marty, Erika, and I have become obsolete. But before we are completely dismissed, the three of us are dazzled and surprised when Freddy books us on a European tour with Madonna. I promptly quit Fiorucci, and together, Erika, Marty, Madonna, and I fly to London.

All of us, even Madonna, fly coach on Air India. We are in dance clothes—sweatpants, leg warmers, sweatshirts, and boots—and stretch in the aisles, like chorus-line gypsies.

We arrive at Heathrow Airport at eight in the morning. We didn't sleep on the plane, so we all feel like shit. London is cold and wet and gloomy. We all check into an inexpensive little hotel in Earls Court, grab some sleep, and then a car picks us up and takes us to the BBC Studios in White City. The next day, January 26, 1984, we are playing *Top of the Pops,* England's number one TV music show.

Once in the dressing room, we are told to wait. The four of us sit there, incredibly nervous. We assume that we'll be filmed in a club setting, but that turns out not to be true. We are led onto a soundstage, and the audience stands around, almost listless.

Madonna, made up with dark eye shadow, dark red lipstick, her hair frizzy, dressed in high-waisted black pants, leg warmers, and a multicolored shirt, her midriff bare, lip-synchs "Holiday" while Erika and I do our usual track-show moves in the background. We feel weird performing in front of an audience who are so uncool that afterward they hardly applaud at all.

We are relieved when the show is over. We go out for an Indian meal, the only edible food in London at the time, and talk about how bizarre the show was, how strange it is not performing live, not having a screaming audience cheering us on.

The next morning, Marty, always the first to know what's hot, drags us to Camden Market, a flea market in a seedy corner of London, with vendors selling everything from leather parkas to baby carriages. Very much London's version of the East Village.

Madonna and all of us buy jeans and shirts and hats. Madonna also buys a pair of plaid pants with little straps connecting the legs together—very punk.

There was no question, in those days, of Madonna being recognized or mobbed in the streets of London—probably the last time in her life when she won't be.

ON JANUARY 27, 1984, we travel up to Manchester by train and perform "Holiday" on *The Tube*, a TV show recorded at the Hacienda. Inside the club, light shows wobble and flicker on a screen. We know raves are sometimes held at the club and are surprised that the audience is so straight. They are all wearing regular clothes, khaki pants, very much like the Long Island crowd, and not hip at all.

Usually during "Holiday," the audience gets into the mood and starts dancing. But not this time. They just stand still and watch, faces impassive. Then, suddenly, they start booing and throwing things at us. I'm hit with a crumpled-up napkin, Madonna with a roll, Erika with something else. We're stunned. It's obvious that this isn't about our music, it's about us.

"Let's get the fuck out of here," Madonna yells, and with cash in hand, we bolt. On the train back to London, we bitch about England and the English. If I had told Madonna then that twenty years later she'd be married to an Englishman, and giving a passable imitation of Lady Marchmain from *Brideshead Revisited*, she would never have believed me and would probably have pissed herself laughing. She hated England that much.

WE TRAVEL BACK to London, then in the morning take the boat train to Paris. Paris, though, isn't much better for us than London. Madonna stays at the Meurice on the Rue de Rivoli. Marty, Erika, and I are stuck in some run-down hotel a few streets away until we complain to Madonna about our accommodations and she eventually relents, letting us stay at the Meurice after all.

We all wander around the city with Marty. He wants to go to Paris's red-light district, the Pigalle, and as always, we follow him there.

In the evening, we record the show in some illegal club in an old gymnasium with an empty swimming pool in the middle of it. We are made to stand on the bottom of the pool and perform, with everyone else standing above us and watching. We are basically performing to a wall, and it's ludicrous.

In the midst of the second song, someone shoots tear gas into the room. We run to the nearest exit, tears streaming down our faces. It's pandemonium, everyone running everywhere.

We spend the rest of the night trying to get the tear gas out of our eyes, complaining that we hate Paris as much as London. The trip gets even worse when we decide to go to Les Bains Douches, a club we've been told is hot, only to be stopped at the door and prevented from entering because the door people don't like the way we look.

The next morning, we fly back to America. I'm happy to be coming home, happy to be back at Morton Street, happy to be back with Danny. I've missed him.

AT THE BEGINNING of February, Madonna asks us to dance in her "Lucky Star" video, to be shot in L.A., and Erika and I fly there together. This is my first trip out there since I was a teenager. I have never seen so many palm trees, so much sun, and so many tanned and perfectly stretched faces in my life.

We shoot the video at the old Charlie Chaplin studio, which is pretty much the same as when it was originally built in the thirties.

I get paid just $200 for dancing in the "Lucky Star" video and don't get any royalties either. However, at the time, I am happy just to be a part of it. The camaraderie between Madonna, Erika, Martin, and me is enough for me. After we shoot the video, we all go to Studio One, above Rose Tattoo, and dance the night away.

But when we get back to New York, it's obvious that things have changed. Madonna has become more businesslike, her new manager, Freddy DeMann is now one of the most important people in her life, and track dates are no longer on the schedule.

Her first album, *Madonna,* is certified gold, and she's in the studio recording her second album, *Like a Virgin*. Soon after, she is signed to play the part of Susan in Susan Seidelman's low budget, $5 million movie, *Desperately Seeking Susan*. The movie is conceived of as a hip screwball comedy centering around a suburban housewife who becomes fascinated by a series of newspaper advertisements "Desperately Seeking Susan." Madonna will play the small supporting role of Susan, a role for which Melanie Griffith, Kelly McGillis, Ellen Barkin, and Jennifer Jason Leigh also test.

Initially, the movie is projected to be a star vehicle for Rosanna Arquette, but, of course, Madonna will walk off with the entire movie—primarily because she is playing herself in every single frame and, as always, plays it to perfection.

Along the way, Erika, Marty, and I are informed by one of Freddy's assistants that Madonna is dispensing with our services. Madonna, of course, assiduously avoids giving us the news herself. I feel a little betrayed. By now, I have cottoned on at last that if I want to continue working with my sister—and I do—I must be prepared for a modicum of betrayal on her part to be woven into the highly colored fabric of both our filial and professional relationships. For now, though, I reason that working with her has been like working on a movie. It feels as if you were a little family, but then filming ends, and the family splits up. I still feel slightly abandoned, another emotion I am starting to associate with my sister, but it isn't a big thing.

Besides, I am a little relieved. The act was getting boring—doing the same steps over and over—and the songs repetitious. I go back to work at Fiorucci. I work in jeans, and Danny in corduroys. I tell him I'm not dancing anymore and won't be away from him night after night. He is clearly delighted. Looking back, I see that warning bells should have rung regarding his possessiveness, but they didn't. Our relationship seems so perfect. I am too happy with him, and happy in particular that he's gone out and surprised me by buying me some paints.

I haven't painted since high school, but thanks to Danny, I start again and rediscover my love of painting. During this period in the West Village, the prewar tenement buildings are being remodeled—the wood-frame windows replaced with new aluminum ones. Piles of old windows are always on the street corners. Danny has collected some of them, and with his approval I use them as canvases. At this stage, following in my sister's footsteps, although not deliberately, I, too, go through a religious phase. I paint religious scenes on the windows. I have no idea whether I am a good painter, just that I am passionate about painting, about being creative.

Meanwhile, *Madonna* the album has sold 1 million copies and is certified platinum, and she follows up with *Like a Virgin*. Madonna has now far transcended the Manhattan downtown scene, and the entire country is starting to sit up and take notice of her. Half the world does, in fact, except, perhaps, me. Danny and I are building our life together, I am immersed in my painting, and I pay little attention to the public adulation Madonna is now receiving and its possible effect on my life. That changes one morning when

I drop into my local Korean vegetable store, run into a friend of mine, tell him I'm back working at Fiorucci, and there is a stunned silence.

"Why the hell are you working when your sister is so rich?" he asks.

I tell him that I am not sure what he means. He explains that she has a record deal and must be making mountains of cash. I tell him, "Just because I'm her brother doesn't mean I get a monthly allowance. I have to work just like everyone else!"

Until then, I haven't given Madonna's financial status any thought. To me, she isn't a big star, just my sister, and just a few months before I was doing track dates with her. I walk back to my little apartment (I haven't yet moved in with Danny) past drug dealers on one side of the street, and flaming garbage cans on the other, and don't give Madonna another thought.

FOUR MONTHS AFTER we get back from L.A., just when I am settling back into life at Fiorucci, she calls again and asks me to join her and Erika and Marty on another European trip, set up by Freddy. But this time, we are also going to Morocco. Of course, Danny doesn't want me to go, but I have an adventurous spirit and am loathe to contain it just to make my boyfriend happy, so in June 1984 I fly to France.

First we perform at a party in Paris for Fiorucci's founder. Then we fly to Munich and do a show there. Afterward, we go to the Hofbräu House and are amazed at how much food—meat and radishes and sauerkraut—is on offer. Then we take the overnight train to Bremen. We've never before been on a train like this—beautiful, with dark wood panels and comfortable beds with cool, starched yellow cotton sheets.

We all love the sheets so much that we pull them off the beds and wrap them round us as if they are togas or royal robes of some sort.

"Traveling on this train is like being in an old Marlene movie or in *The Lady Vanishes*," Madonna says.

"Hopefully you won't disappear tonight," I say, harking back to the plot of Hitchcock's movie.

"Well, if I do, I'm sure you'll come and find me."

"Damn right," I say.

As the train takes us through Germany, we all become giddy with a sense of adventure, the rush of our new experiences, and can't sleep. So we take the divider down between Madonna's compartment and Erika's and sit up all night long, talking. Erika and I understand that our euphoria is temporary, because although Madonna's career is escalating, ours with her is practically over. But for that night, at least, the three of us are caught up in the excitement swirling around her and the romance of roaring across Germany in this elegant train.

From Bremen, we fly back to Paris, and from there, to Marrakech, to make a video for a French TV show. The moment we land there, I feel as if we are on another planet. Being in Marrakech feels like taking a step back into the fifteenth century. Turbaned men ride camels through the city square where snake charmers charm, dervishes whirl, and not a woman is in sight.

Once out of the confines of the Club Med, where we are staying, I am immediately surrounded by young boys offering their services as guides through the souk (market)—a maze of tiny, winding alleys in which it is easy to lose your way. I hire one of the guides, tip him, and he not only leads me safely through the streets, but also keeps the other guides from bothering me. An efficient system.

Marty stays at the market on his own. A couple of hours later, he turns up at our hotel wearing just his boxers and brandishing a set of false teeth.

"Really cool," he says. "Traded them for my jeans."

In the morning, we pile into a bus for the four-hour drive to Ouarzazate in south-central Morocco, in the Saharan desert, where we'll be shooting the video. *Lawrence of Arabia* and, later, *Gladiator* were shot in Ouarzazate, but it seems to me a long way to go just to make a short video.

Freddy, who has gone ahead by plane, is meeting us there. By now, Madonna has acquired another traveling companion, a personal trainer. She is American, with short, curly hair and far too much energy, and she irritates all of us.

Once we leave Marrakech and drive toward the Atlas Mountains, the landscape changes dramatically. No trees, just bare mountains with tiny specks of sheep climbing around. After two hours, we realize we are hungry and ask the driver where we can stop and eat. The answer is nowhere. It's Ramadan and Muslims aren't permitted to eat or drink until sundown. We are about to protest when there is an almighty bang. The bus has broken down.

We are on a deserted mountain road. There are no cell phones, no restrooms. Our driver can't start the bus. He tries radioing for help, but discovers that we are out of range. So he gets out and starts messing with the engine. By now, it's one in the afternoon. We are all hot and sweaty, and it looks as if we're going to be stuck here for hours.

Madonna has a major meltdown. "We're in the middle of the fucking desert. Where the fuck is Freddy? What the fuck are we doing here? I can't believe he did this to me. I'm going to kill him. Christopher, do something!"

I ignore her because I know that if I don't, she'll start yelling at me as well. And if she does, I know it will be impossible for me to stop myself from cracking, "Wonder if Freddy ever sent Michael Jackson through the desert in a bus?"

More bitching and screaming. Her trainer, a touchy-feely girl, strokes her arm. "Stay cool, Madonna. Everything is going to be fine. Let's meditate," she croons.

Madonna slams her hand away. "Get the fuck away from me, it's too hot!"

Madonna may be big in the States and in Europe, but here in Africa she is a complete unknown. So to any outsiders, we are just a bedraggled little group of stranded American tourists, dumb enough to take a bus across the desert.

Finally a tiny, putt-putt three-wheel truck appears. We flag it down. Our driver talks to the truck driver and his friend, and although they speak little English, in a stroke of luck they are driving in the right direction. Money changes hands, and we all get into the truck and discover that it doesn't have any seats. Undeterred, we pile the luggage into the back, along with Marty, Erika, and the trainer. Madonna and I squeeze between the two men in front and sit on the floor with the hot, rusty, and dirty stick shift digging into us. It's now extremely hot and our drivers smell.

We drive for thirty minutes, and as the sun sets, we arrive at a little town just perched at the end of a hill. The town consists only of a café, a gas station, and two small houses. The truck grinds to a halt.

"What the fuck are you doing?" Madonna screeches.

The drivers ignore her. They just get out of the truck and go into the café. As an afterthought, they tell us, "At sunset, we eat."

We end up joining them in the café and have some soup, no doubt made out of one of the goats' heads hanging nearby. Madonna is so hungry that she jettisons her vegetarian principles and eats some goat soup as well. The drivers also just keep on eating. When they've finished, we all pile into the truck again and drive on.

It's nighttime and cold now. One of the drivers turns on the radio, and a pop song blares through the speakers.

He smiles at Madonna and says, "You heard of Michael Jackson?"

"Just shut the fuck up, shut the fuck up, shut the fuck up," she shrieks.

I put my hand over her mouth. "Madonna, just be quiet. We need them to drive us to our destination."

For once, she listens to me and shuts up.

We are out of the mountains now and in the heart of the desert. The sky is pitch-black and a multitude of stars twinkle brightly above us. Just as I begin to enjoy the journey, the truck stops dead.

Somehow, our drivers make us understand that they can't drive any farther, as their license doesn't allow them to drive into the next province. Luckily, a second truck pulls up, and the driver agrees to take us to Ouarzazate.

An hour later, we arrive at Club Med. Freddy is standing outside waiting for us.

Madonna flips out completely. "What the fuck do you think you're doing, Freddy? How can you do this to me? I'm not performing for any fucking French television, fuck this shit. I want to be on a plane right now. I want to go back to New York."

Freddy remains calm. "You're here now; just do the TV thing tomorrow. In any case, there aren't any planes flying out of here tonight."

Madonna stamps her feet. "I'm not doing it, I'm not doing it, and that's fucking that."

She goes on for a good three hours, while Freddy all but

turns cartwheels trying to persuade her to give in and do the show anyway.

During Madonna's tantrum, Erika, Marty, the trainer, and I just sit in the lobby, drinking bottled water. Erika, Marty, and the trainer all marvel at Madonna's high-decibel diva performance. I don't. I grew up with her. Finally, Freddy calms her down, and we all go to bed.

The French TV company is expecting us to film in the desert, but Madonna flatly refuses. Instead, she insists that we shoot here on the pool deck at Club Med. We could be absolutely anywhere on the entire planet.

Madonna declares, "I'm not talking to you, Freddy. I don't want to talk to you for the next five days," but we make the video anyway.

The following day, we get driven back to Marrakech in a broken-down station wagon, with no delays or mishaps. At the Club Med there, we each check into rooms that are sort of tucked in underneath one another. So even though you are in your own room, you are still sleeping above somebody in the room below you, and you can hear everything.

Later that night, everyone but Madonna and me is suffering aftereffects from the goat soup, and all we can hear is people moaning and then throwing up.

By the next morning, the charm of Morocco has worn off.

We fly back to Paris. As soon as we arrive back at the Meurice, Madonna and I get really sick. We drag ourselves to the airport, anxious to get home to America and recover there from our bizarre African adventure.

Back in the USA, Simon Fields, who produced the "Lucky Star" video, offers me a job as a production assistant in his company. I fly out to L.A., stay with Danny's brother, and work for Simon fifteen hours a day, leaving me little time for partying or for hanging out with my sister, whose career is going great guns.

I get my first taste of music videos from the production side. It is by far the worst job I have ever had. Up at dawn, in bed after midnight. Days filled with running errands, delivering props, cleaning up after people, and generally being everyone's gofer. I can't wait for the job to end. While I grow to like the medium, I vow that from now on I will either direct a video or have nothing else to do with it.

In September, I go back to Manhattan and—because I am still painting and interested in art—get a receptionist job at the Diane Brown Gallery in SoHo.

Madonna invites me to see her perform at the first annual *MTV Video Music Awards* at Radio City on September 14, 1984. She has been nominated for Best New Artist Video for "Borderline" and is also performing at the show.

I meet her at Maripol's loft. Maripol is styling and dressing her up as a kind of punk bride. When I arrive, she is fastening rubber bracelets to Madonna's wrists, helping her into white tights, a tight white bustier and skirt, and clasping her BOY TOY belt round her waist. I take one look at the result and—though I don't voice the sentiment—think she looks ridiculous but I know her fans will love the look.

Way in one corner of the loft, a woman with black hair and a leather cap covering her face is sitting on the floor, watching intently as my sister is getting dressed. The woman doesn't say a word, but just gazes at Madonna, transfixed. Finally, after Madonna's outfit is accessorized with a crucifix and a white tulle veil, the woman takes her eyes off Madonna and glances in my direction.

"Cher, meet my brother Christopher," Madonna says.

I smile and, for the first time, take a good look at the woman. It really is Cher. She seems lonely, and I think it strange that she is just sitting there staring at Madonna while she is getting dressed. I haven't got a clue why she's in the room, or how she and Madonna met, and whether or not they are friends, but Madonna is far too busy preparing for her upcoming performance for me to ask.

However, this moment marks the second of the intriguing encounters I have with celebrities I meet through my sister, or simply because I'm Madonna's brother. Basquiat is the first. Cher, the second. The rest, in no particular order, will include Demi Moore, Courtney Love, Lisa Marie Presley, Bruce Willis, Donatella Versace, Kate Moss, Dolly Parton, Johnny Depp, Liza Minnelli, the Spice Girls, Farrah Fawcett, Naomi Campbell, Jack Nicholson, Luciano Pavarotti, Denzel Washington, Mark Wahlberg, Warren Beatty, Sean Penn, Sting, Trudie Styler, Gwyneth Paltrow, and more.

Through all my encounters with celebrities I feel privileged to have access to so many people whom I admire. Often, I meet stars because I am Madonna's date at an event, but she rarely gives any of them more than a cursory glance. Most of the time, she is really bored and wants to leave as quickly as possible. And she is hardly ever impressed by meeting other famous people, so when we do, I make a point of keeping in contact with them on her behalf and because I want to.

That night at the MTV awards, my sister is the star, and after Bette Midler cattily introduces her as "the woman who pulled herself up by her bra straps," Madonna upstages Bette resoundingly.

The audience may be enthralled by Madonna, but I watch the

greenroom TV, see her pop out of a wedding cake, and squirm. As she rolls around the stage, the thought flashes across my mind as to what our father and Grandma Elsie must both be thinking as they see her act on TV. I wonder if my sister is at all troubled at the possibility of shocking or hurting them, but remembering her teen talent show, I doubt it. Nor will I ask her. Since the "Lucky Star" video, we have had little contact, and this evening is not exactly the right moment in which to start. Apart from working ceaselessly to become an even bigger star, she is about to fall in love deeply and, some say, for always.

On the L.A. set of the "Material Girl" video, as Madonna is sashaying down a staircase, decked out in a fuchsia satin replica of the Travilla gown Marilyn wore in *Gentlemen Prefer Blondes,* she comes face-to-face with hot actor Sean Penn.

He is twenty-four, she is twenty-six, their birthdays are just one day apart, and—for both of them—it is love at first sight. Afterward, she will claim that Sean reminds her of pictures she's seen of our father when he was young.

After the video shoot, Sean goes to a friend's house. The friend is reading from a book of quotations, turns to a page, and reads out the following random quote: "She had the innocence of a child and the wit of a man." As Sean later remembered it, "I looked at my friend and he just said, 'Go get her.' So I did."

On February 13, 1985, she and Sean go on their first date together. After that, for both of them, there is no question that they want to be together, for now and always.

THE *Like a Virgin* album sells 3.5 million copies in just twelve weeks, is the first solo album by a female artist ever to be certified for sales of 5 million copies, and knocks Bruce Springsteen off the top of the charts and stays there. And not long after, "Crazy for

You" will become America's number one single, as well. My sister is now a pop phenomenon. I think back to our games of Monopoly and conclude that she could now probably afford to buy Park Place for real.

Meanwhile, I am enjoying my job at the art gallery and am happy with my life in Manhattan with Danny.

That is, until my sister comes calling again.

"Come out to L.A., Chris. Come work, be my assistant. It'll be so cool. I'm going out on tour soon, and you can be my dresser."

Her dresser? "Why not dancer, Madonna?" I say, somewhat flummoxed.

"I can get a thousand dancers, but only one brother to dress me." Well, I may be gay, but taking on the role of dresser seems a step too far, and I tell her so.

"But, Chris, I don't want any fucking stranger seeing me naked. You're my brother. You're the only person I trust. I need you."

My big sister needs me.

The next morning, much to my boyfriend's dismay, I fly to L.A.

FOUR

For there is no friend like a sister in calm or stormy weather.

Christina Rossetti

Two months before the *Like a Virgin* tour begins, I move out to Los Angeles and stay with Madonna and Sean at his home on Carbon Mesa Road, Malibu—a single-level, white stucco Spanish hacienda with a tile roof, built in a dry, arid canyon.

The first thing I notice is that the entire property, small as it is, is fenced in by a big wall topped by metal spikes. As I approach the house via a center courtyard with a disused fountain in the middle. I see that the front door is open and walk in. The living room is furnished with clunky, hand-painted and hand-carved Mexican furniture. Nothing fancy, no particular style at all. Typical of the owner of the house, Sean Penn, my future brother-in-law, who is not into home interiors and wants you to know it. Madonna is at a meeting in Burbank, but Sean sets about making me feel comfortable.

First, a firm handshake. Definite, manly. Different from that of

Madonna's second husband, Guy Ritchie, whose handshake is a trifle unsure. Apart from that, husband number one and husband number two have one marked similarity—Guy and Sean are both middle-class boys from comfortable homes and yet are prone to present themselves as tough street kids. My sister, I believe, has always played the identical game. After all, she is a middle-class girl who propagates the myth that she landed in Times Square with just a pair of ballet shoes and $35. Perhaps this partially explains Madonna's attraction to both Sean and Guy. That and a mutual love of guns.

But unlike Guy in the future, Sean does his best to make me feel comfortable, to be brotherly. A beer? A pizza? A shot of tequila? I opt for the tequila, wanting then, and always, to be more one of the guys than I am. Not that Sean is homophobic. Or if he is, as an accomplished actor he disguises it masterfully.

He spends a great deal of time away from the house, and so does Madonna, so I am often left to my own resources. I'm not particularly comfortable at the house, where my room is Spartan in the extreme, with just a bed, a table lamp, no artwork, no drapes. Madonna doesn't seem particularly at home in the house either. She tells me that she feels isolated, and I don't blame her. She's a city girl, and being stuck out in Malibu—however beautiful the place may be—feels strange to her.

Sometimes we watch movies together, but rarely with Sean, who is usually off somewhere filming. If he is home, he and Madonna never have guests over to the house. From the first, I get the distinct impression that Sean is reclusive and feels happiest hiding out at home with Madonna alone. I stay out of their way as much as I can, except that now and again I cook dinner for her and Sean.

One night, soon after I arrive at the house, I roast a couple of chickens for us all. Halfway through the meal, Sean leans over to Madonna and takes a piece of chicken from her plate.

"Just stop that, Sean," she says, and slaps his hand.

Sean grins at her and takes another piece.

I am starting to deconstruct my sister's attraction to Sean. He is a dead ringer for our father as a young man, is middle-class like Madonna but with a street-kid persona, and presents himself as a bad boy and is a rebel—just like our brothers. Patently a recipe for disaster.

My job as Madonna's assistant is varied and far more interesting than working at Fiorucci. I return calls for her, keep her diary, make her appointments—some of which are with mogul David Geffen, who continually proposes that my sister marry him, whereupon she always refuses.

One of my regular tasks is feeding Hank. Half-Akita, half-wolf, Hank is a gift to Sean from Madonna. When I first arrive at the house, I am confident that feeding him will be easy. I've only heard his bark and haven't yet seen him. But I'm curious why he is always outside the house, in a fenced-off area behind a gate.

Sean quickly enlightens me.

He hands me a heavy black leather suit, a big coat and big gloves, along with a warning: unless I run to the gate and quickly slip Hank's bowl of raw meat through a crack, he'll probably bite me.

Bite me? I take one look at Hank, hurtling toward me like the hound of the Baskervilles on speed, and know that he'll definitely kill me. Easily, and with one chomp. He is massive. Fearsome. A wild animal, not remotely domesticated. But Sean adores him. And he makes no secret of just loving it that Hank scares the shit out of everyone who comes within a mile of him. If he didn't, Hank would long since have been put down.

Sean also loves his friend the writer Charles Bukowski, who lumbers into the house, day or night, blind drunk and puking. The moment he arrives, my sister escapes into the bedroom, disgusted. Strangely enough, Madonna and Bukowski are born on the same date—different years—and she usually admires good writers, but she loathes few things more than an undisciplined drunk. Or a gun collector. Perhaps she, too, has never forgotten Marty and Anthony menacing us with BB guns when we were kids.

As the son of director Leo Penn and his wife, actress Eileen Ryan, Sean is minor Hollywood royalty. Years later, he will reveal that both his parents drank heavily once the children were in bed at night, but never showed any evidence of drunkenness in the morning. In retrospect, I conclude that perhaps with Bukowski, who was almost forty years his senior, Sean was reliving some of the dynamics of his relationship with his father.

UNFORTUNATELY FOR SEAN, he is about to be confronted with a new and unfamiliar fact of life; since meeting Madonna just a few months before, her career has already made a quantum leap and her fame has increased by almost epic proportions. Madonna has been profiled in *Newsweek,* the single "Material Girl" has hit the U.S. charts at number two, and after *Desperately Seeking Susan* is released on March 29 and Madonna receives great acclaim for her performance—which I still can't help thinking is Madonna just being herself—her star is even further in the ascendant.

MY JOB AS dresser for *The Virgin Tour* begins. We rehearse for three weeks in L.A., and I get basic on-the-job training on how to be Madonna's dresser.

On the road, when we stay at hotels, my day begins when, first thing in the morning, I go to my sister's room, check her messages, order sourdough toast and coffee for her, and return her calls. Then I and the rest of the team—including her dancers and the band—go to either the current venue or the next. Madonna always travels first class. She is careful not to show favoritism toward me because I'm her brother. An irony, really, considering that she grew up our father's favorite and didn't protest, but perhaps she now believes that what was glorious for the goose is no longer fitting for the gander. So I fly coach with everyone else.

I arrive at the venue an hour before the show starts. In the dressing room, which on this tour is always in a small tent behind the stage, I inspect all the costumes and make sure that they are all on hand and in perfect condition. If an article of clothing has a hole in it or a hook missing, I quickly sew it up. As Madonna is extremely active onstage and always perspires a great deal, we tour with three versions of every outfit she wears onstage.

Hence we have fifteen pairs of fishnets, ten pairs of gloves, three painted jackets, and three versions of all the other costumes in the show. I make sure that her first outfit is laid out and waiting for her.

Blue lace bra, jean jacket, blue lace top, lace gloves, blue socks, leggings, blue jean skirt. Blue rag in her hair. Silver cross earring for her right ear, silver hearts earrings for her left, chain belt round her midriff. Two crosses around her neck, plus a gilt chain. Blue ankle boots.

I dress her before the show. When she is ready, she has her makeup done, and finally her hair. She will open the show with three songs. She sings the first two, "Dress You Up" and "Holiday," wearing the jean jacket. Then she'll peel it off to do the last one, "Everybody," in the lace top underneath. The rest of the outfit stays the same.

She will have a change of costume every two or three songs, and that change has to be completed in a minute and a half or less. To ensure that the changes happen like clockwork, I hang all the rest of her outfits on the clothes rack in the order she will wear them. I lay her shoes out on the floor and unroll the gloves she'll be wearing in the first change with the fingers folded back and turned inside out so she can just stick her hand through them quickly.

On April 10, 1985, opening night of *The Virgin Tour* with the first of three sold-out concerts at the Paramount Theater, Seattle, Washington, I'm probably even more nervous than my sister. We've rehearsed the timing of the changes over and over, but nothing can compare with the real thing—knowing that Madonna is about to come offstage and that I have to change her entire outfit in seconds.

After "Everybody," she hurtles backstage.

She is wet with sweat and is breathing heavily.

I wipe her down.

She stands still while I remove all her jewelry, then her top, her skirt, the rag out of her hair.

She pauses to take a swig of Evian, and because every second counts, I use the time to check that all the fringes in her next outfit are unknotted.

Then I help her into it: the black bra top, black fringed waistcoat and skirt, and finally the long black gloves.

"What the fuck, Christopher, you haven't pushed out the little finger! Fuck you, you piece of shit," she storms.

I stop dead, horrified.

"Hurry the fuck up, or I'll fucking fire you right now," she screams.

I open my mouth, then close it.

She's due back onstage again in fifty seconds.

I straighten the fringe of her skirt again.

She stamps her foot, wriggles, and one of the hooks holding her bra snaps off.

Rather than take the time to sew up her bra with a needle and thread, I grab a safety pin and pin her bra together—careful not to let her know I'm using one.

"Fuck you, Christopher, I can't fucking believe how slow you are," she screams.

Then she's back onstage, singing and dancing like there's no tomorrow.

While I am left in the tent, close to tears, thinking, *I can't do this job. I'm doing my best but all I get is screaming. I can't do this.*

I hear the applause of the crowd, the cheering, and know that she'll soon be backstage again, screaming and shouting at me. I feel like walking out of the theater and never coming back.

Then I switch from dresser mode to brother mode and realize I can't abandon my sister. I think of the crowds, the fame, and the pressure on Madonna. Thousands of people are out there watching her, the adrenaline is pumping, she's thinking of a hundred different things. Fifteen songs, fifteen dance routines, lyrics, steps, voice, movement, hair, makeup. And how everything—plus the ticket sales, the crew's salary, the audience getting their money's worth—depends on her.

And at that moment, I realize that Madonna really wasn't lying when she said she needed me, because she genuinely does. I am the one person she can rely on, the one person at whom—when the pressure becomes unbearable–she can vent, and the one person who will take it, because I'm her brother, and I feel for her.

I make up my mind there and then that I'll endure the abuse, endure the pressure, and that I won't walk out, because ultimately, in the midst of the show, in the heat of the moment, my sister is at her most vulnerable and I want to be there for her because I empathize. Besides, she's including me in her crazy, fabulous world, and I am relishing every moment.

Some of those positive emotions evaporate when Madonna storms offstage, screaming at me again because her bra's come undone. She rips it off, sees the safety pin, and goes ballistic.

I listen to the torrent of swearwords and, instead of shrinking, flash back to our father scrubbing our tongues with soap because we'd said one solitary F-word. Nowadays, he'd need a whole crateful of soap to scrub Madonna's tongue.

I laugh silently to myself and carry on dressing her. After that, during each show, I block out all the obscenities, all the ranting, and concentrate instead on the change, focus on the job at hand, and ignore whatever she is yelling, unless it has to do with the costumes. Other than that, I learn to make myself scarce and not to react, no matter what.

In a way, this tour is a learning experience for both of us. She has never been on tour before, and I have never been a dresser. That she asked me, who has no experience, to dress her on her first tour is a testament to the trust she now has in me.

I believe that even a dresser with experience would still have found dressing Madonna difficult on *The Virgin Tour.* Other dressers had worked with stars before, but at this point few stars had toured with shows having so many costume changes. And I doubt that the majority sweat so much.

Wiping sweat off Madonna's body—even, at times, off her

breasts—makes me incredibly uncomfortable. Nonetheless, during each and every change, I do just that because she needs me, and because that's part of my job.

After I wipe her body, then dress her, I make sure her hair is in position and her makeup in place, then I push her onstage. And when she comes offstage—in particular after the first set—I always tell her how terrific she was, how wonderful she looks, how much the audience loves her. And she goes back onstage again happy.

The moment the show is over, I bundle her in a towel and then into her car, and the car whisks her back to the hotel. I follow in the tour bus, along with the rest of the cast, who are all still dressed in their costumes.

Once we arrive at the hotel, I go from room to room and, in one of my least favorite parts of my dresser job, pick up all the costumes and take them to the dry cleaner's so they'll be ready for the next performance.

Then I go to my sister's room and we talk about the show and how it went. She tells me what she thinks went wrong, what she thinks went right, gives me notes for the dancers and singers—who screwed up, who didn't. If the show went well, she feels great. I reinforce that feeling. "Really great show, really great crowd, they were so happy to see you," I say, and she is elated.

Along the way, I am getting to know my sister and to love her. I feel protective of her because of the insanity of the world swirling around her, and I want to spare her some of it, if I can.

Witnessing the crowds, the people, the fame, I realize how crucial I now am to Madonna's sense of security, of safety. She is going places, and she needs someone to depend on. Right now, that person is me, and I'm happy to be there for her.

• • •

FROM THE MOMENT we arrive in Portland, Oregon, on April 15, it feels like one of the strangest cities I've ever visited. Outside the Arlene Schnitzer Concert Hall, religious fanatics are picketing the show, milling around with placards proclaiming that Madonna is Satan's spawn, and that she is going to hell.

My desire to protect my sister is intensified when, after we play Portland, Freddy, who doesn't say a word to Madonna about it, tells me that death threats have been directed at her. I freak out. From that moment on, I become hyperaware of what is going on around her, extremely protective, even paranoid. Those emotions will never leave me, and even today, when I see clips of Madonna surrounded by crowds of people, or playing in a massive stadium, I am afraid for her.

After the menacing insanity of Portland, I can hardly believe that we are only at the start of the tour. Madonna performs in San Diego, in Costa Mesa, and in San Francisco, then triumphs in three sold-out concerts at the Universal Amphitheater in Los Angeles, where we learn that *Like a Virgin* has been certified four times platinum.

Then we move on to Tempe, Dallas, Houston, Austin, New Orleans, Tampa, and Orlando, and on May 11—the same day that "Crazy for You" hits number one in the charts—we play Miami. Then we move on to Atlanta, Cleveland, Cincinnati, two sold-out concerts in Chicago, St. Paul–Minneapolis, Toronto, and finally—we end up in Detroit.

By then, in my mind the cities have all merged into one and are interchangeable. But the indisputable highlight of the entire *Virgin Tour* is playing Detroit. When the lights go up, Madonna yells, "There's no place like home." It's a great line, sentimental, humble, and it appeals to her number one fans.

The entire stadium bursts into cheers.

For a moment, she seems deeply moved.

"I never was elected homecoming queen. But I sure feel like one now," she says.

Then she bows her head, as if she really is overcome by tears. Maybe she is, maybe she isn't. Whatever the truth, this is obviously a moment of unrivaled triumph for her. Grandma Elsie is in the audience, and so are Christopher Flynn, Joan, my father, and all our brothers and sisters, aunts, uncles, and cousins. Watching them from backstage, I can see that they are all stunned, proud, and not a little bemused by what has become of the little girl they all thought they knew so well.

Madonna now has living proof that all her dreams have come true. She has made it, she is now a big star, and her life will never again be the same.

Yet amid all the triumph and the applause, the massive career leap she has made during *The Virgin Tour*, some self-doubts still surface.

After the show, in her room late at night, we are watching *Mildred Pierce* together. Suddenly, Madonna switches the TV off.

"Christopher, if Mom were alive, what do you think she would say about me, about the show?"

I hesitate for a second, then, because I won't involve my mother, even the memory of her, in any falsehoods, I tell the truth.

"I don't think she'd like you bouncing around the stage, the crosses, and the overt sexuality."

Madonna looks stricken.

"But I think she'd be very proud of you, anyway," I quickly add.

TWO DAYS LATER, on May 27, Madonna is on the cover of *Time*. "Madonna: Why She's Hot" analyzes her global appeal. The article also includes a long interview in which she rewrites her history and that of our family and sets it in stone.

These are some of her mythmaking phrases: "I was the oldest girl so I had a lot of adult responsibilities. I feel like all my adolescence was spent taking care of babies and changing diapers and babysitting. I have to say I resented it, because when all my friends were out playing, I felt like I had all these adult responsibilities. . . . I really saw myself as the quintessential Cinderella. You know, I have this stepmother and I have all this work to do and it's awful and I never go out and I don't have pretty dresses."

I know it makes a good story, and I applaud her imagination.

Of Marty and Anthony she claimed, "They would hang me on the clothesline by my underpants. I was little, and they put me up there with clothespins." A seeming impossibility, yet a story often repeated by the tabloids, and a testament to my sister's talent for evoking potent visual imagery.

Then there is the oft-repeated tale of her first visit to New York: "I got into a taxi and told the driver to take me to the middle of everything. That turned out to be Times Square. I think the driver was saying, like, 'Okay, I'll show her something.' I think he got a chuckle out of that."

Then: "I got a scholarship to the Alvin Ailey School."

Her mythmaking isn't outrageous, just interesting. And it would continue right through her career. Throughout all that time, our family listens to her reinventing history, but doesn't call her on it. Most of us are far too dazzled by her fame and all the attention it brings us and quite simply don't want to rock the boat.

AFTER THE EUPHORIA of Detroit, we play Pittsburgh, then Philadelphia, Hampton, Virginia, then Columbia, Maryland, followed by Worcester and New Haven, and finally end up where we both started on track dates together, New York. On June 6, 7, and 8, Madonna plays three sold-out concerts at Radio City, followed on June 10 and 11 by two final sold-out concerts at Madison Square Garden.

Among the celebrities at the show are Don Johnson, John F. Kennedy Jr.—then about to start his law studies—and graffiti artist Futura 2000. After the show, all three of them pay court to Madonna in her dressing room. Don Johnson moons around like a lovesick puppy, clutching a large bunch of long-stemmed roses, which seem to be wilting by the minute. John, more handsome than even in his pictures, hovers shyly by the dressing room door. Madonna doesn't even throw him or Don a glance and, instead, focuses on Futura and fondles his hand while they exchange whispers. I get the picture at once; my Machiavellian sister isn't interested in Don, but is set on arousing John's jealousy. Her tactics appear to succeed, as down the line she will have her way with him.

After the last Madison Square Garden concert, a homecoming party is held for Madonna at the Palladium, where she is mobbed. We spend most of the evening behind the velvet rope in the Mike Todd VIP room, reminiscing about the tour and laughing and dancing. I remember feeling a rush of power by association. I am Madonna's brother. The brother of a superstar. I am so caught up in the magic of my brave new Madonna world that I don't care that I am losing myself, and that working with my sister is now my entire life.

None of my friends or family know that I am Madonna's dresser. Most of them assume that I'm just her companion. I never tell them that I actually spend much of my time picking up her sweaty underwear. It's my job, but I continue to be embarrassed by it and would be humiliated if anyone in my life knew.

• • •

I'VE LEARNED A great deal about Madonna and about myself during the tour, and she's made a crucial discovery about herself: by the third song of the show, she is usually already out of breath and exhausted.

Consequently, she decides to train for five months before each subsequent tour. I am convinced that she will tour again as soon as possible. I can tell that onstage is where she is happiest and most secure. A few years later, Warren Beatty will claim that Madonna "doesn't want to *live* off-camera." But for once, he is wrong. For as early on as *The Virgin Tour*, I know that my sister really only wants to live—and only lives—when she is onstage.

After the euphoria of the tour, I go home to Morton Street and land in reality with a thud. I find adapting to everyday life extremely difficult. And it will become more and more difficult after every tour.

I still have to grapple with Danny's jealousy of Madonna, and that he thinks my job as dresser is demeaning. But I don't care. Although on June 24, Madonna and Sean announce their engagement, she and I are getting closer and closer. Moreover, as a result of my work on the tour, she is starting to let me into her life to a much greater extent, and to trust my creative input.

Many years later, she will pay me a backhanded compliment during an interview published in the pages of *Elle Decor*: "It doesn't surprise me in the least that Christopher is good at so many endeavors. Everyone in our family was creative in some way—we all could either dance or paint or play a musical instrument. Christopher, for some reason, could do all three."

SECURE IN MY role as my sister's renaissance man—a jack-of-all-artistic-trades—one morning, soon after the end of the tour, I glance at Madonna in her miniskirt and rubber bracelets and start thinking like her dresser again. But I talk to her like a brother, without fear of being fired.

"Your legs look like fat sausages in that skirt," I tell her. "You're grown-up now; you need a cooler image, more classic, more Katharine Hepburn than Boy Toy."

For a second, I think she is going to slug me.

She thinks about it, then smiles ruefully. "I guess you're right, Christopher. So let's go shop."

I take her to my favorite store, Matsuda, on Madison Avenue near Seventy-second Street.

I pick out a cream silk, man-tailored shirt, grayish brown summer-weight trousers, and brown wing-tip-style shoes. Madonna Part Five is born: a grown-up, elegant woman with style.

Unfortunately for Madonna, her new sophisticated image is destined to be seriously undermined when, in July 1985, nude pictures of her are published in *Playboy.*

At 6 a.m. on July 10, 5 million copies of *Playboy*—containing fourteen pages of black-and-white nude pictures of Madonna—hit the newsstands. The pictures were shot in 1979 and 1980 by two New York photographers, Lee Friedlander and Martin Schreiber, apparently when Madonna posed for photographs in the "Nude" course at the New School. A few days later, not to be outdone, *Penthouse* also hits the stands with a seventeen-page color and black-and-white spread of pictures taken by another photographer, Bill Stone.

The camera has always been Madonna's major ally, and one of her greatest passions. She loves the camera unreservedly, and the camera loves her back. After all, the camera is responsible for capturing and disseminating the multitude of visual images that contribute to her megawatt allure. Until now—apart from paparazzi shots—she has always exercised a ruthless control over the majority of images taken of her. Now, for the first time in her career, she has lost grip, and the media is now flooded with pictures whose rights she doesn't control, and from which she will not profit.

I first hear about the photographs while I am working for Madonna's publicist, Liz Rosenberg, a voluptuous, blue-eyed blonde who is still employed by Madonna today—the only employee in her life, apart from Donna De Lory, who can boast such longevity.

After *The Virgin Tour*—perhaps as a result of my insider status and the trust she now has in me—Madonna has found me a job with Liz, at Warner Records, in Rockefeller Center.

On this morning, I come into work bright and early to find Liz sitting at her desk, feet encased in pink rabbit slippers, just about to pick up her phone, which is in the shape of a large pair of red lips. Liz has a thing for lips. Even her sofa is in the shape of lips—Mae West's by Dalí. Liz's own lips are plump and luscious. She wears red lipstick and generally leaves a perfect bow-shaped stain on the marijuana cigarette she's been known to smoke at four in the afternoon—a brief respite before she resumes work unimpaired. I'm amazed by her ability to do this.

This morning, though, Liz is far from laid-back. In her birdlike voice, she breaks the news to me: "Some magazines have come out with nude pictures of your sister. Don't go and buy them, because we don't want the photographers or the magazines to make any money from us."

"Does my father know?" I ask.

"I haven't told him yet."

I note the use of the word *I*.

Madonna hasn't warned me about the pictures. Clearly she doesn't intend to tell our father herself either, preferring that Liz do the dirty work for her. I blanch at the thought of our straitlaced father arriving at work aware that all his coworkers have probably seen his daughter naked. As for my grandmother, I can't bear to contemplate her reaction. Later, I will find out that when she learned the news, she started crying.

I can't fault Madonna for having posed for the photographs, though. After all, many dancers sit for art classes. For a time, I even considered it myself. After all, if you are a starving dancer, making $10 an hour for taking off your clothes seems like a miracle. There was nothing sleazy about the circumstances under which Madonna posed for the nude photographs, but I am still troubled that she didn't call any of her family, didn't feel the need to warn me or express concern about how our father or our grandmother would feel when they found out. I begin to realize that my sister doesn't seem to care how her behavior or career impacts her family.

Liz's phone never stops ringing, and she fields the calls with the combination of elegance and intelligence that is her hallmark. As for me, I call Danny, and we decide that we ought to take a look at the pictures. After all, the entire country is now obsessed by them.

So on the way home from work, I stop off at the little cigar store on the corner of Christopher Street and Sheridan Square. When I see the *Playboy* masthead, for a second I flip back to my childhood, the tree house, and all my friends gawking over the center spread, which my sister now occupies for other snot-nosed teenagers to pore over her naked body.

I don't open the magazines until I get home, and then Danny and I look through them.

The image of my sister, the serious dancer newly arrived in Manhattan, leaps from the page, not the pop star. For a moment, I am transported back into the past.

My first thought is that the pictures are lackluster and utterly devoid of any artistic merit.

My second thought is that this is the first time I have seen my sister completely naked. In the dressing room, she always kept her thong on. When we were growing up together, or living together as adults, she never walked around stark naked in front of me, nor did she ever sunbathe topless in front of me. In fact, in close quarters, she has always been relatively modest. Aside from her embarrassment at being naked in the dressing room in front of a stranger, at this stage in her career, she hasn't exposed much skin onstage either.

My third thought is that she used to be extremely skinny.

My fourth is that she had a great deal of body hair.

I say as much to Madonna when we finally talk about the pictures.

"Well, I wasn't shaving at that time," she says, laughing.

I laugh, too.

But, although we quickly change the subject, I can sense that she has been deeply embarrassed by the pictures, but is taking great pains to mask her feelings from me.

Nor will she ever utter the thought that I know must be plaguing her: how would our religious mother feel if she could see the pictures?

And although I don't voice the sentiment to her, I am acutely aware that—in the eyes of the world—my sister will now no longer have any mystery about her. And any innocence she may once have had is now gone. She has nothing to lose anymore, nothing more to hide. After all, her privacy has unalterably been invaded. From now on, she will forever invade it herself. From now on, she is free to be as outrageous as she wants. And she will be.

As always, Liz helps Madonna weather the PR storm engulfing her, and when it has subsided, Madonna emerges a bigger star than ever. So-called Madonna experts often claim that my sister is obsessed by Marilyn Monroe and that she modeled herself and her career on Monroe's. They are wrong. Although the release of Madonna's nude pictures may have had the same effect on her career that the publication of Marilyn's nude calendar did on hers, apart from in "The Material Girl" video, Madonna has never identified with Marilyn or modeled herself or her career on Marilyn's. And she has never been remotely self-destructive, which is probably why Madonna has been a star for a quarter of a century and—unlike Elvis and other superstars—didn't die young either.

Part of the reason for Madonna's enduring success, I believe, is Liz Rosenberg. In many ways, Liz, who is ten years older than Madonna, has always been somewhat of a mother figure to her. Liz has sometimes been mistaken for Madonna's mother, and Madonna has once or twice even called her "Mom."

From the start, Liz knows exactly how to treat Madonna: exactly as you'd treat a big baby, saying yes to every little whim, yes to everything, yet at the same time gently guiding her in the proper direction.

In some ways, she has always treated Madonna as her daughter and considered her to be part of her family. And she has been incredibly stoic in the face of Madonna's sometimes unkind treatment of her—sometimes ignoring Liz, other times acting as if Liz hasn't played a part in her success.

After witnessing Madonna doing the same thing over the years to countless other people, me included, I've realized that she doesn't do so out of malice but because, over the years, surrounded by sycophants who always agree with her, she does truly believe she's entirely her own creation, and that, in the manner of King Louis

XIV, who pronounced "*L'état c'est moi,*" she has become a superstar all on her own.

Whether Madonna is prepared to admit it or not, one of the other people most responsible for her success—apart from Liz and Freddy—is Sire Records supremo Seymour Stein.

In fact, while I am working for Liz, a job as his personal assistant comes up, and I interview with him. But just before the interview in his office is scheduled to take place, Seymour switches it to his home.

And while I love his apartment on Central Park West, his collection of jukeboxes, and his American art deco furniture, when he opens the door to his apartment dressed in only a bathrobe, I am utterly unnerved.

He was once married to Linda Stein—the celebrated realtor who was tragically murdered in late 2007. That day in 1985, his first words to me are "Come on, let's talk in my bedroom." This makes me uncomfortable, so I make my apologies and leave. Although I don't get the job, I retain my professional respect for Seymour, as, after all, he had the vision to sign Madonna to a record contract in the first place.

On July 13, 1985, Madonna and I drive to Philadelphia together, and I watch her perform in front of a live audience of ninety thousand, and a global television audience of millions more, at Live Aid. She believes in the cause so much, and I know she desperately wants to take part today. As a nod to the nude-picture controversy, she performs wearing a brocade overcoat. As she struts her stuff, it occurs to me that my sister is now more famous than practically any of the other performers at Live Aid.

But although I hate even admitting it to myself, while no other star is now so world famous, her performance is outshone by the performances of many of the huge stars there. After the show, we drive straight back to Manhattan because she doesn't want to hang out with any of the other stars. During the journey home, we discuss them. I, of course, tell her she was the best, and she probably believes me.

As her publicity machine grinds on, her phenomenal success continues to escalate. *Like a Virgin* is certified for sales of 5 million copies, the first album by a female artist to be so, "Angel/Into the Groove" goes gold, and I fly back to L.A. to stay with Madonna and Sean at their home on Carbon Mesa.

With his wedding to my sister on the horizon, Sean decides that now is the perfect time for us to undergo some hard-core manly bonding.

We are alone in his Mexican-tiled kitchen.

He's wearing blue jeans and a white T-shirt. I'm in a black T-shirt and jeans.

He pulls out a jackknife. "Christopher, let's be blood brothers."

I'm shocked, but fight not to show it. "Be what?" I ask as nonchalantly as possible.

"Blood brothers."

"Oh, sure."

He and the jackknife are now menacingly close to me.

"Show me your thumb," he says, his tough-guy growl even more exaggerated than usual.

I'm left-handed so I hold out my right thumb. Well, I suppose I don't really need it that much. . . .

Sean grabs my wrist with one hand and slices the middle of my thumb with the other. Blood drips out.

I wince, but not much because I don't want Sean to think I'm a pussy.

Then he slices his own thumb.

He presses his thumb against mine and—for a couple of seconds—I return the pressure.

"Now we are blood brothers," he says, and slaps me on the back.

Then he goes off to find Charles Bukowski, who has just finished throwing up in the bathroom.

AFTERWARD, I FEEL good about myself. I've passed my initiation test. I didn't chicken out. I'm one of the guys at last. And Sean and I are now well and truly brothers.

I never tell my sister what we did, though, and I'm guessing that Sean doesn't either. We both know that if we did, she'd laugh like crazy. She just wouldn't understand. After all, this is man stuff.

Six years later and I'm at a party at the old Argyle Hotel on Sunset. Sean and Madonna are now divorced. He's with Robin Wright now, and after his courageous public admission that he was blind drunk through most of the making of *Shanghai Surprise,* I've almost forgiven him for the way he treated my sister. I've also grown to admire his acting immensely. This is the first time I've seen him since the divorce, and I'm glad to see him.

So when he walks over to me, we start chatting.

"How's Madonna?" he asks.

For a second, I consider telling him that she's still in love with him, which I think she is. But I don't and instead say that she's fine.

"Tell her I said hello." There is an awkward silence while Sean shifts his weight from one foot to the other. "Christopher, do you remember that night when we became blood brothers?"

"Sure. How could I ever forget?"

Sean takes a deep breath. "You don't have AIDS, do you?"

I give him an unprintable answer, then walk away.

ON AUGUST 16, 1985, in an open-air ceremony on Wildlife Road, just up the Pacific Coast Highway at the $6.5 million home of developer Kurt Unger, Madonna marries Sean. The invitation reads, "The need for privacy and a desire to keep you hanging, prevents the Los Angeles location from being announced until one day prior." I am living back in New York with Danny again, but fly out to L.A. and meet my grandmother and family at the Shangri-La, the thirties art deco hotel in Santa Monica where they are all staying.

As a wedding present, I give Sean and Madonna a glass window on which I've painted two vines growing together. They both say they like it, but end up not displaying it in their home. Later that year, I will retrieve it from its dark closet and take it back to my apartment.

The following day, Grandma Elsie and my sisters and I all ride in a car to Malibu. Beforehand, we are told that picture taking is banned. Given the ban on photography, I am surprised that the wedding that has launched every paparazzo in the universe on a do-or-die quest to snatch a picture of it isn't taking place indoors. Consequently, to me at least, what happens next is highly predictable.

Helicopters carrying journalists and photographers from tabloids with unlimited budgets hover above the house, taking pictures. Sean growls at the sky above, turns to the guests, and snarls, "Welcome to the remaking of *Apocalypse Now*!" As Madonna later puts it, "I didn't think I was going to be married with thirteen helicopters flying over my head. It turned into a circus. At first I was outraged and then I was laughing. You couldn't have written it in a movie. No one would have believed it. It was like a Busby Berkeley musical. Or something that someone would stage to generate a lot of publicity." For once, that somebody was not my sister. The wedding venue was Sean's decision and his alone.

I know that at this stage in her career, Madonna would never have selected such a remote location for her wedding where photographers could only snatch aerial views of her looking so beautiful on her wedding day. She would have preferred to pose for them. Stunning in a $10,000 strapless gown, with a ten-foot train, and a silver sash with a pinkish tone, embroidered with jewels, designed by Marlene Stewart, *The Virgin Tour* designer, Madonna has, of course, opted to wear white. Lest she be lambasted for being conventional, under her wedding veil she wears a black bowler hat. Sean wears a double-breasted, $695 Versace suit, and, as a nod to nonconformity, leaves the knot of his tie loose.

The ceremony is conducted by Malibu judge John Merrick and takes five minutes. I am sure the words are moving, but we can't hear a single word of the vows because we are deafened by the racket of the helicopters above us. Madonna and Sean exchange gold rings. Then, to the tune of the rousing theme to *Chariots of Fire*, which I can just about hear above the din, Sean kisses her and we all applaud.

Sean makes a toast to Madonna, but we can't hear it. Then he ducks under her skirt and removes her garter. At one point Madonna looks up at the helicopters and flips them the bird, but I know she doesn't really give a fuck. Fed up, Sean charges straight into the house and gets a .45.

Madonna shouts after him, "What's the big deal, Sean! Leave it be! Otherwise, they'll just get pictures of you with a gun. And they aren't going to go away."

She's having a good time. But Sean, still in character, remains in a rage and starts firing shots in the air, while Andy Warhol, Steve Rubell, Cher (in a purple spiked wig), the rest of my family, and I watch, kind of amazed.

Fortunately, Sean is distracted by the announcement that dinner is served, and we all file into an open-air tent on the front lawn. Once inside, we are still deafened by the noise of the circling helicopters, but manage to enjoy Wolfgang Puck's menu of caviar, curried oysters, lobster ravioli, broiled swordfish, and rack of lamb, followed by a five-tier hazelnut wedding cake.

However, my abiding memory of the dinner will always be the image of the helicopters circling above us like ravenous vultures. I know that Madonna ultimately got a kick out of the entire media invasion of her wedding. As always, Madonna more than welcomed any media attention whatsoever. After all, media attention is her middle name. And part of the reason she's a star and has stayed a star is because she's always known how to work the media. Sean, of course, doesn't. In fact, the wedding day sets the tone for the entire marriage: Sean running around with a gun, and Madonna smiling radiantly at the cameras.

FIVE

Brothers and sisters are closer than hands and feet.

Vietnamese proverb

In the five months since Sean and Madonna first met, her career has rocketed from triumph to triumph, scandal to scandal, and I sometimes feel sorry for Sean, who, despite his professed horror for the media, still wants to be a star in his own right. Yet the Madonna juggernaut hurtles on, sometimes with him, sometimes without. As soon as he has weathered the nude-photographs scandal, less than three weeks later Madonna loses a court battle to suppress the release of *A Certain Sacrifice,* a low-budget, one-hour soft-core porn movie made by Stephen Lewicki, which she made in 1979 during her early years in Manhattan.

I am about to call her and sympathize, but then I take another look at the gigantic headline on the front page of the *New York Post,* "Madonna Seeks Nude Movie Ban," and decide that she is probably pleased at all the publicity her suit against Lewicki will engender, and that she may well be suing him just because—with her sixth sense for what the press loves—she knew it would do just that.

In the movie, Madonna is clothed except in one scene, in which she appears topless. But the content is racy. Madonna plays the part of Bruna, a downtown dominatrix who has a stable of sex slaves, and the film also features a rape scene. I'm not in the least bit shocked that Madonna took the part because I understand that she was young then, experimenting with life and doing her utmost to survive in the city. But I know that Grandma Elsie and my father will be horrified by Madonna making such a trashy movie and will wish it had never been publicized. I also feel for Sean. However, none of us ever discuss the movie, which is released later in the year, nor do I ever want to see it.

The fiasco of the wedding behind us, as well as my blood-brother initiation, I decide I really like Sean Penn, my new brother-in-law.

On November 9, 1985, Madonna hosts the season premiere of *Saturday Night Live* and—by parodying Britain's Princess Diana—yet again garners a great deal of press coverage. In Britain, in particular—where, with the release of "Dress You Up" she is about to become the only female artist in thirty years to have three singles in the charts at once—images of Madonna as Princess Diana appear in all the papers. The gods of publicity are clearly smiling on Madonna big-time.

On my next birthday, November 22, 1985, Danny takes me to this French restaurant we always go to on Hudson in the West Village. When we come home to Morton Street and open the door, there are Sean and Madonna and six other people. My first ever surprise party, and Sean, Madonna, and Danny are giving it for me.

Sean and Madonna study my paintings—the religious ones, not the glass ones like their wedding present. Madonna says, "I like them, you should keep on painting," and her encouragement means

Michelina Ciccone, my paternal grandmother, born April 1902.

Gaetano Ciccone, my paternal grandfather, born January 1900.

Silvio "Tony" Ciccone, my father, in 1952.

My mother, Madonna, in 1953.

My mother in her prime, riding a buffalo, 1951.

My sister Madonna, age one, January, 1959.

Madonna, age two, on a swing in our garden at Thors Street, August, 1959.

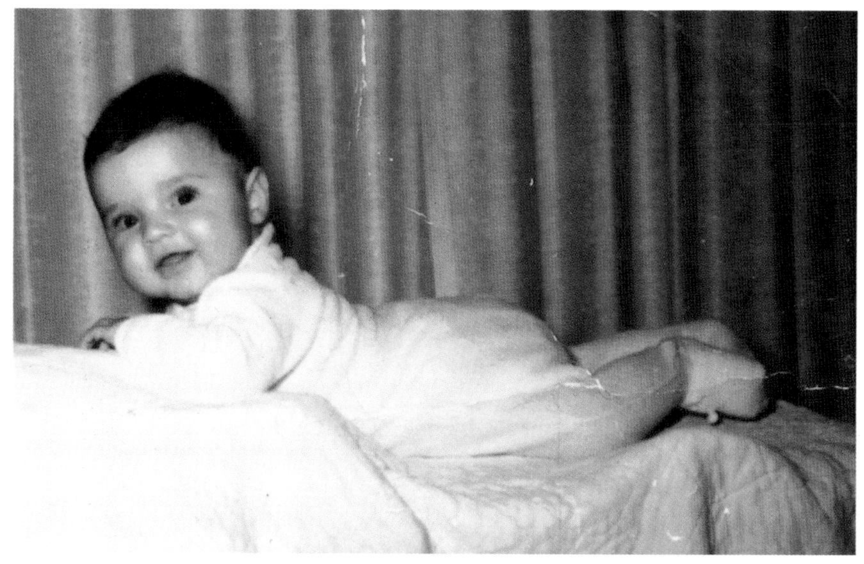

Me showing off my assets, April, 1961.

My mother in the backyard,
just before she was diagnosed
with cancer, February, 1964.

My father in the kitchen, looking young and handsome, April, 1958.

Madonna's first communion, 1967. Her mugging and me annoyed as usual, while my sister Melanie and brother Marty smile for the camera.

The 1967 family Christmas picture—starting with me on the far left, Madonna next to me, my uncle Trevor, Melanie, and then Paula, and in the background, Marty on the left, my uncle Ed, and my brother Anthony at the top of the pyramid.

Madonna's elementary school class picture.

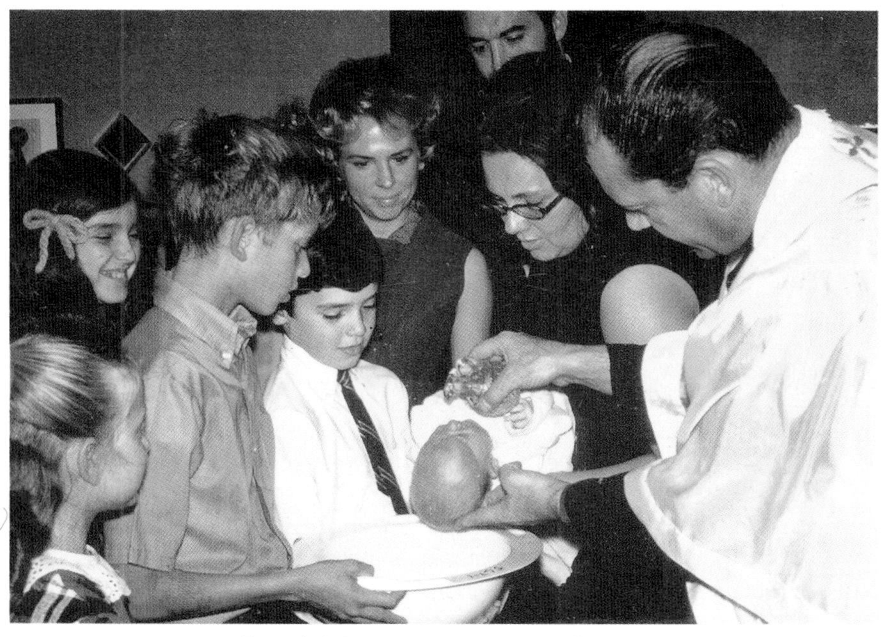

Jennifer's baptism, 1968. Me with the tie,
Madonna with the orange ribbon, and Joan in blue.

A portrait of us in San Matteo, taken in 1970 during our road trip of America. In the front from left to right, Paula, me, Madonna, Melanie—the girls all in their Butterick sundresses—my uncle Chris in the back, Marty, Joan, and my father.

Our house on Oklahoma Avenue.

Madonna and Paula at a 1977 family function—both in couture by Joan.

Just goofing off—from front to back, Mario, Madonna sucking her thumb, me in the beret, and my brother Anthony, 1979.

a lot to me. We drink champagne, play Ella Fitzgerald, and have a great time.

No one else in our family has ever met Danny, and none of them even know he exists. Consequently, I am estranged from all my relatives except for Madonna, and—until tonight—feel cut adrift from my family. But thanks to Madonna and Sean's throwing me this surprise party, I feel as if they have adopted me as a member of their small family, and for the first time since my mother died I am starting to feel safe and secure.

I also can't deny that I am now not only relishing that I am part of Sean and Madonna's family, but that my sister is fast becoming one of America's most famous women. All the star power surrounding Madonna is addictive. I get into restaurants and bars and clubs just by mentioning her name, and when I do, I am treated as a member of royalty. So far, at least, for me there is no downside to Madonna's fame. Nobody bothers me excessively. Photographers call out my name; Madonna's fans all yell, "Christopher, Christopher." My only problem related to my sister's fame is that Danny still isn't won over by her and is continually alienated by all the hysteria and attention that accompany her every move or utterance.

Aside from resenting the ripple effect caused by Madonna's stardom, Danny also loathes sharing me with her. Then, and throughout our relationship, he demands 100 percent of my attention and resents anyone else receiving even a modicum of it. In an uncanny way, Danny resembles Sean. Like Sean, Danny hates throwing dinner parties, hates going to clubs, and prefers to hide away with me alone at our home.

And perhaps it isn't surprising that Madonna and I—being brother and sister, being so close—have chosen to share our lives with such similar men. But while Madonna's relationship with

Sean is destined to founder and die, mine with Danny will endure for over a decade, primarily because he will always play Henry Higgins to my Eliza Doolittle. When we meet, I am a twenty-three-year-old hick from Michigan who is utterly at sea amid the sophistication of Manhattan. Danny, in contrast, is the quintessential New Yorker—urbane, cultured, streetwise. During our years together, he teaches me about good living, Pratesi sheets, Christofle silver, beluga caviar, and Cristal Champagne.

And despite his distaste for Madonna, his resentment of the sway she holds over me, once he gives up his Fiorucci job, he becomes my right hand and takes care of everything at home, so I can concentrate on my job. Moreover, he makes me feel safe, protected—and then there is the high-voltage sexual chemistry that consistently sizzles between us.

ON JANUARY 8, 1986, Sean, Madonna, and I fly from L.A. to Hong Kong to start preparation for the filming of *Shanghai Surprise*, for which, reports claim, they are each being paid $1 million. We check into a hotel on the Kowloon side of the bay. I immediately go out onto the balcony and admire the flickering lights of Kowloon harbor. I photograph the scene and send the picture to my father, telling him it reminds me of the Asian scene that used to hang in the Formal Dining Room of our home in Michigan. Another way, I suppose, of telling him how far we've come, my sister and I.

However, in broad daylight, the scene is not so enchanting. The bay is filthy, and a young woman bathes her baby in it as a dead rat floats by. I take a walk around the city, which seems dominated by fluorescent signs, lighting and advertisements, and evokes one big, brassy red-light district for me. The entire city has the air of a massive shopping mall, only it's far dirtier than the average shopping mall. In fact, Hong Kong is the dirtiest city I've ever known, with big rats skulking all over the place. In retrospect, perhaps I should have realized that those rats were probably an omen.

When I read the script, I understand why Madonna has taken the part of missionary Gloria Tatlock; *Shanghai Surprise* is modeled on the screwball comedies of the thirties—the kind of movie Jean Arthur, Jean Harlow, or Judy Holliday might have made. Where exactly Sean fits in is a bit of a puzzle for me. The part of con artist Glendon Wasey is just not a Sean Penn part, but is flimsy and not in the least bit challenging. I conclude that he has only taken it because Madonna wants him to be in the movie with her and needs him by her side when she makes her debut starring in a big commercial movie. He has agreed to appear in the movie as a gift for her, and I am touched. I'm also hugely impressed when I discover that he's mastered Mandarin—just to prepare himself for his role. Then I realize that his erudition has been slightly misplaced, really, because his character is an American.

Madonna is excited to be visiting another continent—and one so far away from America and Europe. Above all, she is thrilled to be making her first major motion picture. Watching her hang on Sean's every word as he analyzes the character of Gloria Tatlock, I suddenly grasp another reason my sister fell for him: having a Method actor on her team ready and willing to give her acting coaching is clearly yet another good career move for her. I sometimes wonder why my sister doesn't take up chess, because I know she'd become a master.

It's clear to me that she is now driven to prove herself as an actress, to be taken seriously. She has conquered the music business. So her sights are now set on conquering movies. She desperately wants *Shanghai Surprise* to be a colossal success—but not enough to drop her glamorous image and dye her hair brown, wear thick pebble glasses, and go without makeup in all the scenes—which would have been far more in character for her part as a missionary. Instead, she makes certain she looks flawlessly beautiful in every single shot.

The weather is cold, wet, and windy—a drawback because the movie takes place in summer. As a result, Madonna will spend most of the shoot shivering in thin summer dresses. And in the final cut—because the movie was shot in cloudy weather, but the location was lit for summer—Hong Kong and all the other locations look decidedly fake.

In the end, we might just as well have shot the entire movie on a Hollywood soundstage, but then I would have missed the amazing experience of being on location in Hong Kong with Madonna and Sean.

My job turns out to be part assistant, part traveling companion, setting up meetings and shopping for whatever Madonna needs—usually American potato chips, which she craves but can't find in Hong Kong. I end up with little to do but to sit in the location limo and make satellite phone calls to Danny back in Manhattan.

Madonna, Sean, and I are invited to a couple of Hong Kong restaurants, but the Chinese food is far removed from any we've had in Manhattan, smells and tastes different, and we don't go back. Instead, most nights we eat at an English-owned Italian restaurant.

Madonna and Sean, along with former Beatle George Harrison, are executive producers of the movie. That Madonna and Sean have chosen to work with a British production company, Handmade Films, and with George Harrison, is a testament to the professional respect they both have for George and for British movies in general. Madonna is also fully aware that—apart from the negative reception she and Erika and I all had in London and Manchester only a few short years before—Britain is one of her major markets, and her popularity there is at the first of a series of peaks.

In approaching *Shanghai Surprise,* from the first Sean's Method training comes into play. So although Hong Kong is doubling for thirties Shanghai, as we are unable to shoot there, Sean decrees that we go to Shanghai anyway, before shooting starts, to get a feel for what it must have been like there during the thirties.

Madonna, Sean, and I fly to Shanghai together, accompanied by three Chinese government escorts, who monitor our every move. There, we stay at the Metropole, a thirties art deco hotel where the silk drapes are so old that when we pull them, they literally fall apart in our hands.

Madonna and I start each day with a jog, which is unpleasant because the temperature is seven below zero. We are the only people around who are jogging. It is so cold that most of the newly washed clothing people have hung out on sticks in the street to dry is frozen in midair. Everyone else around is bundled up and on bicycles.

After breakfast, we walk all over the city, exploring. Although Madonna isn't known yet in China, passersby still stare at her, simply because she is blond. We look around us and realize that everyone on the street is wearing a green, calf-length, quilted coat with a fake-fur collar, while Madonna and Sean and I are wearing blue ones that have been allocated to us by the government. What with our wearing different-colored clothes, us all having Caucasian features, and Madonna being blond, we must look like freaks to the Chinese.

We wander into a park where some old people are doing tai

chi. One of them comes up to us and says, "New York, New York," over and over. We smile; he's the first person in the park to speak English to us.

In the evening, we all go to the Bund, an art deco riverfront area. There, in a sixth-floor restaurant, we discover that the place is divided into a Chinese bar and an American bar. We peep into the Chinese bar and see that everyone there is drinking orange juice. So we go into the American bar, which is out of bounds for the Chinese. The whole room is dark. We pour ourselves some drinks, then finally find the light switch. The entire bar is covered in dust. Late-seventies disco music is playing. We ignore the dust and quirky American decor and dance. I feel as if I've walked straight into a scene from *Empire of the Sun.*

After a few days in Shanghai, we return to Hong Kong, where Liz Rosenberg joins us. She and Madonna and I take a day trip to Macao, traveling there on a motorized junk. The trip takes around four hours. On the way back, Madonna and Liz spend most of the time throwing up in the bathroom. A couple of days later, all three of us get throat infections. We aren't surprised, though, as there were open sewers in Macao. Down the line, filming will move there, but fortunately I am not required to come along.

Before filming starts, Madonna is still hanging on Sean's every word of advice concerning her acting. But as soon it begins, she stops playing a scene from *Educating Rita* and decides she is Meryl Streep instead. Meanwhile, it is starting to dawn on Sean that he has been cast as Norman Maine, the hapless washed-up star of *A Star Is Born,* destined to be forever upstaged by his wife. It comes as no surprise to me when Madonna and Sean butt heads. Sean is an experienced actor and proud of it, but Madonna is fast becoming a global phenomenon, a brand. Madonna believes she is a talented actress; Sean views her as merely a singer. Conflict continually erupts on the set as to how she should play her part, how he is playing his, her character, his character, this scene, that. Madonna and Sean are about the same height, and when they stand, eye to eye, face-to-face, each trying to win every argument, each trying to get the better of the other, the tension is palpable.

Meanwhile, Jim Goddard, the director, is forced to grapple with the reality that he is not directing the movie by himself; Madonna and Sean are also directing it.

From the first day of shooting, the all-British crew takes an instant dislike to Madonna and Sean. They regard Sean as an arrogant Yank and Madonna as a jumped-up disco dolly. As far as they are concerned, the "Poison Penns"—their sobriquet—are two troublesome brats who are insisting on star treatment without meriting it.

On the second day of filming, publicist Chris Nixon is fired for not having succeeded in preventing the press from taking photographs. Afterward, he says openly, "Penn is an arrogant little creep and his wife goes along with him."

Down the line, during one of the biggest scenes in the movie, in which a bomb explodes and Madonna is supposed to jump into the river, she point-blank refuses to take the plunge. The water is pitch-black with dirt, so I don't blame her in the least. But after the crew is forced to wait while crates of Evian are brought to the set and Madonna, in a navy pencil skirt and pin-striped blouse, is doused in bottled water, they become irate.

Instead of attempting to win over the crew, and taking a backseat to the director creatively, Sean and Madonna are always on the edge of an argument. Worse still, instead of focusing on the movie full-time, Sean is far more concerned with the swarm of world press who have flocked to Hong Kong to cover the movie and whose telephoto lenses are trained on him and Madonna 24-7; he is obsessed with keeping them off the set. When a photographer does manage to infiltrate, Sean smashes his camera.

Sean and I never discuss his hatred for the press covering the movie, but if we had, I would have asked him why—if he didn't want himself and Madonna to be subjected to such heavy media coverage—they decided to make this movie together in the first place. Surely he must have been aware that by opting to make *Shanghai Surprise* with Madonna, battalions of press would continually be snapping at their heels, eager to report every single second. A conundrum, if ever there was one.

When Madonna and Sean do venture out together, the press besiege them, and Sean goes ballistic. To please him, Madonna follows his example and pulls a jacket over her head to prevent any photographers from getting a picture of her. In reality, she doesn't care at all and would welcome the exposure.

Each time Madonna and Sean leave the hotel, there is practically a riot. To Sean, any photographer who snatches a shot of Madonna is, in effect, not just taking her soul, but taking her away from him as well, and Sean feels exploited.

Exasperated, Madonna tells him, just as she did during the media mayhem at their wedding, "Sean, don't yell at them. Let's just get in the car and go. They'll get their shot anyway."

But Sean rarely listens and a brawl invariably breaks out.

Meanwhile, the press is on hand, recording his every move, every tantrum, every fight, Madonna is damned by association, and the legend of the Poison Penns grows by the minute.

Back in London, coexecutive producer George Harrison learns of all the Penn-induced drama swirling around the *Shanghai Surprise* set. He takes the next plane to Hong Kong, hoping against hope that he can defuse the situation and coerce Madonna and Sean into changing their ways regarding the press and the crew.

When George Harrison flies in from London, Madonna introduces me to him, and I am surprised that he seems much older than I expected, and taller, too. Madonna described George as "a sweet, hapless kind of character without a mean bone in his body."

She may well have been underestimating the canny Harrison, who isn't so hapless that he is afraid to read his willful stars the riot act, nor is he sweet enough to sugarcoat his message. The experience of being lectured by a Beatle, I learn afterward, is sobering for both Madonna and Sean, and I am sure that George has not only stressed budget constraints but has also appealed to Sean's professionalism and pleaded with him to tone down his paranoia.

Although I think that George probably handled Madonna with kid gloves—partly because he knows that she, not Sean, is the big box office draw and also because he is aware that all the problems are down to him and not her—later that evening, back at the hotel I can sense that she is feeling uncomfortable, delicate, and slightly insecure about her acting, about how to keep up with Sean, how to stop fighting with him about the press.

She goes to bed early, and so do I.

At around three in the morning, I wake up to the sound of furniture being thrown around in Madonna and Sean's suite next door. He's screaming at her with all his might. Although I am half-asleep, I can make out some of the words.

"I'm the actor, you're not. You should forget about acting. Stick to singing instead, that's what you're good at," Sean screams at her.

"And you don't know a fucking thing about handling the media, you paranoid control freak," Madonna counters.

"Well, at least I'm an actor," Sean growls.

He's really hitting below the belt now. I can't make out all the words, but I hear him smash his fist against a wall. Then the sound of a table sent flying. I am about to break down the connecting door between our suites when, all of a sudden, it flies open. Madonna—in the black satin pajamas with white satin piping from Harrods that I gave her for her last birthday—runs into my suite. Sean is in hot pursuit, snarling with rage.

For a second, I am reminded of Hank, his guard dog.

Just in time, I slam the door right in Sean's face—and lock it.

Madonna falls into my arms. Her face devoid of makeup, usually so pale, is flushed and she's crying.

I put my arm around her and lead her over to the sofa. I hold her while she sobs. Meanwhile, Sean is banging on the door, yelling her name.

He keeps on thumping at the door for a full five minutes, yelling, "Open the fucking door, Madonna, open the fucking door."

My first instinct is to open it and beat the shit out of him. But I know that will only escalate the situation. So instead, I hug Madonna.

We listen in silence as Sean yells and bangs.

Finally, Madonna falls asleep in my arms. Soon after, I fall asleep as well.

In the morning, she's gone.

When I see Madonna again on the set later that day, her makeup is immaculate, her hair perfect, and she is smiling her bright, confident smile. Sean comes over to me, but I ignore him completely.

Until last night, I was his biggest defender. No matter how weird I thought our blood-brother ceremony was, I felt that it meant something, that we had really and truly become blood brothers. From then on, I always defended him no matter what everyone said about his tantrums and press paranoia. Not just because I felt honorbound, but because I did really feel that we were brothers beneath the skin.

Here in Hong Kong, I was Sean's only defender amid a cast and crew who generally despise him. But that no longer holds true. Now I am neither Sean's defender nor his friend. Although I don't say this to Madonna, I wish that I weren't his brother-in-law.

Remembering Sean's admission that he was drunk during *Shanghai Surprise,* it becomes eminently clear to me that once again my sister and I have made similar choices: we have both fallen in love with men who have, at one time in their lives, become violent from the effects of too much alcohol.

Filming in Hong Kong ends. Sean and Madonna fly to Berlin, where his movie *At Close Range* is being premiered. He stays there for a few days while Madonna flies ahead to London. I fly in from Hong Kong in time to meet her.

At Heathrow, I am escorted to the tarmac. Madonna, in a black scarf and dark sunglasses, along with a bodyguard and her trainer, disembarks. A police escort is at the end of the Jetway and walks with us to customs.

After the officers have finished with everyone's bags, the police throw open the door between the customs hall and arrivals. A posse of photographers lie in wait for us. All hell breaks loose. The hall is ablaze with exploding flashbulbs and the glare of TV cameras. Fans scream and photographers yell, "Over here, Madonna, over here."

As we walk past the barrier, fans and photographers jump over and surround us. With the bodyguard and the trainer, I form a protective circle around Madonna. We try to edge our way to the curb and our waiting limo.

The police are being less than helpful, and although they make a halfhearted attempt to clear the way for us, it takes us a full fifteen minutes to make it to the exit.

I push cameras out of Madonna's face. What seems like three hundred photographers keep right on snapping.

I can see Madonna's about to crack.

I hold her more tightly. "Stay close, Madonna, I'll get you out of here," I say.

Finally, we get to the car, a black Mercedes. The door is already open. Madonna and I jump into the back. Cameras are shoved against the car windows. A massive thump, and the car shakes. A photographer has jumped on the roof. Another on the hood. Five or six are banging on the windows.

"Madonna, Madonna, talk to us."

She slides down in her seat. I hold her close. We are both near hysteria.

Another loud thump and a photographer lands on the back of the car.

"Get me out of here, get me out of here!" Madonna screams.

But the driver can't move because we are surrounded.

"Just drive," Madonna yells.

We inch forward, and I feel a little bump.

A photographer has slid off the roof and onto the road.

We pull away.

I look back.

He is on the ground.

All the other photographers start to snap his picture.

He tries to get up.

"Lie back down again," the other photographers yell.

He does, and they take his picture.

As the car pulls out of the airport, we look out of the back window at the crowd of screaming photographers behind us, and the thought flashes through my mind that we are a long way from flying Air India, economy class, eating curry in Soho, and buying jeans in Camden Market.

"Great," says Madonna. "A whole month in London, and that's what we've got to look forward to!"

When we finally get to read a British newspaper, we discover the reason for the airport riot. While we were in Hong Kong, leaks from the set were pouring into the British tabloids. Now Madonna and Sean are big news. In Britain, the Poison Penns are now the target of every single paparazzo in the country.

Moreover, we now understand exactly why George arranged for Sean to fly ahead separately.

"If he'd have been at Heathrow today, he'd have slugged them all," Madonna says. And she's right.

But no matter how much I now despise Sean, after that terrifying airport experience I feel a flash of empathy for him. After all, I only had to endure the full force of the paparazzi for a few hours, but Sean is condemned to endure it for as long as he and Madonna are married.

MADONNA AND I arrive in Holland Park, where George has rented Madonna and Sean a house, and me an apartment, and just as we stop, a group of cars skid around the corner in a screech of burning rubber.

The ever-resourceful paparazzi have caught up with us.

The exterior of the house is rather like an Elizabethan chalet. We duck inside before the media grab a shot of us. The inside is furnished seventies style, with shag carpeting and a sunken living room overlooked by a big glass window stained with an illustration of a rainbow.

I am relieved that Sean isn't here. Madonna and I spend the evening together. We chat about how difficult the movie has been for her, but neither of us broaches the subject of her abortive relationship with Sean, or that upsetting night in Hong Kong.

Outside, it is cold and wet. I go home to my rented apartment to bed and leave Madonna, protected by her bodyguard, waiting for Sean.

THE NEXT MORNING, followed by a bunch of paparazzi that have slept outside the house in their cars all night, we drive to Shepperton Studios, where we are due to start filming the movie's interiors. For the next months, the routine is the same: Every morning the media lie in wait for us outside our house. Each night after shooting, they follow us home again. They spend the night in their cars outside and follow us to the studio again the next morning.

And so it goes for most of our London stay.

Finally Madonna explodes: "I've had enough of being a fucking prisoner."

So we book a table at one of London's foremost restaurants, Le Caprice. Then we hatch a plot. Madonna enlists a male and female extra, and the following evening they cover their faces and dash out of the house and into a waiting Daimler.

The Daimler roars away, with the paparazzi in hot pursuit.

"It worked! It worked!" Madonna exults.

Then the three of us duck into the black Mercedes parked outside and are promptly driven to Le Caprice, where we spend a relatively peaceful evening without the paparazzi recording our every moment.

However, when we leave the restaurant, we are besieged by the waiting paparazzi and realize that someone must have tipped them off. But at least we've had a few untroubled hours in a paparazzi-free zone.

EACH DAY, THE British press attack Madonna and Sean in viler terms. So far, the *Daily Mail* has lambasted her as "the Queen of Slut Rock playing at Garbo, but playing it oh so badly." The *Daily Express* has posed the rhetorical question "Will Madonna and her man ever clean up their act?" Countless other scathing articles have appeared in the British press, and Madonna is hurt and bemused.

"Christopher, I don't understand why people are writing this kind of shit about me," she says.

I can't blame her for being puzzled. After all, until now the British press have been among her strongest allies and have always been kind to her. But, thanks to Sean, who isn't half as much a star as Madonna now is, they have all turned against her.

Finally, George Harrison calls a press conference to defend his stars. On the afternoon of March 6, 1986, at the Roof Gardens—a stylish sixth-floor restaurant above Kensington High Street, London, where pink flamingos stalk around ornate formal gardens—seventy-five members of the British press gather to meet Madonna.

Sean was originally scheduled to take part in the press conference as well, but at the last minute, it was decided that it was far more politic for him not to attend.

Madonna and George sit side by side at a small table. Four bodyguards hover nearby. George is in a blue-and-white shirt and a blue suit and chews gum. Madonna is in a black dress with white cuffs, her hair is down, and her lipstick is bright red.

She looks exceptionally beautiful.

George starts the conference by welcoming the assembled

members of the British press, then asks for order. I stand on the side and watch as Madonna fields the first question: "What kind of a boss is George Harrison and were you a Beatlemaniac?"

The question is benign, and so is Madonna's answer: "I wasn't a Beatlemaniac. I don't think I really appreciated their songs until I was much older. I was too young to really get caught up in the craze. But he's a great boss, very understanding and sympathetic."

So far, so good. Madonna and I have been lulled into a false sense of security, unaware of the fearlessness of the British press when faced with a global superstar, and of their capacity for asking direct if impertinent questions. George clearly is, hence his decision not to subject the hotheaded Sean to their interrogation. By the third question, "Is it fun working with your husband, Sean Penn?" the writing is on the wall. Initially, Madonna deftly sidesteps any problems by giving a bland answer: "Of course it is. He's a pro. He's worked on several films and his experience has helped me."

The next question is more of a zinger: "Has it caused any personal problems off set? Do you row at all?"

George jumps in before Madonna can answer. "Do you row with your wife?"

The journalist is temporarily silenced. The questions become more general, but only for a few moments, then they are again aimed at eliciting comments from George or Madonna on Sean's tantrums.

Did they expect the kind of coverage they received? Would George work with Sean again? "Sure, I happen to like Sean very much," George counters.

Madonna stays silent until a journalist asks why Sean isn't at the press conference.

I give a silent answer: *If Sean were here, most of the journalists in this room would have been toast by now.*

George says, "Because he's busy working."

Madonna backs him up with "He's in more scenes than I am," which is true.

Then the press go directly on the offensive. A journalist asks, "Madonna, I wonder if either you or your husband would like to apologize for incidents which have involved bad behavior on your behalf."

Madonna draws herself up to her full height. "I have nothing to apologize for."

George laces into the press. When a journalist challenges him with "We have loads of film stars over here, but never have had these sorts of fights," Madonna comes to her own defense and I'm proud of her.

"When Robert De Niro comes to the airport, are there twenty photographers that sit on his limousine and don't allow him to leave the airport?" she asks.

Things become increasingly ugly when George says, "We expected nonanimals," and a journalist leaps up and yells, "Talking of animals, is it true Sean Penn has been on the set giving orders?"

George counterattacks. Then the journalists bring up the incident at the airport and say, "It wasn't the press that was at fault."

Madonna looks genuinely upset.

I want to sock the journalist. I stand up and say, "I was in the car. He got up and then lay down again for the photographers."

Madonna mouths me a silent *Thank you.*

In the face of the unrelenting British media onslaught, she is calm and polite, and the tide of public opinion begins to turn in her favor.

But when *Shanghai Surprise,* which ends up costing an estimated $17 million to make, premieres in August, then goes into release at four hundred U.S. theaters, the reviews are abysmal, with *Time*'s critic declaring, "Madonna seems straightjacketed by her role and Penn, for once, looked bored," and Pauline Kael in *The New Yorker* dubbing the movie a "listless bore of a film."

But instead of becoming downhearted or depressed by the reviews, Madonna refocuses her attention on her music career, which just zooms from strength to strength. "Live to Tell," the theme to Sean's *At Close Range,* is released and hits number one in the United States. Madonna is featured on the cover of *Rolling Stone.* "Papa Don't Preach" (the lyrics of which, despite speculation to the contrary, are not rooted in anything to do with our father) is released and hits number one on the U.S. charts for two weeks, while "True Blue" stays there for five.

I eventually see *Shanghai Surprise* and am embarrassed at how bad it is. Madonna and Sean have zero on-screen chemistry. Not that I am surprised, because offscreen there is little tenderness between them either.

Clearly, neither of them ever examined their own performances. Overall, the movie is a victim of the creative control Sean and Madonna exerted over it.

However, Madonna flatly refuses to take any responsibility for the movie's failure.

"It's all Sean's fault," she tells me, in a voice that brooks no contradiction.

After the fiasco of *Shanghai Surprise,* Sean and Madonna start living separate lives. With at least fifteen paparazzi routinely hanging out in front of the New York apartment on Central Park West that they have recently purchased, Sean spends as much time as possible in L.A.

Madonna flies out to L.A. intermittently to be with him, but they end up fighting all the time primarily because Bukowski is always around the house, still drunk as a skunk. Madonna wants him out of the house, and Sean doesn't.

Anytime Sean does come to town, the three of us hang out at the Pyramid, a dark, dingy little bar on Avenue A between Ninth and Tenth, where Madonna, Erika, and I once did a track date. But before we can reminisce and marvel at how far we've come, the moment we get inside the door, Sean has to fight for Madonna's attention—just as Danny often has to fight for mine. Madonna and I have both fallen for possessive, jealous men, and we pay the price.

Whether or not Sean likes it, he's compelled to face that we are on her territory now, and everyone wants a piece of her, and he's not the main event. And when he and Madonna leave the bar, photographers are waiting outside, ready to grab a shot of her. Everything surrounding Madonna is frantic. The press is pulling them apart. Moreover, she is now far more famous than he is. She overshadows him completely, which must feel emasculating. I can't help being aware of the irony that the man who has always aspired to be the James Dean of his generation has now been relegated to the role of a surly underling trailing around in his wife's starry wake.

OCTOBER 1986. MADONNA calls me and breaks the devastating news that Martin Burgoyne, one of our oldest friends and her first road manager, is very sick with AIDS. Although not too much is understood about the disease at this time, we already know a few people who have AIDS and both of us understand the tragic implications. Madonna pays Marty's medical expenses at St. Vincent's Hospital. Madonna and I go to the hospital together to visit him one day. While she is with Marty, I wait outside his room. When she emerges, her face is stained with tears. He dies within a month. He was just twenty-four years old.

Apart from giving Marty as much financial support as possible and easing his last days, Madonna has already established an impressive track record in raising money for AIDS research and braves a media storm by participating as a model at the AIDS benefit fashion show at Barneys New York that will benefit St. Vincent's AIDS research clinic. Right up until the midnineties, her personal involvement in fighting the disease and raising money to benefit AIDS sufferers remains passionate and unimpeachable.

Like Princess Diana, she has no fear of AIDS, and her commitment to its victims will help raise public consciousness of this harrowing disease.

At the end of the year, the release of Madonna's "Open Your Heart" single and video—in which she simulates a kiss with an underage boy—causes yet another high-octane Madonna-style controversy. The video of *The Virgin Tour* wins a *Billboard* Music Award for the Top Music Video of 1986, and she wins the AMA award for Favorite Pop/Rock Female Video Artist for "Papa Don't Preach" and makes a surprise appearance at the Shrine Auditorium and collects the award in person. Accepting awards—apart from the elusive Grammy, which she still hasn't won—is becoming an everyday occurrence for her.

When rehearsals for her next tour—*Who's That Girl?*—begin, I agree to be her dresser again. Better to be on the road than here in Manhattan, where AIDS is now decimating the gay men in the city and a creeping sadness is pervading our once carefree existence.

Danny is, of course, deeply opposed to my touring again with Madonna. But he hasn't got a chance of stopping me. Despite that I've been with him for four years now, and I love him, I still want what I want. Unlike *The Virgin Tour*, this will be a world tour, so I'll get to visit Europe and Japan. And since Sean is pretty much out of the picture, Madonna and I are closer than ever, and I really want to help her weather this tour.

Whenever anyone comes out with the usual crap that Madonna's success is due to luck, I am always outraged. Through the years, I witness the rigors of her pre-tour preparations. The moment a tour is scheduled, she starts training with a vengeance. When the *Who's That Girl?* tour begins, she will run six miles in the morning, then do a two-hour show in the evening. Her self-discipline is impressive, her stamina superhuman, and it's far from easy to keep up with her.

By the time the *Who's That Girl?* tour kicks off, she's lost the slightly plump look she had on *The Virgin Tour* and is now sleek, with a sinewy, muscled back. Her body is lean, but still soft and feminine. She is much more athletic, sure of her body, sure of herself.

Who's That Girl? is far more theatrical than *The Virgin Tour* and has a Spanish theme. She has recently released "La Isla Bonita," which hits number four in the U.S. charts and will remain an enduring favorite among her fans. Not every scene is Spanish-oriented, though. When Madonna sings a medley of "Dress You Up," "Holiday," and "Material Girl," she wears rhinestone-studded harlequin glasses, and her dress, decorated with dice, charms, and plastic toys, is extremely difficult for her to wear as it is boned for support. She keeps bitching that she "can't dance in these fucking bones," but still does. The dress is also extremely tight, and when I disrobe her, her body is covered in red marks as if she were a medieval martyr scourged in the service of her faith.

By now, I've got the change of clothes and the whole backstage operation down pat. I am braced to ignore all the tirades Madonna unleashes on me practically every time she storms offstage. I know how to cope on every level, and she trusts me implicitly, secure in the knowledge that she can rely on me completely.

I still have to pick up the dancers' clothes after the show, collect baggage at the airport, and have the costumes delivered to each room. I hate it, but grin and bear it because I love every moment of working on the show, traveling everywhere, and making sure that backstage everything goes smoothly.

Despite how proficient I've become at my job, despite how much my sister needs me, she still takes great pains not to show me any favoritism. While we are on the road, she always has a four-room penthouse suite, but as far as she is concerned, although I have been working for her longer than anyone else on the tour, I still don't rate a suite. Even her personal assistant has a better room than I do. The rest of the people on the tour, though, treat me with great respect, making sure to defer to me—simply because I am Madonna's brother. I have become accustomed to my role, and I am content.

On *The Virgin Tour* we were playing arenas seating no more than fifteen thousand a show. On *Who's That Girl?* we are playing stadiums seating eighty thousand. Our track dates—always great fun—are far behind us. Even *The Virgin Tour* seems, in retrospect, to be kids' stuff. Now that Madonna is playing stadiums, she is making millions of dollars a night, much more is at stake, and life on the road is now more serious.

The *Who's That Girl?* tour opens on June 14, 1987, at Nishinomiya Stadium, Osaka—the first of Madonna's five concerts in Japan. More than twenty-five thousand fans flock to the show, each paying around $45 a ticket, many dressed in identical black leather and sunglasses, presumably believing this to be Madonna's current style. Although troops are called in just in case of trouble,

I discover that Japanese fans are civilized and well behaved. During the show, instead of standing up and screaming, they are orderly, sit with their arms folded, and never stand up and yell. When the show is over, they don't jostle to get out, but exit by row, and if anyone leaves something behind, it is immediately turned over to lost property. Both Madonna and I feel relatively safe in Japan.

In Osaka, we hear about a great noodle shop, so Madonna hides her hair under a scarf, puts on men's trousers and a men's shirt, and together we sneak out of the hotel. The restaurant is packed, we eat in the middle of crowds of people, but no one recognizes her.

One night, all of us—Madonna and me, the dancers, Liz and Freddy—visit a geisha house, in a huge hall, all dark wood and pretty. We sit around a twenty-foot-long dining table and are served a ten-course dinner. Once we have finished eating, six geishas appear, singing, dancing, and playing all different instruments.

Madonna, in particular, watches the geisha performance like a hawk. In the future, the geisha costumes, the makeup, the music, even the movements, will be appropriated for her performances and videos.

After our geisha evening, we decide that we want to experience more of the mysteries of Japan, so our guide suggests we go to Kyoto. There, we visit a Shinto temple, surrounded by light blue bamboo trees, and little hills covered with fur coats of moss. Madonna and I feel elated that we have finally encountered the mysterious Japan we've glimpsed before in Kurosawa's movies, but the impression is slightly mitigated when we take the high-tech bullet train back to Osaka.

Sean doesn't join us on any of the Asian tour legs. Instead, Madonna spends much of her time with a straight dancer on the tour, Shabadu. I don't know whether she is cheating on Sean, and I don't know the nature of her relationship with Shabadu, but I can't imagine that after the show she would have any energy left over for sex.

On June 27, 1987, the nineteen-city U.S. leg of the *Who's That Girl?* tour opens at Miami's Orange Bowl, and sixty thousand fans brave a tropical downpour to see Madonna. We are staying at the Turnberry Club, where Madonna, as always, has the penthouse. Sean, clearly on his best behavior, fills the suite with white lilies and white orchids and spends a couple of days with her there. They sunbathe in their private rooftop solarium, but even though they are staying in the honeymoon suite, I can tell that this is the swan song for their marriage, and that Madonna is only making an effort because, on July 7, Sean will begin a sixty-day jail term for assaulting a photographer who snapped a picture of him on the Los Angeles set of his latest movie. I feel momentarily sorry for him, then decide that—judging by his past antics—jail might do him some good.

AFTER MIAMI, WE move on to Atlanta, Washington, Toronto, Montreal, Foxboro, then Philadelphia, and on July 13, at Madison Square Garden, Madonna performs an AIDS benefit concert in Marty's memory, during which more than $400,000 is raised on behalf of amfAR, the American Foundation for AIDS Research.

We both miss Marty, and I know the concert is emotionally draining for Madonna. Yet the show must go on and we both know it, so immediately afterward we move on to Seattle, then Anaheim, Mountain View, Houston, Irving, St. Paul–Minneapolis, Chicago, East Troy, and Richfield.

The physical demands of the tour on Madonna are grueling, yet we rarely fight. Madonna sometimes complains about her voice and her throat and how tired she is. She has been working for weeks, singing, dancing, projecting her megawatt personality to the audience, with never a hint of tiredness or boredom, so if—now and again—she is close to exhaustion, I can hardly blame her.

I don't sympathize with her much because I know that while my sister might trawl for sympathy, she isn't really comfortable when she gets it, nor does she want to spend any time playing the role of victim. So instead of commiserating with her, I give her a quick hug and crack, "I know, Madonna. But just think of what you're earning." She perks up immediately.

On August 7, Madonna is scheduled to play Pontiac, but causes an uproar when she goes on the *Today* show and cracks to Jane Pauley that Bay City is "a smelly little town." After the show, she calls me in a panic asking me if I can remember the name of the plant near Grandma Elsie's house. I do, and she incorporates that information into her apology to the forty-two thousand fans who attend her performance in Pontiac, and all is forgiven.

After the show, we travel home to our father's house for a barbecue. This is Madonna's day off and she'd much prefer to be spending it in her hotel suite. I'm relieved, though, to be out of my room, but then it isn't nearly as nice as her suite.

My father has invited everyone from the tour to the house, and we all travel there by bus. My father barbecues. Joan makes upside-down pineapple cake. Madonna is civil to her, but distant—as she always is in front of our father. Fortunately, she and Joan are never alone together, so Madonna never has the opportunity to give vent to the ever-present bitterness she feels toward Joan.

Someone has tipped off the press about our visit, and some of them are lurking in front of the house. Madonna is wearing sunglasses, blue jeans, a white shirt, and little Moroccan flats, with her hair pulled back with a headband. I am in my usual T-shirt and jeans. She looks tired and definitely doesn't want the press to get a shot of her today, so we stay in the yard. She's also clearly bored.

Some of our neighbors come over, including my first "girlfriend." She becomes a little worse for wear and starts crying about how much she still loves me and how she wishes we were married. Madonna and everyone else—with the exception of my father and Joan—laugh themselves silly. The old girlfriend has no idea that I am gay, nor, at this point, do my father and Joan.

My dad tries his best to give us all a happy day. We play volleyball, eat a lot, talk about old times, but I know Madonna and I both feel the same: far removed from our past. We find it impossible to go back and spend the afternoon by our childhood sandbox and my old tree house and pretend this is fun when it isn't.

MEANWHILE, DANNY HAS quit Fiorucci and we are both living off my salary (around $50,000 for this tour), so he has to put up with my working for Madonna again. And on August 6, he comes with me to the Times Square premiere of the movie *Who's That Girl?* in which she plays an ex-con named Nikki Finn.

Madonna looks beautiful in a vintage Marilyn Monroe dress decorated with gold bugle beads. A crowd of more than ten thousand love-struck fans cheers for her. Before she goes into the theater, she says a few words to the crowd over a microphone that's been set up for that purpose: "This is a real irony. Ten summers ago I made my first trip to New York and I didn't know a soul here. I told the taxi driver to drop me off right here in the middle of Times Square. I was completely awestruck. And now here I am looking at all of you people and I'm completely awestruck. Thank you, and I hope you like the movie."

Her pride is palpable, and however exaggerated the story of her first visit here, the essence is true, and she deserves to be proud of all she has achieved. After all, who else could bring Times Square's traffic to a halt during rush hour? Her sheer star power is immense.

Going into the movie, she is happy. Coming out, she is not.

The movie, yet another screwball comedy, is awful, and much too late, she's realized it. Although the screening is in front of an invited audience of friends and associates, and everyone laughs politely in the obvious places, I find it difficult to join in. Even Madonna must have read the writing on the wall and confronted the truth that this abysmal movie is destined to fail.

She has never asked my advice regarding whether to take a particular movie part. It's beginning to dawn on me that she probably doesn't involve any of her business associates, such as Freddy, Liz, or Seymour, in her moviemaking choices either. Just as she reached for success in the music business with untrammeled self-confidence and an almost insane optimism, blinkering herself to the possibility of failure, she seems to be straining for movie stardom without having any perspective on her acting talent or the roles she takes.

She sees herself as a latter-day Judy Holliday and hasn't yet realized that Judy was a genuinely funny actress—who won an Academy Award for her performance in *Born Yesterday*—and that she is not. She hasn't learned her lesson from *Shanghai Surprise,* and it seems unlikely that after *Who's That Girl?* flops, she will be prepared to step back and make a dispassionate evaluation of her acting talent, or lack of it.

The U.S. leg of the tour ends a couple of days later, on August 9, at Giants Stadium, East Rutherford, New Jersey, close to the New York State line. On *The Virgin Tour* we started the tradition that on the last night of the tour, we play a practical joke on one of the tour members. I decide that I am going to play one on Madonna. When I dress her in her Spanish skirt and bolero, I stuff the end of a roll of toilet paper into her shorts. She marches onstage trailing it. The moment she hears the crew and the band laughing, she realizes and pulls it out just before the audience sees it. She doesn't talk to me for two days, and I guess I can't blame her.

A lot of my friends come to the last night of the American tour, but I don't want them to discover that I am merely her dresser and not her personal assistant, which is what I routinely tell them. During the scene in which she throws her glove into the pit and I have to scramble around, find it, and hand it to her, I hide my face so my friends won't recognize me. Not the proudest moment of my life, but being my sister's dresser is somewhat degrading and is not an appropriate job for an adult male, and I just don't want to advertise that I'm doing it. Not that I ever regret being Madonna's dresser, because, after all, I am part of a huge artistic enterprise and have the opportunity to travel the world and, above all, help my sister.

The European leg of the tour opens on August 15, in Leeds, England, before we move on to Wembley Stadium in London, where Madonna performs three sold-out concerts. In Frankfurt, she also plays to sold-out crowds, and in Rotterdam, as well.

In Paris, on August 28, Madonna presents Jacques Chirac with a check for $85,000 to benefit AIDS charities in France. In Paris on August 31, at the Parc de Sceaux, Madonna plays to one of the biggest crowds of her career so far, 130,000 fans. We have a police escort to and from the show. When I look out in the audience, I can't quite believe that all these people are here to see my sister.

Sean already seems like a distant memory. In Italy, when we take our daily jog, three cars drive in front of us, five cars trail behind us, and at least fifty fans and press all jog beside us. It would have been great to be able to jog through these ancient streets of

Rome without the circus following us. Worse than the crowd is that we are spluttering from exhaust fumes streaming out of the cars in front of us.

Madonna and I kid each other about how Sean would have handled the situation, agree he would probably have liked to kill everyone in sight, and we laugh about it. Instead of drawing a gun, I go up to them, ask them to pull up, and they do. Madonna and I jog on, unfazed. Both of us have long accepted that the press and fans are part of the package, and the truth is that we are both attention junkies and revel in it.

On September 4, in Turin, in front of a cheering audience of over sixty-five thousand, Madonna wows the crowd with her mastery of the Italian language. First she asks them, *"Siete già caldi?"* (Are you hot?), then announces, *"Allora, andiamo!"* (Then let's go), and finally makes the crowd roar in approval by declaring, *"Io sono fiera di essere italiana!"* (I'm proud to be Italian). Afterward, there is a riot and the police hustle us out of the auditorium. Both of us are a little scared, but we get back to our hotel without further problems.

The tour ends on September 6 at the Stadio Communale in Florence. A month later, *Forbes* will name Madonna the top-earning female entertainer of 1987. Looking back on the *Who's That Girl?* tour, I conclude that she's earned every penny.

I ALSO THINK that her performance as secretary to a mogul in David Mamet's new eighty-eight minute play, *Speed-the-Plow,* which opens on May 3, 1988, at Manhattan's Royale Theatre, is good. I tell her so after seeing the play on opening night. She is pleased, seems happy, but says she can't get used to playing to an audience that listens in silence and doesn't scream at intervals. As the run of the play continues, Katharine Hepburn, Sylvester Stallone, and Sigourney Weaver all come to see her. Nonetheless, she tells me she is often bored doing the same thing night after night. In her own show, she can alter steps or lyrics whenever she feels like it, but not in a play. In the end, she concludes that she prefers music extravaganzas. I concur.

After Sean is released from jail in mid-September 1987, having served thirty-three days of his sentence, he and Madonna attempt to resuscitate their marriage, but fail. She files for divorce, but later withdraws the petition and decides to try to save the marriage after all.

She lends me $200,000—on which she does not charge me interest, but which I agree to repay within two years, and do—so that I can buy a studio on Fourth between Eleventh and Twelfth, an open space with fifteen-foot ceilings that offers a fine view of Chinatown and the Brooklyn Bridge, where I begin to paint regularly. I consider painting my vocation and, if I had to enter my profession on my passport, would unhesitatingly list it as "artist," and definitely not "dresser."

Speaking of art, on May 8, 1987, Madonna takes me to a dinner at the Met in honor of their Egyptian exhibition. Lauren Hutton, one of the first supermodels and the star of *American Gigolo,* sits next to me looking incredibly handsome. We start talking and click. We exchange numbers.

She invites me to her loft above an old theater on Jones Street and the Bowery. She's got a big refectory table with all her magazine covers spread out on it. During our many conversations about life, love, and modeling, she tells me she's really into art and that she longs to paint, so I advise her to buy a canvas and go ahead and paint. I explain that no one needs to see the result, and if she doesn't like it, she can paint over it.

The following week she invites me to the apartment again,

where she's now got an eight-foot-long, ten-foot-high blank canvas, and every conceivable paint supply. I am about to ask her what she's playing at, why she wants to paint so big, and how she got the canvas into the loft in the first place, when she hands me a blue line drawing of a cross section of a pregnant woman, with a fetus inside her.

"I wanted you to see this drawing," she says.

The drawing is stunning, beautifully executed, almost perfect.

Lauren tells me she wants to paint the same picture on the canvas and asks if I will help her by starting the painting for her. I am hesitant, but agree. She goes out shopping for a couple of hours.

During that time, I copy the drawing onto the canvas and am so involved in painting that I don't even hear her coming back to the loft again, nor do I realize I have nearly completed the painting.

She strides over to the canvas, takes one look at my painting, and flips out.

"How dare you finish my painting! How could you do this to me? What have you done? What have you done? I wanted to do all the painting, but you've gone and done it again. You must be lashing out at Madonna."

What the hell is she talking about?

"You're crazy," I tell her. "Paint over it. I don't care. And don't call me again until you've come to your senses. Madonna has nothing to do with this."

Besides, I've only done what Lauren asked—I've painted a copy of the drawing onto the canvas.

Then I walk out in amazement.

Five days later, she calls me at my studio and apologizes for blowing up like that, but says that she still thinks I'm lashing out at Madonna. I ask her what she did with the painting. She says, "I took it up to the roof and burned it." I say, "You're nuts," and hang up the phone.

A few weeks later, Danny and I are strolling around the Village, and on a rack I see a postcard featuring the identical drawing Lauren showed me. I pull it out of the rack and flip it over. On the back, a credit: Picasso, from his blue period. I should have known. I resolve to study Picasso's work more closely. And although Lauren contacts me later and suggests lunch, I never see her again.

Down the line, my study of Picasso will pay off. Two years later, Madonna tells me she wants to start collecting art and will I help her? I find out that a Léger is about to go on the market, get a transparency of it, and show it to my friend Darlene Lutz, an art history major who used to work with Maripol. I tell her I know nothing about the artist or the painting, but think it is great and ask her to research it.

She does, and I take the transparency and the information to Madonna, tell her the painting is amazing, perfect for the apartment, and that I think she should have it. She listens, and with her approval I bid $1 million on her behalf and win the painting for her.

Soon after, she expresses interest in Tamara de Lempicka because she's read a book about her and is fascinated by her. I tell her that Lempicka fits exactly into the apartment's deco style, and Madonna starts collecting her work. From then on, my role in Madonna's life expands further; along with Darlene Lutz, her official art adviser, I am now her unofficial one. I regularly browse through all the catalogs, visit all the galleries, and, with Darlene, generally bid at auctions on her behalf.

After the Lempicka, Madonna buys Frida Kahlo's *My Birth*, and my favorite of all her collection, Dalí's *Veiled Heart*.

Picasso's *Buste de femme à la frange*, depicting Dora Maar, comes on the market. I tell Madonna, and she authorizes Darlene and me to attend the auction and bid on it.

The painting is beautiful. Darlene and I sit in Sotheby's auction room, knowing that Madonna doesn't want us to bid more than $5 million. I am desperate to win the bidding for her. It opens at $2 million. I bid three. I am outbid by a million. Then I bid again, and there is silence. The auctioneer announces, "Sold to the gentleman with paddle number 329." Everyone in the room applauds. The painting is mine. Or rather, Madonna's. The moment is so exhilarating, so surreal. I sign the contract with Sotheby's, walk out as if I am floating on a cloud.

I call Madonna. "You've got it, babe, you've got it. It's fucking beautiful."

She cries, "Yippee." Then a second later, gives a big sigh.

I know exactly what she's thinking. "It's worth it, Madonna. You've got a really great Picasso."

Madonna decides that the Picasso should be hung over her rosewood desk. I supervise the crew of guys hired to hang it. A few days later, she comes back into town and sees the painting for the first time.

"I think it's beautiful, and I love it," she says. "And I don't feel bad about spending the money, because you were right, it is worth every cent."

Over the years, with Darlene, I will spend around $20 million of Madonna's money on art for her—which collectively, by 2008, has no doubt increased in value by over $100 million.

• • •

MADONNA NEVER VISITS me in my art studio until one evening when, a few months after I first move in, she arrives there with JFK Jr. Clearly her ploy of making him jealous during his visit to her dressing room has worked. I'm not surprised. She hasn't told me that they are romantically involved. But by bringing him to the studio, she clearly wants to let me know that she and John are an item. I also get the feeling she wants to impress me, and she does. I am more than impressed. I am knocked out. I can hardly believe that I have a Kennedy in my studio. John is handsome and polite, but it's clear that their relationship is casual, light and fun.

Later, Madonna calls me and says, "I feel like I am repeating Marilyn and the president."

I can't believe she's serious. I tell her, "Go ahead and enjoy yourself. You aren't Marilyn, and he's not the president."

After she hangs up, I ponder whether she is using John's luster to enhance her own mythology. Then I remember that although John, bowing to his mother's wishes, is assistant DA here in Manhattan, he is also an aspiring actor and is set to make his professional acting debut a few months later in *Winners* at Manhattan's Irish Arts Center. He may well feel that dating Madonna is more appropriate to his theatrical aspirations.

In the end, they date briefly, hang out for a while, work out at the gym and go jogging in Central Park together, then part. However, they remain friends, and when John founds a new magazine, *George,* Madonna even agrees to pose for the cover.

SIX

This above all: to thine own self be true,
And it must follow, as the night the day,
Thou canst not then be false to any man.
William Shakespeare, *Hamlet*

By now, Danny and I have settled into an annual holiday routine. His family know he is gay and accept me completely. The highlight of our relationship comes every Christmas when, on Christmas Eve, we drive in my old used green Range Rover—along with two of his brothers who live in Manhattan—to his parents' place in Queens, where we will spend the night. His parents always decorate the house in true American Christmas style—too much of everything. But I love being there and would never dream of commenting on it. I am far too content, as I feel that I am now part of the family.

Each year, I bring Grandma Elsie's meat pie, which I've made and everyone loves. Then on Christmas morning, I fly to Michigan and spend Christmas with my family. Even though Danny's family are New Yorkers and my family are Midwesterners, there is very little difference between them, other than that Danny's family are comfortable with his sexuality, and my family—with the exception of Marty, Melanie, and Madonna—are totally in the dark about mine.

On the afternoon of Christmas Day 1987, my father decides to confront the issue at last. He asks me to come out to the garage and help him change the oil on his old Ford F-150. Not an odd request, as I am a Detroit boy, born and bred.

We are alone.

As I slide under the truck to empty the oil, my father goes quiet, then asks, "Are you a homosexual?"

I drop the wrench and knock my head on the front bumper as I sit up. "What?"

An extremely pregnant pause.

"You don't have a girlfriend. You don't ever talk about girls . . . and I'd like to know if you're, well, gay?"

I consider my options. I am twenty-seven years old and am in a committed and loving relationship with a man. Why be afraid to admit the truth?

The image of Marty floats before my eyes, taunting me. I grit my teeth and erase it.

"Yes," I say, "yes, I am."

I hold my breath, waiting for my father, a church deacon and a conservative Catholic, to explode in rage and disappointment.

Instead, to my vast relief, he starts laughing. "I should have guessed a long time ago, but it only crossed my mind lately."

I am immensely surprised by his benign reaction, surprised, and I feel a bit strange. But glad I won't have to keep my sexuality a secret anymore.

We go back to working on the car together.

I assume we will now live happily ever after. My father, me, and his knowledge of my homosexuality.

I return to New York. A month passes. Then a letter arrives from my father, in which he says, "Christopher, after our discussion, I've thought about this for quite a while. And I don't think you are well. So I think you should see a psychiatrist to help you with this problem. And I'd be happy to pay for it."

I am appalled. I had been fully prepared for my father to react this way when I first told him that I'm gay, but not now, not a month later. The first time around, he played the tolerant liberal, but now his true feelings have come out and I am deeply disappointed. For while I understand his position on homosexuality, what really hurts me is that he is suggesting that I am mentally ill and, thereby, Danny as well. And by doing so, he is relegating my love for Danny to being merely a symptom of our dual sicknesses.

I write back, "Dear Dad, fuck you. I am not mentally ill and I will not 'seek help' to cure something that doesn't exist. I am the most stable of all your children. The only one who has been in a relationship for more than two years. You've never seen me naked in *Playboy* and I haven't fathered any children out of wedlock. If you'd like to vent your morality, I suggest you look to your other children.

"Until you come to terms with my life and choices, don't bother calling or writing. Good-bye. Our relationship is over."

A part of me understands my father's position, but I don't accept it. It hurts me, particularly because Danny is being dismissed as an illness. So I choose him over my father.

My father and I don't speak for a year. I am surprised and touched when Joan calls a few times and tells me she knows what is going on with me and Dad, that she supports me, but I need to understand his point. The Catholic view, etc. I listen but am not convinced.

A year later, out of the blue and to my great surprise, my father calls me and says, "I don't want this to come between us. I want you in our lives. I can accept you for what you are and I love you."

I am incredibly moved by this and pleased that my father has come to accept me. And I tell him I love him, too, and apologize for the letter I wrote to him. He then invites me and Danny home for the following weekend.

Danny and I fly to Michigan. It's late spring and the weather is ideal. Leaves and flowers have bloomed and I'm happy to see the six massive cottonwood trees that line the front yard. My parents are there to greet us, and much to my dismay, I find that we will be alone with them the entire weekend.

All weekend, my father is overaccommodating, telling jokes, acting exactly as he would have with one of my sister's boyfriends. He's trying really hard.

I say, "Dad, you're embarrassing me."

He certainly is, but at the same time I'm deeply touched that he loves me so much that he is willing to put aside all his hitherto die-hard beliefs and prejudices. In fact, he has gone the extra few miles to demonstrate his acceptance of me and my sexual choices, because had I brought a girl with me for the weekend, he would never have allowed us to sleep in the same room together. Later, he even went so far as to ignore Madonna's exalted status, both in the world and in our family, and banned her and Carlos Leon from sharing the same bedroom because they were unmarried.

Yet with me, he has pulled out all the psychological stops and has even instructed Joan to make up the bedroom next to his and hers for Danny and me. I know that the walls are practically made of cardboard and that my parents will hear every single sound through them. I suggest to Danny that we have sex, but are unable to because we can't stop laughing. We bounce up and down on the bed instead, doing our best to make my parents uncomfortable.

Despite our mischievous moment of immaturity, the weekend goes great. Afterward, my father and I begin speaking regularly and the subject of my being gay doesn't come up again.

Sometime later, Danny and I get an invitation from Melanie to her upcoming wedding in Michigan. I know all my family will be there. We accept. A week later, I get a call from my father asking if I am bringing Danny with me. I tell him that of course I am. He tells me he wishes I wouldn't because many of our distant relatives don't know about my sexuality.

I say, "You know what, Dad, I'm coming and Danny is coming. Melanie invited us both and that's that."

I realize that it is taking my father longer to accept my sexuality than I thought. At the wedding, I introduce Danny as my friend and my father avoids us. We don't kiss in front of anyone or hold hands. I've got the message. It's going to take a little more time.

IT'S 1988, AND Sean is making a heavy, serious movie, *Casualties of War,* and is completely out of step with Madonna, her life, her art, and, in particular, her friends. He's also far from amused by her latest playmate, the self-avowed lesbian, hip comedienne Sandra Bernhard. Whenever I see Sandra and Madonna together, Sandra seems enthralled by Madonna, almost worshipful. Whereas in my estimation Madonna is just playing around with her. She and Sandra hang out at clubs all over the city, sometimes with Jennifer Grey, who has just split from Matthew Broderick, and the three of them celebrate Sandra's birthday at The World together. Madonna and Sandra pose happily for press pictures together. Clearly aware that the cameras are on hand to immortalize the tableau, Sandra rests her head on Madonna's shoulder, while Madonna runs her fingers through Sandra's hair.

On July 1, 1988, Madonna makes a surprise, unscheduled appearance on *Late Night with David Letterman* on which Sandra is guesting. The reason, of course, is publicity; *Ciao Italia: Live from Italy* has been released on home video and, just weeks after her *Letterman* appearance, catapults to number one. Her way of promoting herself, though, is quintessential Madonna.

By prior arrangement with the producers, in the middle of Dave's interview with Sandra, Madonna suddenly materializes on the set, challenging Dave, "Let's talk about me and Sandra."

Letterman asks how she and Sandra spend their time and whether he could hang out with them.

"If you get a sex change," Madonna cracks.

I can tell she thinks she is being funny.

It gets worse.

Sandra tells Letterman that she and Madonna hang out at the Cubby Hole, a notorious lesbian bar in the Village.

"I think it's time to fess up, get real," says Madonna. "She doesn't give a damn about me. . . . She loves Sean. She's using me to get to Sean."

That ridiculous statement aside, she is clearly working to give the impression that she and Sandra are having a gay affair. I believe that isn't true. I feel Madonna is just working the PR factor.

She and Sandra carry on their double act when, in June 1989, they perform Sonny and Cher's "I Got You Babe" at a benefit for saving the rain forests. I attend and don't find them nearly as funny as I know they think they are.

Nineteen eighty-eight ends with Madonna signing a two-year film contract with Columbia Pictures and being cited in the 1988 *Guinness Book of World Records* for selling 11 million copies of *True Blue*, which hit number one in twenty-eight countries.

By now, Madonna is spending most of her time in her Manhattan apartment on Central Park West. At first, I was really disappointed that she bought that apartment because, to me, the building—a 1915 brick building, built in the arts and crafts style—is ugly.

She and Sean have tried and failed to get into the San Remo and the Dakota, so this place seemed a good second best. Besides, she wanted to live by the park. The apartment is on the sixth floor, facing the park, but as the years go by, the trees grow taller, obscuring the view completely. Not that Madonna cares too much. She far prefers New York to L.A., and until she moves to London, Central Park West is her favorite home.

Now that she is on the verge of divorcing Sean—which, true to family tradition, she and I never discuss—Madonna asks me to design and decorate her New York apartment so she can live in it permanently. As far as she is now concerned, I've clearly proven myself and won her trust—she gives me a credit card with my name on it, charged to her account, and doesn't even set a budget.

So I go furniture shopping for the apartment, buy a couple of simple sofas, some chairs, not in any particular style, a dining room table, and some stools. Without realizing it at the time—thanks to my sister, as ever, the instrument of my fate—I am becoming an interior designer.

Eventually, she will buy the apartment next door, join it to the first, then later add a third and a fourth, all of which I design.

The first time around, I decorate the apartment's entrance in a muted gray; a 1930s Fresson print by French photographer Laure Albin-Guillot, entitled *Nude,* hangs on the wall above a gilded, late-nineteenth-century Russian chair.

Léger's *Les Deux Bicyclettes,* the first major artwork I encouraged Madonna to purchase, hangs above the wood-burning fireplace. My sister loves fireplaces and also has one in her bedroom, opposite her theatrical burl-maple bed with copper trim, which is lit by a burnished-copper, oval ceiling light fixture that I designed for her.

I also design the barrel-vaulted hallway, in which hang many female nudes, including *Nude 1929* by George Platt Lynes, and a series of nude distortions by André Kertész. I also design Madonna's rosewood desk, and her stainless steel kitchen, complete with microwave, in which she likes to make popcorn. Rice Krispies Treats represent the rest of her culinary repertoire. Generally, when she entertains, either I cook or she hires a caterer or in more recent years, a French macrobiotic chef. On those evenings, the rooms are lit by her favorite gardenia-scented Diptyque candles.

While I am designing the kitchen, Madonna asks me to create a breakfast nook rather like a booth in a 1950s diner, which she feels is perfect for small, intimate gatherings.

In January 1989, I get a call from Liz asking me to fly to L.A. Apparently, the previous night, Madonna and Sean had a big fight, and Madonna needs me. I call Madonna at once and ask how she is. She says she is okay, but her voice is small and I know she isn't. Without going into great detail, she tells me that Sean has been violent and abusive to her again.

"If you want me to kill him for you, I'd be happy to," I say.

She gives a weak laugh and tells me she is staying at her manager Freddy's Beverly Hills home and feels relatively safe.

"But you aren't going back to your own home?" I ask.

She tells me she isn't because she wants to avoid Sean and that she needs to find a new house for herself right away. She asks if I'll help her. I tell her I am happy to.

The next day I fly out and check into the Bel Age Hotel. She picks me up in her black 1988 convertible Mercedes 560SL, a car she loves. But because she is rigorous about protecting her skin, during the ten years she owns the car she never takes the top down.

When we meet, she looks pale and wan, and I can tell that she hasn't slept for days. She seems depressed, but when I ask her if she wants to talk, she squares her shoulders and tells me that she doesn't. "No, let's concentrate on houses," she says.

Over just a few days, I look at more than twenty-five houses for her. The last is on Oriole Way. Although it is perched on the edge of the Hollywood Hills, it has the air of a Manhattan penthouse, and I sense that Madonna will be happy there. The house is ready to move into, and just needs furnishing.

I tell her about it, show her the house, and she signs the papers immediately, and I set about furnishing her new home.

She has total confidence in my taste and tells me to buy whatever I want, money is no object. So I go to the Design Center, aware that they never sell anything straight off the floor. But, as I suspect, when I tell them the furniture is for Madonna, they immediately go against their policy and sell me whatever I want to buy for her.

Then I shop Melrose Place for antiques—primarily Italian, including eighteenth-century chairs and a pair of candelabra—and all over town for sheets, towels, dishes, soap, potato peelers, everything. Two weeks later, Madonna moves into the house and is delighted by what I've wrought for her in such a short time.

On January 25, 1989, Madonna signs a deal to make a $5 million, two-minute commercial for Pepsi, which also includes Pepsi sponsoring her upcoming tour. She is slated to appear in the commercial, and "Like a Prayer," her upcoming single, will play in the commercial as well. It's a perfect financial deal and a great way of launching "Like a Prayer." Michael Jackson had previously made a similar deal with Pepsi, so I assume Freddy has suggested and brokered the deal for her.

On February 22, 1989, during the Grammy telecast, Pepsi takes the unprecedented step of running a television commercial *for* the commercial. And on March 2, an estimated 250 million people worldwide tune in to see Madonna in the commercial itself. I imagine that Pepsi feels it got its money's worth out of her.

Soon afterward, Madonna's "Like a Prayer" video bursts upon the world, featuring Madonna dancing in a field of burning crosses, simulating stigmata and seemingly crying tears of blood, and kissing a black saint. To me, what happens next is predictable.

On April 5, 1989, Pepsi announces that it is dropping its ad featuring Madonna and "Like a Prayer" because of boycott threats sparked by the religious imagery in the video.

I visit her at Oriole Way and she shows me the video.

"Can you believe it—they canceled my video!" she says.

"Well," I say as gently as possible, "you have burning crosses in it, you are pretending to have stigmata, and you are kissing a black saint. Didn't you think that might be a problem?"

"But I don't understand why."

She really has no idea that what she has done is eminently shocking because she simply didn't do it to shock. She isn't upset about the ad being canceled—because, after all, Pepsi has already paid her $5 million for it—but is genuinely surprised.

Soon after, I come to the house again to see Madonna and almost pass out in shock. Her lips are enormous.

"Did somebody sock you?" I ask.

"No, I just hurt my lips."

Concerned, I ask how.

"I don't know," she says. "Perhaps I've got an allergy."

Of course, she's lying, but I don't suspect. I haven't yet heard of collagen. If I had, I would have fully understood her reasons for wanting to acquire sultry, sensuous lips: she is about to meet one of the most notoriously libidinous men alive, Warren Beatty.

Madonna is determined to win the part of Breathless Mahoney in *Dick Tracy,* the upcoming movie based on the comic strip that Warren Beatty's producing and directing. Breathless—a femme fatale who schemes to lure Dick from his loyal girlfriend, Tess Trueheart—is the perfect role for Madonna and she knows it.

Initially, Sean Young was cast in the part, but she backed out, claiming that Warren had made sexual advances to her. Undeterred, he set his sights on casting either Kim Basinger or Kathleen Turner in the role. Then Madonna threw her hat in the ring. Warren, however, was far from a pushover. Through the grapevine, he let it be known that he was now considering Michelle Pfeiffer for the part. Madonna countered by offering to play it for union scale, just $27,360—plus a percentage of the box office take.

Warren still held out. Then he and Madonna had dinner together at the Ivy, and the deal was done—just as I believe Warren had always intended. According to *Desperately Seeking Susan*'s director Susan Seidelman, as far back as 1984 Warren had asked to view the dailies of the movie and was palpably intrigued by Madonna. Madonna, too, had always had a yen for Warren. I flash back to her bedroom in Michigan and remember that when Madonna and I were teenagers, while I only had maps hanging over my bunk bed, Madonna had a poster of Warren Beatty. And when his seminal movie *Reds*, the story of revolutionary John Reed, who wrote *Ten Days That Shook the World,* is released in 1981, she insists that we go to the movies and see it together.

They finally meet for the first time in 1985 when Sean introduced her to him at a party.

Madonna tells me she has the Breathless Mahoney part, and that she's dating Warren, as well. Not a surprise to me, as he is notorious for becoming involved with his leading ladies, including Julie Christie, Diane Keaton, and Natalie Wood. As for Madonna, she will be intrigued by the ghosts of girlfriends past and will find following in the footsteps of Brigitte Bardot, Vivien Leigh, Joan Collins, Carly Simon, Barbra Streisand, Susan Strasberg, Britt Ekland, and a legion of other legendary—and not so legendary—beauties who have loved and been loved by Warren not only challenging, but also massively erotic.

Madonna is a big star now, bigger than Warren, sure of her status, but curious about what hanging out with him will be like. Above all, my sister being my sister, she's acutely aware that being Warren Beatty's girlfriend is wonderful for her mythology, her status in Hollywood, not to mention its positive effect on the final cut he, as director, will make on *Dick Tracy.*

As for Warren, he is fifty-two now, and a romance with the biggest female star in the universe—more than twenty years his junior—is clearly a canny career move for him.

Meanwhile, true to form, Madonna doesn't allow her liaison with the playboy Warren Beatty to distract her from the main event: her career. Filming begins on *Dick Tracy* on February 28, 1989, around the same time she makes the "Express Yourself" video—which is filmed on a $5 million budget, the highest in music video history—and still summons up the energy to take part in an AIDS Dance-a-Thon benefit at the Shrine Auditorium.

At the height of her romance with Warren, Madonna tells me that he wants to meet me. I'm both flattered and immensely curious. I accept Warren's invitation to join him and some friends for dinner at his house on Mulholland Drive, overlooking the San Fernando Valley. I arrive at the lower driveway. There is no security. I ring the bell at the gate and Warren's assistant opens it and shows me into a large area between the dining room and a glass veranda, with a roof opening up to the sky.

A long table set for twenty people is covered with a simple tablecloth, no table decoration, and set with rather ordinary china. *Cozy* is not a word I'd apply to the house. There are no plants, no art, no photographs on display, everything is austere. A Sinatra song—redolent of hot women and cool sexual conquests—plays in the background, but other than that, there is no sense whatsoever that this is the home of a legendary lothario whose conquests number many of the world's most desirable women, including my sister. Warren's soulless house doesn't betray an iota about the nature of his charm, his capacity to seduce practically everyone who crosses his path.

Then I shake hands with him and within ten seconds experience perfectly the full megawattage of his all-embracing allure.

His hand is big. He slides it into mine slowly. Then applies slight pressure. He keeps hold of my hand a split second longer than is usual. The moment has a distinctly sexual feel to it.

He stares straight into my eyes, says hello, and I say hello back.

"So, Christopher," he says in his deep, slow, measured voice, without hardly skipping a beat. "Can I ask you something?"

I nod, already enraptured by him.

"What is it really like being gay?" he asks, as intently as if he has been yearning for half a lifetime to meet me and pose that question to me. "And do you feel you had a choice, or do you think you were born gay?" he adds, as he guides me over to a couch and we sit down there together.

Within moments, I am pouring out all kinds of intimate details about my sexuality to him.

"So has it been difficult for you—being gay?" he asks, gazing intently into my eyes.

By now, Debi Mazur, Jennifer Grey, and a few of the tour dancers are also in the room, standing near the couch, but Warren makes me feel as if he and I were the only people there.

I am totally won over, sucked into the maelstrom of his irresistible persona, instantly under the sway of his lethal charm, and I've only known him for about ten minutes.

Warren's potent spell over me does momentarily weaken when—on our second meeting—he again asks me similar questions about my sexuality. And on our third. And on our fourth. I am left with the strong impression either that Warren is obsessed by homosexuality, or else that asking so many questions about it is simply his tactic for putting me at ease, and he is just being charming to me because—in the eventuality that I become his brother-in-law—he wants me on his side.

Back to our first meeting chez Warren. Dinner conversation is light; Warren drinks little. His chef serves us run-of-the-mill California cuisine. Madonna, in a short black skirt and black top, sits next to Warren, but isn't the least bit kittenish and definitely doesn't cling to him.

"Wa-a-ren Batey," she whines halfway through dinner, "I'm getting bored."

Of course she is. Warren has been expounding on his friend Senator Gary Hart's chance of making it to the White House, and my sister always gets bored unless the conversation centers on her, her next tour, or her next album.

Warren, however, isn't the least bit insulted. Instead, he smiles indulgently. I can tell he's amused by Madonna, but that their relationship is more father and daughter than highly passionate fling. Throughout dinner, they rarely touch. In all the subsequent times the three of us are together, I never see Warren and Madonna kiss or cuddle or even hold hands.

Chocolate mousse is served. My sister wolfs it down, stands up, announces, "I'm done," and then walks out of the dining room.

I am transported back to Monopoly. I am nine, she is eleven. I succeed in buying Park Place, but because I am not yet aware of the natural scheme of things in my little world, I refuse to relinquish it to her. Now I'm going to win, and I'm glad.

"I'm done," my sister declares, throws her pawn—always the top hat, whereas I always get the iron—onto the board, and flounces out of the room.

The game instantly ends.

Years later, and nothing has changed. Warren, however, remains unperturbed.

He makes no attempt to control Madonna. And she knows better than to try to control him. She understands only too well that countless women before her have tried and failed. She has no intention of making the same mistake.

Whatever else her machinations entail, they clearly succeed on a big scale, because one morning, when we are in the kitchen having coffee, she tells me Warren has asked her to marry him.

I put down my mug, completely surprised.

"So do you think I should, Christopher?"

"Well, do you love him?"

"I think so. What do you think?"

I hesitate. She exuded more passion for Sean and will in the future have more for her boyfriend John Enos and Carlos Leon, the father of her daughter.

So I tell her that I like Warren and think that he will make a great father, but I don't say much else because—despite his devastating charm, his political clout, and his vast power in Hollywood—I sense that my sister isn't truly in love with him. She likes him, admires him, and they have fun together, but love doesn't come into the equation.

In the end, she stalls the question of marriage, and the fun goes on.

THE THREE OF us go to see k. d. lang perform at the Wiltern in L.A. Warren drives us to and from the show in his gold 560SEL Mercedes, which I covet. I vow to one day own the identical model in black, and eventually I do.

After the concert, in the car driving home, Warren ponders, "Why is it that women with extremely strong voices are always nuts?"

An interesting question and, perhaps, a backhanded compliment to my sister.

I'm extremely curious about Warren's relationship with his own sister, actress Shirley MacLaine, three years his senior, but he never mentions her. When I tentatively ask him if he ever hangs out with her, there is a long pause.

"We live in separate worlds," he finally says.

THAT SUMMER DANNY and I lease our usual house on Fire Island—a three-bedroom, 1950s cottage on the bay. Fire Island is twenty-six miles long, a quarter of a mile wide, and runs along the southern coast of Long Island and is dotted with small, separate communities. The farther east you travel from New York City, the more "rugged" and gay the communities become—culminating in Cherry Grove and the Pines, which are completely gay.

Cars are banned here, so the residents use small wagons to transport luggage and groceries around its narrow boardwalks. Fire Island is beautiful and the only place in the world where I feel completely at ease being a gay man. I invite Warren and Madonna to come out there for lunch, and—to my surprise—they agree. I tell them that they can either drive to Sayville and take the ferry from there to the Pines, or take a seaplane from East Twenty-third Street in Manhattan. They opt to take the seaplane.

I go to meet them at the dock. They disembark from the plane looking green with nausea. Both of them say, "We are never ever doing this again. Why didn't you tell us?"

Apparently, space in the plane was really tight, and it flew so low that it bounced all the way from Manhattan to the Pines.

Once they've recovered from the trip, we have lunch and then go swimming.

By now it's midafternoon. The island is swarming with people.

The word that Warren and Madonna are in town sweeps through the island like wildfire. They are probably the biggest stars ever to visit in more than fifty years. After that, my status on Fire Island really soars.

At the end of the day, I take Warren and Madonna to the ferry, which takes them to Sayville, where a car will take them to Manhattan in comfort. Danny and I walk back to the house, smiling, knowing that everyone knows we just had Madonna and Warren Beatty to lunch.

MADONNA CARES ENOUGH about Warren to want to buy him a birthday gift. She shows me a 1930s Lempicka-style painting of a man sitting in a cockpit, entitled *The Aviator*, and asks me if I think he will like it. Aware of Warren's fascination with Howard Hughes, I tell her I think he will and she buys it for him. He hangs it just outside the foyer of his house, and it is now the only piece of art to hang in his home.

DURING THE MAKING of *Dick Tracy,* I visit Madonna on set. She is shooting the first scene, set in Breathless Mahoney's dressing room, when Breathless first meets Dick and asks if he is going to arrest her. In a sheer, black, floor-length robe, which affords the illusion that—aside from small black panties—she has nothing on underneath, Madonna is at her most beautiful. Her makeup, too, is flawless: translucent skin, bright red lips, and her hair in platinum curls.

As we chat on set, her hairdresser is teasing her hair. I ask Madonna how the movie is going for her.

"Difficult. Nerve-racking, really. I feel like the baby on set."

I tell her I sympathize.

"I'm playing a bad girl."

I attempt to raise an eyebrow. "So what's it like working with Warren?"

"Amazing. He's being so helpful and patient. Not like working with Sean."

On many nights, after dinner, Warren, Madonna, and I go clubbing together. Throughout her career, Madonna has always made a point of checking out all the clubs—in particular the black clubs, where the new dance trends usually begin, so she can monitor what everyone is doing.

Hence her discovery of voguing. By maintaining contact with the club world, keeping a toe in the water, and staying on top of the current trends, Madonna has consistently remained at the top of her game. Of course, her club forays end when she discovers Kabbalah, but around the time of her relationship with Warren, she is still going to clubs, catching dance trends at the top of the wave, then incorporating them into her albums or videos.

The three of us often go to Catch One, a black club with a drag-queen room. The club is in the kind of L.A. district where you leave your car outside, but have to pay a guy to watch it—otherwise it won't be there when you come out.

We also often go to Club Louis on Pico, a tiny place run by Steve Antin, an actor, with a bar rather like someone's living room, decorated with seventies posters of black guys with Afros. Very cool. Madonna and I really love it there, and so do countless other celebrities.

We spend the night on the dance floor, doing steps from our old track-date routines, making up new ones along the way. My sister dances with me, and if any of our dancers come with us, we all dance together. On the dance floor Madonna isn't self-centered. She doesn't want to dance alone, but in step with me and anyone else we are with; we all end up dancing the same steps together.

Meanwhile, Warren sits on the sidelines, sometimes smiling, other times frowning, always watching, always indulgent, and unthreatened by being around so many gay people.

I say, "Come on, Warren, come and dance with us."

He grins that half grin and says, "No, thanks, you guys do it better than I do. Dance away."

He is the only straight guy in the room, and I think he likes it that way. He doesn't have a problem with all the gays dancing together. He is far too sure of his own masculinity for that.

Nor does he react to my gayness by deriding me or by suggesting that my sexuality emasculates me. He always treats me with the utmost respect, makes sure never to overlook me, and never comes between Madonna and me. All in all, I really like and admire Warren.

Meanwhile, my sister is cheating on him.

I KNOW LITTLE about the other man, just that he is Latino.

She has told me that she doesn't trust Warren; she is convinced that he is being unfaithful to her, but she has nothing tangible on which to base her suspicions.

From what I know of him, I think she is wrong and that he isn't fooling around.

Warren is perceptive enough to sense that Madonna has other fish to fry, and that, as far as she is concerned, he definitely is not the only game in town.

At this stage, we are rehearsing for the next tour, *Blond Ambition.* Madonna has promoted me to artistic director, although she still wants me to dress her, and I am more involved than ever in planning the tour. In the four-month run-up, I stay with her at Oriole Way, where I have my own room.

We run together every day and afterward work fourteen hours a day and hang out together when we're not working.

Warren rarely comes to rehearsals. Many times at the end of the day, when we are in the kitchen, talking about the show, Madonna tells me Warren is coming over later. By the time he makes it, I am usually in bed. The next morning, Madonna and I go running. When we get back, he has already left.

One night, I wake up thirsty at around three in the morning and go to get a glass of water. The house is dark and the limestone floors are cool beneath my feet. The house is shaped like a U, with the master bedroom at the end of one side of the U and my bedroom at the end of the other. In between, there is the office, the library, the living room, and the kitchen. To get to the kitchen, you have to go past the office. As I walk down the long hall to the kitchen, out of the corner of my eye, in the shadows, I see Warren in the office. It looks to me as if he is rifling through my sister's wastebasket.

I quickly walk on into the kitchen and pour myself a glass of water, making sure to create a lot of noise.

When I walk past the office again, Warren is gone.

The next morning I decide to keep the whole Warren-in-the-office incident to myself. But deep down, I think that Warren, operator that he has always been, has had the sense to recognize his equal in Madonna. An accomplished philanderer, he has met his match and knows it. All that is left for him is to unearth the evidence. And that, I believe, is apparently the explanation for his going through Madonna's garbage: searching for proof of her infidelity out of an understandable desire to know the truth.

Whether he finds it is debatable. What is incontrovertible is that as soon as Madonna starts being filmed for *Truth or Dare,* his relationship with her starts to spiral downward. Warren exhibits great disdain for the project, and—with the exception of one short scene—refuses to take part in it. His refusal earns him my further admiration.

EACH MORNING BEFORE rehearsal, Madonna and I go for our usual six-mile run. On the way back to Oriole Way, we run up an extremely steep hill. One morning, I get to the top of the hill and feel light-headed. I don't say anything to Madonna, drive with her to rehearsals, but all morning keep forgetting things and, in general, feel extremely weird. I find it difficult to catch my breath.

By lunchtime, my thoughts are in turmoil. So I go to see David

Mallet, the tour director, and tell him I don't feel well and that I think I need to go to the hospital—adding that he mustn't tell Madonna, as I don't want her to freak out.

I go to Providence Saint Joseph Medical Center, on South Buena Vista right by Warner Studios, and take an ECG. The results show that I am in the midst of an arrhythmia attack. My heartbeat is off-kilter and blood is failing to reach my brain properly. I lie on the table, worrying about how rehearsal is going without me.

A freckle-faced nurse pops her head into the curtained area I'm in and with a look of surprise and curiosity says, "Madonna is on the phone for you. Is it *the* Madonna?" I tell her it is and ask her to bring me the phone, which she does.

Madonna asks me what's going on.

I tell her that I have a problem with my heart and that further tests are pending.

She tells me not to worry about coming back to rehearsals, and that she'll call back to see how I am.

Then she carries on rehearsing.

Fifteen minutes later, the same nurse comes up to me and—with utter disbelief—announces, "Warren Beatty's on the phone! You're pretty popular!"

I smile wanly and get on the phone with Warren.

"Christopher, tell me exactly what's going on."

I tell him, and without skipping a beat, Warren says, "I am going to call my cardiologist. He'll call you back in five minutes."

He does.

I see the cardiologist the next morning, and he diagnoses me with mitral-valve prolapse. Whatever is or is not going on between Warren and my sister, Warren is there for me, he comes through. I think he is cooler than ever. (Six years later, the same thing happens to me again, but my heart problem is reclassified as a stress-related electrical issue—at that time in my life, hardly surprising.)

The last time I see my sister and Warren together is at the Washington premiere of *Dick Tracy*. Afterward, they and the dancers and I all come back to the hotel together. I go downstairs to have a drink, and Warren and Madonna go upstairs together. After that, their relationship just fizzles out. They have been an item for just fifteen months. No fireworks, no recriminations herald the end of their romance. Just a slow, gentle fade-out.

I last see Warren about four years ago when we have lunch together at a little Japanese restaurant high above Beverly Hills, close to his home on Mulholland. He advises me about a script I've written, I advise him regarding renovations on his home, and then he asks me about Madonna.

For a while, we chat about her. But during the entire lunch, Warren, cool as ever, never once mentions current my brother-in-law Guy Ritchie. All during my lunch with Warren, I wish that Madonna had married him instead.

Warren's successor in my sister's life is not a big-time Hollywood tycoon, but a twenty-seven-year-old actor, Tony Ward—who appeared in the Pepsi video and has also made gay as well as straight porn. Not that Madonna has ever been remotely interested in porn. The image she so painstakingly projects in her book *Sex* is just that—an image concocted for commercial purposes. She never has any porn around any of her houses. Like Warren, though, Tony is incredibly sexy, and I fully understand Madonna's attraction to him, though in this case I don't share it.

As the eighties end, Madonna is showered with accolades. MTV's viewers vote her Artist of the Decade, *People* lists her as one of "20 Who Defined the Decade," she overtakes the Beatles on the list of all-time consecutive top-five U.S. singles (she has sixteen of them in a row), and she is named the world's top-earning female entertainer. Madonna's legend will unquestionably endure far into the next decade.

SEVEN

What counted was mythology of self, blotched out beyond blotching.

Wallace Stevens

THE DAY BEFORE the opening of the *Blond Ambition* world tour, Marine Stadium, Makuhari, Tokyo, Japan, April 12, 1990, Madonna marches onstage bitching about the sound system, stomping around and yelling "You motherfuckers," all classic Madonna, all captured on camera by Alek Keshishian for his documentary *Truth or Dare*. I hesitate, though, to apply the word *documentary* to my sister's performance in *Truth or Dare* because it really is a performance, comprising the best acting of her whole career. And anyone who thinks that *Truth or Dare* reveals the real Madonna is on the wrong track—just as she always intended them to be.

The title, *Truth or Dare*, is a grave misnomer, because anyone seeking the truth about the real person behind my sister's artfully constructed facade won't find it in this "documentary," except in the Marine Stadium scene and in a second authentic Madonna moment, which comes when she is having breakfast with Sandra Bernhard. Dressed in a silk kimono, she is relaxed and natural.

Sandra asks her about her childhood after our mother died, and Madonna tells her how—for five years after our mother's death—she used to have nightmares that someone was strangling her, broke out in sweats, and fled to our father's bed for comfort. Sandra asks how she slept in her father's bed, and Madonna cracks, "Fine. I went right to sleep after he fucked me." Then she laughs at her own "joke" and adds, "No, I'm just kidding."

The scene perfectly illustrates Madonna in one of her more aberrational moments when—in her head—she is so above everything and everyone that she thinks she can say whatever she wants. I never mention it to her again. I am far too angry with her.

As to the rest of *Truth or Dare*—which in Britain is retitled as *Bedtime with Madonna*—this travesty of reality starts with Madonna bemoaning that the end of the tour is nigh. "I'm just getting rid of the depression of what I feel when the tour's over with. . . . I know I'm going to feel something later."

Consequently, she says, she is becoming emotional. In reality—and this is an exact quote from Madonna, as she told me when the tour ended—her primary emotion was "Thank God it's over."

In general the end of a tour is never remotely emotional for Madonna, just for the tour dancers, who have been harboring the fantasy that they have been growing closer to her daily—and will always remain so. However, during these last days of the tour, they are slowly starting to realize that once the tour is over, they will never see her again face-to-face.

In this first scene of *Truth or Dare,* Madonna appears to be extremely thoughtful and weighing her words. In reality, she is far more likely to blurt things out, without giving them any thought at all. Yet here she is obviously calculating what to say next and is clearly reciting her words, as if she has memorized them from a script.

The phone call to my father, inviting him to the show—which begins, "Listen, I realize I haven't talked to you in a while. You know I hope everything's okay and everything, but I have no idea what night you guys are coming to the show, what night. . . . Well, who wants to come and when?"—is also a setup, filmed with my father's permission. In real life, Madonna's assistant Melissa would have made that call, not Madonna.

When she pulls the petals off a daisy and wistfully poses the question about Warren—"He loves me, he loves me not"—that moment is contrived for the camera. At this stage in their relationship, Madonna doesn't care much about Warren at all anymore. Nor would she ever berate him the way she does on camera or call him "pussy man." In real life, she would be far more polite, far more respectful. As for Warren, he makes it clear from the start that he hates the concept of *Truth or Dare*. He definitely is not himself in the few scenes in which he consented to take part. After Madonna secretly tapes one of their more intimate phone calls and later tells him she plans to include it in the documentary, he sends in his lawyers and the call is cut.

During the scene in Toronto, when we play the SkyDome on May 27 and 28 and her manager, Freddy DeMann, and I learn that the police might arrest Madonna for obscenity, I am seen giving her the news. The scene is staged from start to finish. The director urged me to tell Madonna on camera, and despite my better instincts, I agreed. In reality, I would never have mentioned the police threat to her until after the show, and would have dealt with the situation myself.

The backstage scenes in the Palace, Michigan, when Madonna plays there from May 30 to June 2, are also contrived. In my experience, Madonna would not have allowed Marty backstage, or her childhood friend Moira McPharlin. Nor would she have socialized with the dancers' families. She's too focused on the tour to be even remotely interested in anyone's family when she's on the road.

During the second show in Detroit, she announces, "There's no place like home. There's nobody like this man. There's nobody like my father. I worship the ground that he walks on." Our father comes onstage, she bows down to him, and she gets the audience to join her in singing "Happy Birthday" to him, and in that she is sincere.

The poem Madonna recites in praise of her assistant Melissa Crowe, which plays extremely well in the movie, may be heartfelt, but not long afterward, Melissa quit working for her because she'd had enough.

After Melissa stopped working for Madonna, I wanted to stay in touch with her as we were good friends, but Madonna decreed that I couldn't. As far as she is concerned, once employees are out of the loop, they are banished for all time. And anyone who has the temerity to talk to them is branded a betrayer.

HERE IS THE full truth about *Blond Ambition* from my perspective.

Madonna calls and says, "I'm going on tour, and of course I want you to dress me, but I think you ought to design the stage and art-direct the show as well."

Stunned silence from me.

"You designed my New York apartment and the Oriole Way house, so you should be able to design my show as well."

I am really pleased, but mildly disappointed that I still have to be her dresser. But at least I can now tell my friends that I am art-directing Madonna's show. And the pay is now $100,000—much more than I've been paid for the other two tours.

My responsibilities now include overseeing and supervising the costumes, the tour book, the look of the stage, and, of course, dressing Madonna. By now, her team are all aware that I have a great deal of influence over her, so if they want to tell Madonna something they're afraid to say to her face, they ask me to be their intermediary. I end up carrying a great many messages between her and everyone else.

Before the tour begins, we meet with Gaultier and look at design concepts, including the iconic bustier. He sends us a number of designs for it, and Madonna and I make the final selections. Next, the bustier, and everything else we pick, has to be made in triplicate. Everything has to be double-sewn with elastic threads and supports in various places, including for her chest. Her shoulder straps are strengthened, and all snaps are replaced with hooks or zippers, so none of the clothes come apart onstage.

I suggest that we set this version of the song "Like a Virgin" in a harem. However, the costume for the scene proves to be a problem, as the thread is really heavy gold metal, and the costume is hard for her to wear. All six versions we have made eventually corrode beyond recognition.

Madonna sings "Like a Virgin" on a red velvet bed with two dancers on either side, and the song ends with her simulating masturbation. My feelings about the scene alter from night to night. Either I laugh uncontrollably or have to turn away in disgust. I may have seen the scene at least fifty times, but it remains difficult for me to watch. I may be my sister's art director, but she is still my sister.

I AM WITH her while she conducts the dancer auditions. Although I have learned to keep my mouth shut, at intervals Madonna does question me about the stage and in particular dancers. Oliver

Crumes is her pick, her straight man for the tour. In *Truth or Dare,* she treats him like a child. They spend a great deal of time together each night after the show, but I don't know whether their relationship went any further.

A FEW DAYS before opening night, director Alek Keshishian comes to Tokyo to start filming *Truth or Dare,* but initially he has a rough time, because Madonna will only let him shoot certain things and is wary of strangers. So he ends up pumping me for advice on how to handle her.

A short summary of what I told him: "You can't just bounce into the room and do your thing. You have to enter the room carefully and first check Madonna's mood. Check her face. Say hello and see in what tone of voice she answers.

"If she says 'Hi, how are you?' that's a better sign than if she just says 'Hi.' If she doesn't look at you or doesn't even say hi, you know it isn't a good day. You must never get in her face. You must make her feel as if all your ideas, in actuality, came from her."

He takes my advice; she relaxes with him and gives him almost total access. Now he is shooting everything. Far more than I think he should be.

On the road, Madonna makes a stab at treating the dancers as if they are her family and even calls it "mothering"—but it isn't really conventional mothering. She keeps them close enough and devoted enough to remain loyal to her, and useful, but isn't genuinely loving and nurturing. At times, she reminds me of Joan, keeping her brood in order.

When we play Detroit and Alek shoots backstage, I hover around her, but I don't pick anything up or wipe the sweat off her body. Alek asks me to do all of that, but I refuse point-blank to either dress or undress her on camera. Now that I am art director, more than ever I don't want my friends or family to think of me in the role of her dresser.

For Madonna, one of the most embarrassing and incriminating moments during *Truth or Dare* is Moira McPharlin's backstage visit in Detroit. Moira is invited specifically so that Alek can film her face-to-face meeting with Madonna. If he hadn't wanted to film it, the meeting would never have taken place, as Madonna always avoids that kind of one-on-one interaction, particularly when she is in the midst of a show.

Before she meets Moira, whom she hasn't seen since tenth grade, Madonna reminisces on camera about their childhood, claiming that Moira taught her how to use tampons and how to make out. Moira vehemently denies both claims. Madonna launches into a whole riff about experimenting sexually with Moira, and Moira denies it.

Madonna grants Moira a brief one-on-one audience. Clearly uncomfortable with the cameras, Moira asks Madonna to sit down, but Madonna says, "I can't now, I'm really sorry." Moira tells her that four years ago she wrote her a letter asking her if she would be her unborn son's godmother. Madonna hastily says that she remembers, but that she got the letter a long time after the fact. Moira tells her that she has unexpectedly gotten pregnant again and asks Madonna point-blank to be her unborn child's godmother. Madonna visibly squirms.

Moira tells her she wants to name the child after Madonna and asks Madonna to bless the child in advance, and Madonna is momentarily speechless. Normally, handling awkward situations is my role, and Madonna would just issue the order, "Deal with it," and I would. Until now, she has never had to dirty her hands, but with Moira she has no choice.

Madonna escapes from Moira as quickly as possible, promises

to call her, but is clearly put out. After all, Moira has overstepped the mark—she has put Madonna on the spot, which Madonna hates, and the camera has recorded it. Her focus on the film has made her impervious to Moira's feelings, and I find that depressing.

WHILE WE ARE in Pontiac, Melissa calls me and tells me that Madonna is going to visit our mother's grave the next morning and asks if I want to go. I say I do. She tells me to be in the lobby at eleven. She gives me no clue that our visit to our mother's grave will be recorded on film. If she had, I never would have gone.

Instead, at eleven, I get into the limo. My sister, in black leggings and top, and extra-dark glasses, is already in it waiting for me. She's extremely quiet. I assume she is merely tired after last night's performance. In fact, she is either planning her next scene for *Truth or Dare* or anticipating it and feeling slightly guilty. Or perhaps both.

We drive for one and a half hours to Calvary Cemetery in Bay City. The limo pulls off a lonely paved highway and onto a bumpy dirt road that seems to lead to nowhere. I have a vague memory of traveling down this same road when I was a small child, but neither Madonna nor I have been back to the cemetery in years.

We drive through the graveyard gates, one of which is swinging off its hinges in the light breeze, and arrive at the small cemetery, which, to me, seems overgrown and unkempt. Headstones are arranged in no particular order, and it takes Madonna and me half an hour to finally find our mother's grave. Just as we do, Alek and the crew pull up in the film van.

My heart starts pounding. I am furious. "What the hell are they doing here?" I ask.

"Oh, didn't you know?" Madonna says, wide-eyed. "They're shooting this."

"Have you lost your *mind,* Madonna?" I know she isn't going to answer, so I walk away from her.

"Please, Chris, please don't."

I just keep on walking.

Madonna starts to come after me, then stops. Even she knows better.

I am sick to my stomach.

The cameras power up.

I fight my urge to rip the camera out of the cameraman's hands and smash it over Madonna's head.

Then her performance—which in the completed movie unfolds with the sound track of the song "Promise to Try," which she cowrote, playing over it, as well as a montage of Madonna on the tour—begins.

I lean against a nearby tree, white with rage, and observe my sister's on-camera shenanigans.

For a while, she wanders around the cemetery, recreating our search for the grave. She places a bunch of flowers on our mother's gravestone, kneels, and kisses it.

In a voice-over that she recorded afterward, but made sure not to let me know about, she recites, "I hadn't been to the cemetery since I was a young girl. I used to go after she died. My mother's death was a whole big mystery to me when I was a child; no one really explained it.

"What I remember most about my mother is that she was very kind and very gentle and very feminine. I mean, I don't know, I guess she just looked like an angel to me, but I suppose everybody thinks their mother is an angel when they are five. I also know she was really religious.

"So I never really understood why she was taken away from us; it seemed so unfair. I never thought that she had done something wrong, so oftentimes I thought it was what I had done wrong."

Then, in probably the worst moment of all for me, she muses, "I wonder what she looks like now? Just a bunch of dust."

More theatrics ensue as she lies down next to our mother's grave.

"I am going to get in right here, they are going to bury me sideways," she declares.

The camera is switched off, then Madonna turns to me and says, "Okay, now it's your turn, Christopher."

Her voice says it all: light, bright, with a subtext of "no big deal."

She and Alek expect me to now also visit our mother's grave strictly for the benefit of the camera. That isn't ever going to happen. I make Alek put the camera back in the trunk.

I turn my back on him and Madonna.

I ask him and Madonna to leave me alone at the grave.

After a good deal of cajoling, they finally move away and leave me alone to pay my respects to my mother in relative peace and privacy.

I spend some time sitting by her grave, wishing she were here. Then, full of sadness, I trudge back to the limo.

Madonna and I ride back to the hotel together in silence.

That night, I find it impossible to sleep. That my sister used my mother's grave as a movie location, her death as the impetus for her performance, wounds me deeply.

I am horrified at the lengths my sister is prepared to go to promote herself and her career. I fear she no longer has any boundaries, any limits. Everyone and everything is grist for her publicity mill, fodder for her career—even our late mother.

And if she does still feel genuine grief for the loss of our mother, she has long since buried it under the weight of her mammoth ego, obliterating it with her legend, her superstardom. Perhaps today's spectacle is her way of coping with her grief. Perhaps.

All I know is that to Madonna nothing is sacred anymore. Not even our dead mother, whom she has relegated to the role of mere extra in her movie. Yet to me, nothing is more sacred.

I never mention the graveyard scene to Madonna again. There is no point because I'm sure that she will never understand why her behavior has upset me so much. Instead, I sublimate my anger. Fortunately, the demands of the tour are such that I have little time to brood on my feelings or talk to my sister about anything meaningful. From Pontiac, the tour moves on to Worcester, then to Landover, to Washington, to Nassau Coliseum, to Philadelphia, and ends up at the Meadowlands Arena, East Rutherford, where Madonna performs two sold-out concerts, followed by a third in memory of Keith Haring, who died earlier in the year, that raises $300,000 for amfAR.

On June 30, 1990, the European leg of the *Blond Ambition* tour opens in Gothenburg, Sweden. On July 3, 4, and 5, Madonna performs three sold-out concerts at the Palais Omnisports de Paris. While we are there, we stay at the Ritz on the Place Vendôme.

Gaultier has agreed to exhibit my paintings at his gallery on the Faubourg Saint-Honoré. He has selected twenty of my religious paintings, and I am elated.

Tonight is the opening. Due to nerves, I take a long time to get ready. By the time I go downstairs, Madonna is already in the lobby, yelling for me.

Outside, the hotel is besieged by paparazzi and screaming fans. Madonna and I are escorted out the back door, into an alley behind the Ritz. Our car is waiting for us.

We leave in a convoy of three cars, each with a security guard in it. The first car leaves ahead of us. We follow him. A third security car follows us. As we turn out of the back alley, the paparazzi spot us, and the chase begins.

Our driver drives so fast that he almost runs into the security car in front, until he gets the picture and races ahead even faster. We are now in the Alma tunnel, the same tunnel in which Princess Diana would die. And our driver is driving faster and faster.

The press honk their horns.

Our driver steps on the gas. We hurtle through the tunnel.

"Slow the fuck down!" Madonna screams.

She shrinks down in her seat. I put my arm around her. We are both petrified.

I am convinced that we are going to crash.

Madonna keeps yelling at the driver to slow down.

He ignores her.

Finally, we are out of the tunnel and, with a screech of brakes, stop outside Gaultier's gallery.

When we climb out of the car, still shaken by the chase, Madonna is mobbed.

She smiles and waves and walks ahead, leaving me in her wake, feeling mildly annoyed.

Once inside the gallery, she glitters at the cameras and only gives my art a cursory glance.

I fight back the urge to say, "Madonna, tonight is about me."

Tonight was, indeed, meant to be my night. With the passing of time, and a degree of maturity, I accept that—no matter how talented an artist I might be—if I were not Madonna's brother, Gaultier would probably not have given me this show. And even if he had, if Madonna didn't attend, none of the press would have bothered to cover it. That night twelve of my paintings sell.

FROM PARIS, WE move on to Rome, where Madonna's second show is canceled due to a union strike, and less than stellar ticket sales—perhaps due to Catholic groups having condemned *Blond Ambition* as blasphemous. Undeterred, we move on to Turin and from there fly to Germany, where we play Munich and Dortmund, and then, on July 20, 21, and 22, Madonna performs to three sold-out audiences at Wembley Stadium, where, as always, the fans are among the most enthusiastic in the world.

After London, we play Rotterdam and then fly to Spain, where we play Madrid, Vigo, and Barcelona. On August 5, the *Blond Ambition* tour ends at the Stade de l'Ouest, in Nice. When HBO broadcasts the show live, it is seen in more than 4.3 million households, becomes the most-watched entertainment special in the network's eighteen-year history, and wins the Grammy for Best Music Video, Long Form.

Back in America, *I'm Breathless: Music from and Inspired by the Film Dick Tracy* is certified 2 million, Madonna performs "Vogue" at the seventh annual *MTV Video Music Awards*, where the video wins three awards, and on September 7, Madonna is honored with "The Commitment to Life" award and performs "Vogue" at the benefit for AIDS Project Los Angeles. Until now, I have no reason whatsoever to doubt my sister's sincerity regarding AIDS charities and her all-embracing allegiance to the gay world in general.

On October 27, 1990, Christopher Flynn, our first ballet teacher and Madonna's mentor, dies of AIDS. Madonna does not attend his memorial, but I understand and accept that she does not want to upstage the other mourners. I am sure she mourns for Christopher, though. Both of us do.

• • •

MADONNA ENDS THE year by releasing "Justify My Love," which, on December 3, 1990, premieres on *Nightline. Rolling Stone* crowns her "Image of the Eighties." *The Immaculate Collection* is released and stays at number one in the UK for nine weeks. In the United States it is certified two times platinum, and *Forbes* names Madonna the top-earning female entertainer of 1990, citing her income as $39 million. The magazine also votes her "America's Smartest Business Woman."

I realize that *Forbes* was right when, on May 7, 1991, just as *Truth or Dare* is about to be released, the *Advocate* publishes an interview with Madonna in which she outs me.

In an apparent ploy to garner support for the movie by ingratiating herself with her gay fans, she says, "My brother Christopher's gay, and he and I have always been the closest members of our family.

"It's funny. When he was really young, he was so beautiful and had girls all over him, more than any of my other brothers. I knew something was different but it was not clear to me. I just thought, *I know there are a lot of girls around, but I don't get that he has a girlfriend.* He was like a girl-magnet. They all seemed incredibly fond of him and close to him in a way I hadn't seen men with women.

"I'll tell you when I knew. After I met Christopher [Flynn], I brought my brother to my ballet class because he wanted to start studying dance. I just saw something between them. I can't even tell you exactly what, but then I thought, *Oh, I get it. Oh, okay. He likes men too.* It was an incredible revelation, but I didn't say anything to my brother yet. I'm not even sure he knew. He's two years younger than me. He was still a baby. I could just feel something."

I was incensed. From my point of view, my sister has evidently decided that outing me to the readers of the *Advocate* is the perfect promotional tool for the movie. Let's face it, *Truth or Dare* deals—directly or indirectly—with sadomasochism, lesbianism, rape, a hint of incest, a dead mother, so why not a gay brother as well?

After all, Madonna used my mother's grave as a movie location, so why not use my sexuality as a publicity opportunity? I realize another reason. The gay community had been her original fan base in the early eighties. Now, though, some gay fans were starting to feel that she had become far too mainstream, too hetero. Her answer? Her way of winning them back? "My brother Christopher is gay."

At the time, though, I don't ruminate over her motives for outing me. I just know how outraged I am. Without asking me, without giving me a say in the decision, she has taken it upon herself to out me. I know that she hasn't for a moment considered whether my homosexuality is public knowledge, the reality that our grandmother doesn't know about it, and neither does our extended family nor anyone outside our circle of friends. Besides, it has always been my choice whether, when, or where to come out, not Madonna's. But why should I be surprised? She didn't stop at exploiting our grief at our mother's death, so why should she stop at exploiting me?

"How could you possibly have done that to me, Madonna!"

A moment's silence, during which she chews her gum.

"Don't see why you're upset, Chrissy."

She knows I hate being called Chrissy. She knows my name is Christopher. If the subject weren't so serious, I'd call her Mud, just to piss her off.

"I mean, everyone knows you're gay. I don't see why you give a fuck," she goes on.

Half an hour of trying to explain, trying to make her understand that it should be my decision to go public or not, not hers, but to no avail.

"What's the big deal? You *are* gay, aren't you?"

I try not to make as big a deal of it as I'd like. She quite plainly doesn't understand what she's done. How can you fight with someone who doesn't understand?

A week after the *Advocate* appears, I get a call on my unlisted phone number from the *Enquirer,* telling me that they are about to publish a story that I have AIDS. I'm monogamous. And so is Danny. Although I have been tested before and know I am not positive, I get tested again and send the *Enquirer* the results. I am negative. They drop the story.

In July 1991, Madonna films *A League of Their Own*. Madonna being Madonna, she can't help inciting controversy by airing her feelings on Evansville, Indiana, where the movie was shot, and complaining that the house she rented didn't have cable. No fewer than three hundred residents of Evansville join in protest against her. It's hardly the most virulent protest she's encountered in her long and protest-filled career, so she emerges unscathed.

Rosie O'Donnell is in the movie with her. Rosie and Madonna become friends. I think they primarily bonded because both of their mothers died young, though I know Rosie never incorporated her dead mother into her act.

In November 1991, I have my second art show—this time at the Wessel and O'Connor Fine Art Gallery, on Broome Street, SoHo. During this period, my work centers around academic single-line drawings of limbless torsos. Although it doesn't occur to me at the time, my choice of subject—helpless and passive—is extremely telling.

I invite Madonna to the show. She comes and it's a replay of the Gaultier opening. She walks in and the entire room stops, then everyone clusters around her. I hope against hope that she will now move toward me and view the paintings with me, but she doesn't. Instead, she just stands in the middle of the room, reveling in the attention of the crowd. I keep smiling, because she has at least taken the trouble to support me by coming to the exhibition. And I suppose that half of Madonna is better than none. I know all of that and accept it, but, even when I sell eight of my paintings, three of them to David Geffen, it isn't easy. While I've always had confidence in my own artistic abilities, living in my sister's shadow often makes me question whether my art really is any good, or whether my success is merely predicated on her fame.

AT THE END of the year, on December 10, Madonna is honored with the Award of Courage by amfAR.

In Madonna's private life, Sandra Bernhardt is still on the scene, but Madonna and I both find her a little too negative, down in the mouth, not a happy person. Nonetheless, Madonna still invites her to her 1991 New Year's Eve party. Sandra brings her then girlfriend, Ingrid Casares, with her. A butch version of Audrey Hepburn, Ingrid is boyish, fawnlike, with big, slanting doe eyes. She's tall, thin, and extremely cool. For the past year, ever since Ingrid met Sandra after one of her shows, Ingrid and Sandra have been an item. But the moment Ingrid meets Madonna, as far as Ingrid is concerned, Sandra is history. And Madonna will embark on the deepest, most enduring liaison of her entire life.

Ingrid and I become close friends, and even today, however much harm she may have done to my relationship with my sister, I still love her as best I can. She has helped in my career as a music video director, is fun to be with, and, above all, is a true original.

Born in 1964, in Little Havana, Miami, Ingrid is the daughter of wealthy parents—her father owns RC Aluminum, which makes windows for high-rises—who fled Cuba during the revolution.

A convent schoolgirl, and a brilliant basketball player, Ingrid grew up a typical Coral Gables rich girl. She went to the University of Miami, first began using cocaine at fifteen or sixteen, and by 1994 has struggled to treat the problem several times. Along the way, she took a degree in English and PR, then moved to L.A., where she became a model booker for Wilhelmina and met Sandra.

Since then, she has worked as image consultant for Emilio Estefan's Crescent Moon Records—whose artists include Jon Secada and Albita—and was co-owner of the Miami clubs Liquid and Bar Room. In the late nineties, she tried without success to open a club in Manhattan. She has always been a hard worker, but she has nonetheless aroused the ire of feminists such as Camille Paglia, who has written of her, "She's turned herself into Madonna's flunky and yes-girl. I think Madonna's dependence on Ingrid Casares is a self-stunting illness. Madonna should go to the Betty Ford clinic to break her addiction and detox from Ingrid."

At the time of Madonna's first meeting with Ingrid, the woman in Madonna's life was Sandra, but—whether or not their relationship was physical—Madonna couldn't control Sandra. A woman with her own career, a definite personality and opinions, Sandra has never been Madonna's puppy dog. Ingrid, however, is quite another story.

Madonna has never taken well to criticism. At the time of her first meeting with Ingrid, she is well primed to find a permanent yes-woman. Now that she is a star, she has no patience with anyone who disagrees with her. Ingrid never will.

A snapshot: Madonna and Ingrid are breakfasting in Madonna's Miami home. Madonna is reading *Vogue*. She comes across a picture of an actress and says to Ingrid, "Look at her—she's so fucking ugly."

Ingrid takes a brief look at the picture.

"I don't think she's that ugly."

"Yes, she is."

"You are so right, Madonna," Ingrid says, "she *is* so ugly."

Ingrid is the perfect echo for Madonna. Never an instigator of conversation, she has a knack for taking on her environment and the opinions of the most important person around her—Madonna. She is the perfect chameleon, never challenging, never confrontational, and incredibly skilled at asking or answering questions, saying exactly what Madonna needs to hear.

Ingrid knows exactly how to make herself indispensable to Madonna. Ingrid's a great networker and collector of gossip and, from the first, is happy to pass information on to Madonna. She is always available, and as she is independently wealthy, she always pays her own way. She is at the house early in the morning, ready to work out with Madonna; Ingrid is a big fish in the small Miami pond, ready and willing to shop with Madonna or for her. She can find clothing Madonna wants, and if Madonna is in the mood for a man, Ingrid will find one for her.

In actuality, until Madonna marries Guy—who Ingrid tells me doesn't like her—Ingrid is the man in Madonna's life. Or perhaps *boy* would be more accurate. Ingrid looks like a boy, but because she is a girl, she is happy to do girl stuff with Madonna: get her nails done with her, have a massage or a facial with her. And she's discreet, which is of paramount importance to Madonna.

Above all, Ingrid is no competition for Madonna. She doesn't compete with Madonna for men, nor does she compete with her for women. For more than fifteen years, Ingrid will endure in Madonna's life, as Ingrid doesn't need Madonna for money, keeps her mouth shut, and adores her without question or limitations. It wouldn't have surprised me at all if my sister and Ingrid were having intimate relations. But Madonna never confirms or denies it.

I have no real problem with Madonna's relationship with Ingrid. In a way, it's a match made in heaven. Ostensibly, Ingrid and Madonna have nothing in common, except one thing: they are both in love with Madonna. At least, Ingrid definitely falls in love with her at their first meeting and, to this day, remains enthralled.

When Madonna and Ingrid are out in public, Ingrid always hovers over Madonna protectively. Madonna rarely reciprocates. Now and again, she does flirt with Ingrid only slightly, just enough to keep her on the hook. If they are out in a club, Madonna will give Ingrid a big kiss on the lips or cheek, and for the next five months Ingrid will live on that moment. But when they watch movies together, for example, they don't sit on each other's lap, although Ingrid sometimes sits at Madonna's feet, as if she were Madonna's slave. To some extent, she is. And Madonna knows exactly how to keep her in line. Many times, when they are going to a party together, at the last minute Madonna will inform Ingrid that she can't ride with Madonna in her car because there is no room. Ingrid will be devastated.

One night, the three of us are at a big dinner together. Ingrid goes to take her place next to Madonna.

Madonna shakes her head. "No, Gridy, you can't sit next to me tonight."

Ingrid makes a face, then quickly masks it with a small smile.

She takes her place at the other end of the table.

But as the evening progresses, she slowly makes her way back to the seat near Madonna. When the moment is right, she sits down next to her, just as she intended in the first place. Then she is happy.

In general, I find it painful to observe Madonna demeaning Ingrid, and Ingrid unresistingly acquiescing.

In January 1992, Madonna and photographer Steven Meisel start shooting her *Sex* book in Coconut Grove, Florida. From that time on, Ingrid and Madonna hang out together in the $4.9 million, six-bedroom, four-bathroom Coconut Grove mansion, which Madonna rents during the shoot and then buys.

I dislike the book—which is published on October 16, 1992—intensely. Before production on it begins, I tell Madonna she should have Helmut Newton shoot the pictures and only publish five hundred leatherbound, numbered copies.

"Make it special, unique, a collector's item," I say.

"This is how I wanna do it," she says.

And that's how she does it.

In the United States the book sells a record five hundred thousand copies in just one week, and in Europe sells more than one hundred thousand copies in just two days, so on a commercial level she was obviously right.

The Coconut Grove house was built in the thirties and was originally part of the Vizcaya estate. Madonna asks me to decorate it for her, so I fly down to Miami, where the first person I meet is Ingrid, who has come over to check out the house on Madonna's behalf, along with Eugene Rodriguez, the broker for the property.

The former owners of the house replaced the original thirties Spanish interior with Italian light oak wood and had everything built in, even the beds. Horrifying. I set about restoring the house. It ends up having six bedrooms, new bathrooms—Madonna's is black-and-white marble—a large living room with a carved ceiling, a long dining room with coral keystone arches, a gym, an office, and a media room. All in all, a great place to hang out.

Sylvester Stallone lives on the same street, and Madonna and I laugh at the vanity of his CASA ROCKO insignia emblazoned on his mansion gate.

Although the house is intended to be Madonna's vacation home, she often uses it year-round, primarily because she is at her most relaxed at the Coconut Grove house. The press has no access. We hang out by the pool, I cook a great deal—pastas and salads—and Madonna, Ingrid, and I, along with various other people, all watch old movies together—*A Clockwork Orange, 2001, Laura, Bringing Up Baby.*

Often, a New Age priestess, Elsa Patton—a tall, heavily made-up blonde who drives a late-model Rolls-Royce—comes to the house with her daughter, Marisol, and sprinkles blessed water around all the doors. Now and again, she takes Madonna and Ingrid out on Madonna's small speedboat, *Lola Lola,* and gives them a ritual baptism in the ocean.

Once Elsa conducts one of her iconoclastic rituals on me—a treatment that Madonna has regularly, which Madonna explains to me is designed to cleanse the soul. I lie on the bed, wearing all white, and Elsa rubs hot oil with rosemary and other herbs and spices into my body. Then she goes into a trance and starts talking to me in a strange language. This takes precisely thirty-five minutes. When she's done, she says I have to keep the oils on for the next twenty-four hours. I think I smell like a roasted chicken and shower the oil off immediately.

But Madonna believes implicitly in Elsa and her treatments. When it comes to religion and rituals, Madonna's policy—to be on the safe side—is to cover all bases. In Coconut Grove, she has containers of spiritually cleansed water by the doorways, a nineteenth-century Italian dark-mahogany-with-ivory-inlay prayer bench that I gave her for Christmas, rosaries hang throughout the house, and a small shrine to our mother.

Elsa and Marisol are frequent visitors, and Madonna's soul is repeatedly cleansed. On reflection, I suppose it isn't a big leap from there to Kabbalah.

Although Ingrid is very much a part of Madonna's life now—rather like Cleopatra's handmaiden, or a windup doll that can speak, but whose battery has wound down, or, if she does speak, is an ever-willing echo—Madonna still has relationships with a series of men.

She has a brief relationship with Vanilla Ice, but breaks it off because she considers him less than her intellectual equal, and I agree. Then she starts seeing the actor John Enos, who appeared in *Melrose Place,* a genuine man's man. Like my brother Marty, John Enos is the kind of man both Sean and Guy long to be. He changes the oil in his car, drives a fifties pickup truck, which he restored on his own, and has a basement in his house set up as a shooting range. He is tall, happy, quite good-looking, and is one of the owners of the Roxbury nightclub in L.A.

Despite being so masculine, John is, like Warren, totally comfortable with gay men, and we often hang out together. In yet another attempt to bond with the man in my sister's life, I go with John to Tattoo's By Lou in South Beach, where I have the tattoo of an anchor and the word "mother" tattooed on my shoulder. While we don't mingle our blood together like Sean and I once did, John and I are definitely buddies and I like and admire him. A year later, Madonna, John, and I go to a party up in the Hollywood Hills, along with Guy Oseary, who works for Madonna's company, Maverick Records, and is straight. Marky Mark—Mark Wahlberg—is also at the party. I dance with a guy on the dance floor, and Marky mutters something under his breath. Guy Oseary comes to my defense and starts tussling with Marky. Things look as if they are about to get ugly. John makes a move toward Marky. Marky takes one look at him and sprints out of the house. Enos follows in hot pursuit, yelling, "Come back here, you pussy, I'm gonna beat the shit out of you." But Marky just keeps on running.

However much a man John is, he still isn't man enough for Madonna, who starts cavorting around with her twenty-two-year-old bodyguard, Jim Albright. It only takes me an hour with Albright to conclude that the attraction might be purely physical.

Ingrid, Madonna, Jim, and I take *Lola Lola* across the bay to Key Biscayne. The water in between is shallow. We've ridden the boat out that way many times, and I know you have to take a certain route. I tell Jim, but he doesn't listen.

On the way back, I again tell him what route to take, but he insists on steering the boat in the direction he wants. Seven hundred yards from the dock at the end of our garden, the water is only around two feet deep. I try to direct Jim, but he ignores me.

Two minutes later we are stuck on a sandbar.

Madonna yells, "Goddamm it, Jim, why the fuck didn't you listen to my brother?"

I call on the cell phone for a boat to tow us out.

We sit in the boat, waiting.

After twenty minutes, Madonna stands up. "I'm not waiting here anymore." She starts to climb out of the boat and into the water.

"Don't, Madonna," I say, and tell her about the nurse sharks that normally lurk around the bay. "Six or seven feet long, and not particularly docile, so it's not a good idea to go wading."

She sits down in the boat again.

The sun is beating down on us. In a replay of our Moroccan trip, she starts bitching about the heat.

Finally, a boat pulls up to tow us home.

"You're driving, Christopher," she says.

And that's the last I see of Jim Albright.

MADONNA AND I spend Thanksgiving and Easter in the Coconut Grove house, and during the year, she often throws parties there. Her parties are relatively sedate and usually end with everyone sitting in the living room playing some stupid game she has suggested.

On one occasion, David Geffen, Rosie O'Donnell, Ingrid, Madonna, John Enos, and I are all in the living room. Madonna suggests we play a game—a hybrid version of truth or dare—in which we pass a lit match around and whoever is holding the match when it goes out has to answer a question.

The questions?

"If you have to kiss anyone in the room, who would you like it to be?"

"Who is the most beautiful person in the room?"

"If you have to have sex with anyone in the room, who would you like to have it with?"

The others answer: "Madonna." "Madonna." "Madonna."

My answer: John Enos.

All the focus in the room is on Madonna, every question is about her, every answer—and they all go along with it. She is the be-all and end-all, the alpha and the omega, of all our existences, and we endlessly trumpet our allegiance to her.

In Coconut Grove, Madonna now owns three Chihuahuas—Chiquita, Rosita, and Evita—all selected for her by Ingrid. But Madonna is not a dog or cat lover. She won't walk the dogs and views them as little more than live-in accessories. She allows them to run all over the house and, even though they shit everywhere, pays scant attention to them.

I FIND OUT in April 1992 that Madonna is still seeing Jim Albright. John Enos also knows and is not happy about it. But he is so besotted with her that he doesn't end their relationship.

She says of him, "He's way too available and way too mainstream, although he's extremely handy around the house."

One incident in particular rankles John. Madonna takes Good Friday off. Enos assumes that he will spend the day with her. Instead, she tells him she wants to hang out in South Beach with Ingrid and have lunch with her there, just the two of them. As it happens, Sean was also in South Beach with Robin at the time.

Poor John. Not only does he have to cope with Madonna and Albright and her intense relationship with Ingrid, but also her continuing fascination with her ex-husband, Sean Penn. Then there is Guy Oseary, now her manager, with whom she has had a long-running flirtation.

Madonna's breakup with John is inevitable. Afterward, he dates a glittering array of sexy women: Taylor Dayne, Heidi Fleiss, and Traci Lords—all a testament to his masculinity.

ON THE CAREER front, both Madonna and I are more than surprised when Oliver Crumes, Kevin Stea, and Gabriel Trupin, dancers from *Blond Ambition,* file a lawsuit against Madonna for invasion of privacy, fraud and deceit, intentional misrepresentation, and more, basically accusing her of exposing their private lives in *Truth or Dare.*

I have little sympathy for them; all the dancers were aware, from the first, that they were being filmed for *Truth or Dare,* and no matter how much I might dislike the graveyard scene in the film, all the dancers knew exactly what they were participating in. Nonetheless, Madonna eventually chose to settle with them.

THROUGH THE YEAR, Madonna and I remain extremely close. We both relish seeing legends perform, then meeting them afterward, and often go to their performances together. On February 24, 1992, we see Pavarotti at Lincoln Center. At intermission, we go backstage to visit him. In his dressing room, he is spread out on the couch, his big body all covered in warm, wet towels to soothe his voice, his head popping out of another towel. A translator is on hand for his conversation with Madonna.

"The show is great," she says.

"It's an honor," Pavarotti says.

"Grazie."

"You're Italian! Isn't that great!"

"Shouldn't the whole world be?" she says.

ON AUGUST 26, 1992, Madonna, Ingrid, and I go to see Peggy Lee sing at Club 53 at the New York Hilton. Peggy is wonderful, but can barely move onstage. She's seventy-two and infirm, but is still an incredible performer. She is wearing a wig, attached to her head by a large diamond brooch, which seems to be pinned into the top of her skull. It's an odd sight, but quickly forgotten when she belts out "Fever," which Madonna will cover on her *Erotica* album. After the show is over, Madonna presents her with a bouquet of red roses. Then Peggy is wheeled out in her wheelchair.

IN DECEMBER 1992, Madonna's *Dangerous Game* is released. I tell her this is the best movie that she has ever made and that I think she can act. This time, I mean it. Soon after, *Body of Evidence* comes out, and I am once again tremendously embarrassed for her.

Despite the debacle of *Body of Evidence,* which critics universally pan, Madonna now has tremendous compensations—financial and otherwise—in her career, particularly after she signs a $60 million, seven-year contract with Time Warner, with whom she forms a new multimedia entertainment company. Her reviews for *A League of Their Own* are positive—and I agree with them.

True to form, she also fans the flames of controversy by modeling topless at the Gaultier amfAR benefit at the Shrine Auditorium, but the cause is good and the show raises $750,000 for AIDS research. I am glad that my sister still does so much for the fans who made her and against the sickness from which so many of our friends have died.

EIGHT

"Wouldn't it be awful if this was—was the high point?"

F. Scott Fitzgerald, *This Side of Paradise*

In early 1993, Madonna calls and tells me she's going on tour again and wants me to work on it. She is also looking for a new house and asks me to come out to L.A. and help her.

I fly out, stay at Oriole Way, spend a couple of weeks looking at houses with Madonna. We look in Bel Air, in Pacific Palisades, in Beverly Hills. We never let the brokers pick us up from Oriole Way, though. Madonna can't stand real estate brokers and I know they don't like her very much either, for when it comes to real estate, she is an extremely particular and difficult customer.

Consequently, Madonna always drives us to the prospective houses. She likes to drive and enjoys being behind the wheel. She drives a little fast and is not a smooth driver, a little jerky. She doesn't particularly care about cars, except for a classic white convertible Mercedes with a red leather interior that she owns—an older model that she first has in L.A., then ships down to Coconut Grove.

So we drive to meet the brokers. Each time, we walk up the drive, but don't go inside the house, because it takes Madonna one glance at an exterior to know she isn't interested in a particular house—which bugs a lot of brokers, as she is depriving them of the chance to pitch it to her.

But then we see Castillo del Lago, the former home of gangster Bugsy Siegel—coincidentally the subject of Warren's movie *Bugsy*—which overlooks the Hollywood Reservoir and doesn't feel as if it is in L.A. at all, but more like a palazzo in northern Italy. Madonna loves it and so do I. The twenty-thousand-square-foot castle has five bedrooms, seven bathrooms, stands on four acres of land, and—with its 160-foot lookout tower—feels secure.

Madonna buys Castillo del Lago for around $5 million, and I start renovating it, working 24-7. Madonna doesn't give me a budget, and I end up spending $3 million on renovations, the interiors, fixtures, and fittings. Then she has second thoughts. She sends me a letter in which she writes, "I don't know how long I can live in this culturally bankrupt town," and tells me I am spending too much money on Castillo. I probably am, but I'm having a great time doing it. Besides, every expenditure is necessary and accounted for.

We meet and discuss the budget. I explain what I need to carry on the renovation. To my surprise, for the first time ever while I am working on one of her houses, Madonna questions my judgment, and I find it disconcerting. Ultimately, she leaves me completely to my own devices, and Castillo del Lago ends up being the most enjoyable interior job I have ever done for her.

Part of the renovation of Castillo del Lago includes transforming the house's two turrets, and its massive retaining wall. I hit on the idea of copying a little church in Portofino that Madonna and I visited at the end of *Blond Ambition* and both loved, which is painted in alternating white and terra-cotta stripes. I tell her my idea. She says, "Are you sure it won't look like a circus tent?" I promise her that it won't, particularly after it has aged. She tells me to go ahead.

On the largest wall in the living room, we hang a Langlois nude of Selene and Endymion, which was first commissioned for the Palace of Versailles, which I had originally mounted on the ceiling of the Oriole house. With Madonna's imprimatur, I fly to London and spend a fortune on fabrics and furniture. On Lillie Road, I find sixteen William and Mary chairs—an expensive purchase, but well worth it—and buy them. Madonna loves them. They travel with her on all her moves and she still has them to this day.

Madonna and I are together all the time now, and—in shades of the past—whenever I wake up in the dead of the night, she is sitting on the floor in her library, reading books such as Paulo Coelho's *Alchemist.* Despite the intervening years, her patterns are still the same. Only the surroundings and the lifestyle are grander.

With the house under way, she asks me to meet with Freddy about my role on the tour. I tell her I want to direct as well as design. I ask to be relieved of my old dresser duties, and she says she will think about it.

I have long forgiven her for outing me. She is trusting me to do her house, and the chances are that she is now about to trust me to direct her tour. She is relying on me, I am part of her world, and I am perfectly content.

When I arrive at Freddy's and he gives me the good news that Madonna has decided that I can direct *The Girlie Show,* he also gives me the bad. She has certain conditions.

On tour, she will give me my own car and driver and will fly me first-class. However, she will not pay for me to stay in hotel suites. I am annoyed because even her assistant stays in a suite.

My sister stands to make millions from this tour. I ask Freddy why he is haggling with me over a few thousand.

"I have to, it's my job and she insists," he says.

The remark is cryptic, but I think I know what he means. Although Madonna fully accepts that I merit the job of director and has willingly agreed to give it to me, strangely enough she partly resents her generosity to me. Refusing to allow me to stay in hotel suites is an expression of that resentment.

When we arrive in London and I am shown to my room—a single one, at that—I complain to the tour manager. He gets me a suite instead. My sister finds out and sends me a rather nasty letter of complaint. I go to see her in her suite, and for the first and last time, I resort to a tear or two. I tell her that I am so sorry if she feels I took advantage of her and ask her to forgive me. For the rest of the tour, she books me into suites. I win the battle, but the point is still taken. She is thinking in terms of costs, not human beings, and definitely not of me and all the years we have worked together. Or perhaps I am now getting too close to her, and she is beginning to pull away.

Starting in July, we begin rehearsing the show at Sony Studios on West Washington in Culver City. I am still designing Madonna's house, but I am also supervising the crew, designing the stage set, handling all the dancers, maintaining peace onstage, and—above all—directing Madonna.

To my surprise, though, at rehearsals she listens to me, and follows my advice on dance moves, costumes, lighting, and staging. We are together 24-7 and there are no more conflicts. Our creativity is perfectly in tune and I am having the best time of my life, although I have never worked harder.

At first, I do have some problems with the crew—about a hundred roadies who assume I am only around because I'm Madonna's brother. She doesn't disabuse them of that notion. It takes me two weeks to win their respect, but in the end I do.

In the evenings, Madonna and I talk about the show and, for inspiration, watch Bollywood musicals, Thai dancing, Burt Lancaster's *Trapeze,* Marlene Dietrich, and Louise Brookes. We decide on a burlesque circus theme for the show and that we will use five different choreographers. Gene Kelly is one of them.

He is to choreograph the "Rain" number, but from the first it is clear that he is uncomfortable with our dancers, whom we have picked for personality, and not because they are classically trained ballet dancers. He doesn't understand the show's concept of grand spectacle and burlesque with heavy sexual overtones.

I take Madonna aside and tell her she needs to come and watch Gene's number, as I don't think he is working out and we need to fire him.

She sits in on the number and strongly disagrees with me: "No, I think Gene will be fine."

I shrug and bide my time.

A week later, she marches up to me and says, "Christopher, I've just watched Gene's number again. I don't think he's working out. I think we need to fire him."

"Really? Are you sure, Madonna?"

She nods, shamefaced at having single-handedly conceived of such a terrible fate for this venerable American icon. "Will you break it to him?" she asks, somewhat tentatively.

"No way, Madonna. Your idea—you tell him!" I say firmly.

"I'll get Freddy to do it."

Exit Gene Kelly, with no hard feelings, I hope. Madonna, on the other hand, is not sentimental and never has been.

• • •

In June 1993, just before the tour begins, Danny and I celebrate our tenth anniversary. In commemoration, I design two matching platinum bands for us—one set with square-cut rubies, one set with square-cut emeralds—and have them made at the venerable Harry Winston. I have also translated to Latin and had engraved on the outside of the rings the words "As I am yours, you are mine."

During our ten years together, once Danny has conquered his drinking issues, the only cause of dissonance between us has been my relationship with my sister. Although she and Danny are on friendly terms, and when I am working on the Coconut Grove house, he comes to stay there with me, but in private he tells me that he thinks she is using me.

He says constantly that she is sucking the life out of me. I counter with "You are wrong; she's giving me life." He hates Madonna because he holds her responsible for tearing me away from the secure little world we've created together in New York.

I try to bring him into my world, but he simply refuses. He doesn't want to meet me on the North American leg of the tour; he hates L.A., doesn't drive, and won't join me out there. As much as I can, I encourage him to work again. He has always expressed an interest in architecture, so I offer to send him to NYU to study it. I get the applications, help him prepare all the forms, but a week before the interview he decides he doesn't want to go to college after all. He prefers to stay in our perfect little bubble, and to hell with the outside world.

Apart from his distaste for Madonna, he is also uncomfortable with many of my friends because he feels they take me away from him, as well. And when one of my lesbian friends begs me to father her child, and I consider it, he nearly has a fit.

I pay all our living expenses, but in the house we definitely live Danny's way. I cook most of the time, we regularly throw dinner parties, and I firmly believe that our relationship is for life, although the gulf between my life with Madonna and my life with him is growing ever wider.

ON JUNE 1, 1993, Madonna and I see Charles Aznavour and Liza Minnelli at Carnegie Hall. After the show, we are whisked backstage and into Liza's dressing room. She is seated in front of her makeup mirror, dressed in the same red-sequined gown she just wore onstage. *"Hello,"* she blares in her distinctive voice, "I'm Liza!"

"I'm Madonna."

"I know, I know," says Liza, "I'm a massive fan of your work!"

"So am I," Madonna says, hastily adding, "I mean of yours, of course."

Madonna turns and introduces me.

"You were amazing," I say to Liza.

Liza gives us both a broad, toothsome grin. The dressing room door opens. Her grin immediately fades. A group of fans enter. Liza's grin glitters again, only this time not at us. Madonna and I exchange glances. The audience is over. We tiptoe out of the room, leaving the fans to Liza and vice versa. One more legend under our belts.

On September 25, *The Girlie Show* opens at Wembley Stadium. Then the show moves on to Paris, where Madonna gives three concerts at the Palais Omnisport, to Frankfurt, and on October 4 to Tel Aviv, Israel.

On our day off, we take a trip to Jerusalem, where Madonna and I vist the Church of the Holy Sepulchre together. We see how in the Catholic Church every sect of Catholicism has its own section. We are both scared by the intensity of religious feeling in Jerusalem. Madonna says, "Everyone wants a chunk of this city. It would be so hard to live here and find peace."

THE EUROPEAN LEG of the tour ends in Istanbul on October 7, then we fly back to America. Since we left, I have inhabited Madonna's world, utterly and completely. With her, I live out all my creativity and travel to other countries, as well, which fascinates me and feeds my desire for inspiration and adventure.

She and I are closer than ever, but that doesn't stop her from forming her habitual on-the-road relationship with a so-called straight man—this time with Michael Gregory. And because I am lonely, and as I have done on every tour, I follow suit and develop an on-the-road relationship, this time with a dancer I'll call Richard. We form a close, platonic relationship, and from Richard, I receive a little of the affection to which I am accustomed at home. Our relationship is not sexual or romantic, but nevertheless intimate.

Before the London opening of *The Girlie Show*, all the dancers give me thank-you cards. I keep just one of them—a black-and-white thirties photo of ballet dancers—the one from Richard, on which he has written, "Thank you so much for being my friend. Working with you has been wonderful. You're an amazing director. All my love, Richard, xx."

When I arrive back from Europe, I spend a couple of nights with Danny at our New York apartment. As Madonna is only going to do three shows—two at Madison Square Garden and the third in Philadelphia—and will leave straightaway for Asia, I don't bother to unpack my suitcase.

After the show in Philadelphia, on October 19, 1993, Madonna and I drive straight back to Manhattan. I get home to the apartment at around two in the morning. There I find Danny sitting on the floor, holding Richard's card. One look at his face and I know I'm in trouble.

He throws the card at my feet and accuses me of cheating on him. He demands that I confess then and there. I tell him I have nothing to confess. He insists that I swear that I won't be unfaithful to him again. I tell him that I won't swear that because, if I do, I'd be lying, because I haven't been unfaithful to him in the first place. I tell him that what happened with Richard and me was only friendship, that I am not in love with Richard.

Danny rounds on me and says, "You decide right now. Tell me that you will never be unfaithful to me again, or leave."

I am utterly dumbfounded.

We spend the next couple of hours arguing.

At four, Danny finally goes to bed.

I sit on the kitchen floor till the sun rises, asking myself if I can go on. Do I want to remain on this isolated little planet with just Danny for company and never experience the wider world again? Or do I want to carry on exploring, living, being part of the world I crave, rather than watch from afar while life goes by me?

As dawn breaks, I decide. I grab my bags and move to my studio.

In the morning, I call Madonna and tell her what has happened. We rarely talk about our feelings in our family, so I know better than to expect her to offer me her shoulder to cry on; still, I secretly hope that she will care enough about me to be slightly sympathetic.

"Don't worry, I never liked him anyway," she says.

For a second, I am speechless.

Then she goes on, "Don't worry about it. Everything will work out."

End of discussion. Back to work again.

No suggestion that I come over for breakfast or sit with her on the plane so we can talk.

Nothing.

Ten years of my life, gone.

At this moment, the loss of my mother is at its most profound. There is no one for me to turn to, no one to understand. No one.

I concentrate, instead, on retaining my professionalism—and succeed. On October 21, we play the Palace of Auburn Hills; on October 23, we play Montreal; then we fly to San Juan, Puerto Rico, where, on October 26, Madonna performs in front of twenty-six thousand fans and, by pulling the Puerto Rican flag up to her crotch, ends up being condemned by the Puerto Rican House of Representatives for desecrating their flag. Fortunately, we are allowed to leave the country.

From there, we fly to Buenos Aires, then perform in São Paulo and in Rio, where Madonna appears in front of a sold-out crowd. In Mexico City, Madonna puts on three shows, flying in the face of religious groups that have fought to bar her from their country, but have failed.

By the time the tour moves on to Australia on November 17, where Madonna performs in Sydney, then in Melbourne, Brisbane, and Adelaide, I am starting to be somewhat distracted from my breakup with Danny.

After New York, Richard and I have embarked on an intimate relationship after all. Although I am on top of the world professionally, I am still acutely aware that my personal life has come crashing down on me.

When I arrive in Tokyo, where *The Girlie Show* tour ends with five sold-out concerts, all I can think of now is Danny. However much Richard has succeeded in saving me from the dark days, now that I am confronting the reality that I am about to return home to

My maternal grandmother, Elsie, Madonna, and Joan's mother, Rose, taken after Madonna's Like a Virgin *tour came to Detroit in May, 1985.*

Madonna in a Shanghai restaurant, prior to the shooting of Shanghai Surprise, *which premiered in August, 1986.*

Madonna, the day before the Dick Tracy *premiere, 1990.*

Madonna and Gaultier in Tokyo before Blond Ambition, *1990.*

Carlos and me at Madonna's 1996 birthday at the Delano, Miami.

Same event, with Gianni Versace.

The Planet Hollywood opening in Cannes in May, 1997—me, Demi, Naomi, and Kate.

Madonna pregnant with Lola, with me in background, in the kitchen at the Oklahoma Avenue house in Michigan in 1996.

Madonna and Marty at the notorious "butter" Thanksgiving, 1996.

Dan Sehres and me, at a party at the Atlantic in 1997.

Me and Daniel Hoff on his birthday, 1997.

Madonna with Guy Oseary, Evita, and Chiquita in Miami, Thanksgiving, 1997.

Me and Niki Harris, 1997.

Lori Petty, Me, Gwyneth Paltrow, and Chris Lee, Halloween, 1999.

John Enos and me, Atlantic Restaurant, 1998.

Alek Keshishian, Daniel Hoff, Ingrid Casares, and Kate Moss at party in New York, 1998.

Ingrid, Madonna, Stephen Dorff, and Chris Paciello at a party at Ingrid's Miami club, Liquid, in 1999.

New Year's at the Versace Mansion, 1999—Ingrid spoon-feeding Madonna as usual.

Madonna and Carlos visit my father's vineyard in 1995. From left to right, me seated, Jennifer, my nephew Levon, Madonna seated on a chair in the center—just like a queen. Standing behind her from left to right, Melanie, Anthony's girlfriend, Anthony, Joan, my father, Carlos, and Paula.

Ciccone Vineyard and Winery in Traverse City, Michigan, 2003.

America without Danny there waiting for me, I feel as if I have thrown away my last chance at love, the best man I'll ever know, and I'm distraught.

I think back on my life with Danny and decide that I want to compensate him for all the years we have spent together. I send him almost a quarter of my savings—$50,000—funds I've been saving for the last fifteen years.

I tell Madonna, and I am deeply moved when she writes me a long and comforting letter. Addressing me as "My dearest tortured brother," she says that it's nice to discover that "indecision, self-doubt, the inability to be alone, and masochism is a familial trait and nothing exclusive to my own genetic structure."

She confesses that not a day goes by without her experiencing those same feelings. With a degree of insight that surprises me, she tells me that she feels I have outgrown Danny and that she understands how break-ups are particularly hard for us because we never got enough love as children.

"You need to be around a man that disagrees with you loudly . . . I'll race ya! Let's see who gets there first."

She is right on all counts. Moreover, she has demonstrated such sisterly love toward me that I am deeply touched. I guess that's how it is with siblings—we disappoint the hell out of each other one moment and shower each other with unconditional love the next.

YET HOWEVER POSITIVE and encouraging and sisterly Madonna is, I still feel my life has somehow ended. In contrast, hers is beginning again, and she is moving in a new and dramatically different direction; she plans to get pregnant. She doesn't yet have a father in mind, so she launches on what she calls "The Daddy Search."

She tells me she's reached a crossroads in her life when her maternal instinct is starting to kick in. I believe that she wants and needs someone of her own, something of herself to carry on when she's gone, and I surmise that she wants to be the mother she never had, and to have her child experience the maternal love she never received herself.

She is determined to find a father for her child, and her search becomes a running theme between us. Going to a sperm bank is unthinkable for her, as the press would find out in two minutes flat. She decides to select a man to father her unborn child, whether she marries him or not.

We come up with the term *Daddy Chair.* Every now and again I will ask her, "Who's sitting in the Daddy Chair today?" She requires the ideal Daddy Chair candidate to be smart and good-looking. She has no strictures about race or religion. She just wants a father for her child and is casting around for the perfect fit for the Daddy Chair.

For a while, Enos is in the running. Then she goes to a Knicks game at Madison Square Garden and fixes on Dennis Rodman—the six-foot-seven basketball player, famous for his tattoos and multicolored dyed hair. The next time she's interviewed on television, she makes sure to mention how much she wants to meet Rodman. Three months pass, but Rodman doesn't contact her. My sister isn't a quitter, so she engineers an assignment to interview Rodman for *Vibe* and flies down to Miami to meet him.

In his autobiography, *Bad as I Wanna Be,* Rodman claims that the moment the interview ended and the photo shoot began, he and Madonna were "just all over each other," and that they went straight to bed. According to Rodman's book, she tells him exactly what she wants with no preamble: that he father her child. Along the way, she tells me she's frustrated by the fact that the NBA schedule doesn't coincide with her ovulation and that Rodman's estranged girlfriend still seems a factor. "In any case," she says, "it's nice to have to chase someone around for a change."

The "estranged girlfriend" turns out not to be estranged from Rodman at all. Her name is Kim and Rodman is double-timing Madonna with her. Nor does Rodman exactly fit into the somewhat louche lifestyle Madonna and I have embraced with so much gusto. We decide to throw a party at the Coconut Grove house to celebrate her birthday. I arrange for Albita to entertain us and also invite a bevy of drag queens: Madame Wu, Damien Divine, Bridgette Buttercup, Mother Kibble—the crème de la crème. Madonna invites her coterie of basketball players, including Rodman.

As soon as the drag queens flounce into the party, a Capulet/Montague scenario unfolds. The basketball players turn their backs and stay away from them. The drag queens follow suit. With both factions now firmly ensconced in opposite corners, the party might have passed without incident, except that Madonna and I make what turns out to be the fatal mistake of going inside the house for a few moments. When we come out again, we are met with mass squealing coming from the pool. The basketball players have pushed all the drag queens into the water.

Eyelashes float on the surface of the pool, wigs bob about in the water, along with all the drag queens, some of whom can't swim. I dive in and pull a few of them out while Madonna looks on, trying hard not to laugh too loudly.

Then she throws the basketball players a look. "I don't think they like drag queens," she cracks.

Rodman's days are numbered, and my sister launches another casting call for the Daddy Chair.

Soon after, Danny asks to see me. We meet at my New York studio and talk about reconciling. He tells me he wants to fight to save our relationship, and we explore the possibility of getting back together. Then the subject inevitably turns to his financial situation. I feel bad for him, so I give him another $50,000. A few days later, his mother writes to me saying that I owe Danny alimony. I don't answer her letter. Nonetheless, I still love Danny and am distraught about our breakup.

I SPEND SOME time in Miami trying to forget, then fly back to New York where I attempt my first one-night stand—safe sex, naturally. I don't enjoy it. I always have had the sense that when I'm involved with someone, I become a better person. I know I need to be in a relationship. Random anonymous sex leaves me feeling lonelier than before.

ON APRIL 26, 1994, *Madonna: The Girlie Show—Live Down Under* is released on home video and laser disc. It will be certified gold, signifying sales of five hundred thousand copies. The following January, Madonna will release her second book, *The Girlie Show,* for which I took many of the photographs and get paid $100 per photo used. I am beyond caring. Haunted by all my memories of Danny, I find living in New York intolerable, so I move to a duplex in L.A. I have two friends move in with me, as I am not accustomed to living alone anymore—nor do I want to.

By now, Madonna is focusing on an acting career and doesn't plan to tour in the near future. Norman Mailer has recently named her "the greatest female living artist," in *Esquire,* and she has little left to prove in terms of her music.

Through Ingrid—who introduces me to Gloria and Emilio Estefan, who both love my work on *The Girlie Show*—I am offered the opportunity to direct a video for the legendary Cuban performer Albita.

I have never directed a music video before, but although I'm nervous, I jump at the chance. As always, I relish the challenge of mastering a skill without any help or guidance. So I agree to do the video, and it's a success.

After seeing an Yves Klein exhibit of anthropometries—body prints of blue-paint-coated nude models made directly on canvas—I persuade my friends to let me paint their bodies, then I press their body parts strategically against my walls and doors. Along the way, during a party at my home, one of my friends pulls his pants down and kneels on Madonna's prayer bench from Coconut Grove—the one that I gave her and that she discarded, as she generally did most of my presents—and I paint his butt, then press it against the wall. Soon, the walls of my apartment are covered with the imprints of butts. I also decide to take Polaroids of my friends' backsides.

I am probably partying harder than I should, a direct result of living in L.A., a city that doesn't inspire me but has manifold temptations, including, in my case, cocaine.

I start doing the drug once a week, on Saturday nights, when I might share a gram with four other people, dance my ass off at a club, have a few drinks, then go home to bed. Not a massive amount of coke, but nonetheless I am beginning to form a pattern of destructive behavior.

Madonna isn't particularly happy either and sends me a letter in which she sounds surprisingly depressed: "I have no interest in working lately. It's not like me but I just wanna have fun—read, watch movies, see my friends—what's happening to me??" Although I don't tell her, I think her problem is that she hasn't yet found a suitable candidate for the Daddy Chair.

• • •

In the fall of 1994, Madonna meets Carlos Leon, a personal trainer, in Central Park. Soon after, she asks me to redesign her Manhattan apartment because she is now planning to start a family. Moreover, she tells me that Carlos fits the Daddy Chair perfectly—and that he is an aspiring actor.

I say, "Great, another actor."

"Shut up; he's sweet," she says.

I meet Carlos, and she's right. He is sweet. He's also handsome and sexy. But she's not sure he fulfills the intelligence requirement of the Daddy Chair.

I meet him, spend time with him, and decide that he is a fish out of water in Madonna's rarefied world, but he's far from stupid. Down the line, I will observe him on the red carpet with her, and my misgivings about the permanency of their relationship crystallize.

I am sure that Madonna has prepared him in advance for being in the spotlight—the screaming, the shoving, the adulation surrounding her. But he is scared and out of his depth. I can also tell that she is rolling all over him, metaphorically speaking. And I find it symbolic that he lags behind her on the red carpet. He allows other people to get physically between him and Madonna and doesn't stand his ground. He's a decent guy, but I fear that in the end Madonna's insatiable need for attention is going to suck the life out of him.

She has now bought six apartments in the same New York building and joined them together. I design a spiral staircase, add a huge gym, a media room, an additional master suite, and a rose-marble steam room.

Her relationship with Carlos progresses. In January 1995 we spend a few days in London, where she is singing "Bedtime Story" at the British Music Awards, and I design the set and direct her performance. We build a grid; she stands on it; light, smoke, and air rise up; and her hair blows in the air. She now resembles an angel, soaring through the sky, and she is terrific.

Soon after, she signs to play Evita in Alan Parker's movie of the same name. I am delighted for her, as I know she has always dreamed of winning that role, a role I consider ideal for her.

I have a new boyfriend now, Kamil Salah, a lean and handsome young man of Tartar descent, a salesperson at Prada in Manhattan. For the next two years, we see each other sporadically. Like Carlos, he is really sweet, and Madonna likes him. But, just as she once observed, I need a man who is more his own man, and not overly compliant or obsequious. Kamil sets no boundaries, and I know that they are necessary for me if the relationship is to endure. In the end, the challenge isn't there, and we split, but remain good friends.

In mid-2006, I receive a call from Kamil. I know he is about to publish his book, *Celebrity Dogs*, and I am excited for him. When he calls, my first thought is that he is going to tell me about the plans for the party his publisher is giving for the book launch.

Instead, he tells me that he has colon cancer and that it has spread to his liver. I am in Miami and take the next plane to New York to go see him. He is clearly terminal, but I do my utmost to talk to him in the most positive terms about his prognosis. We spend two days together, then I have to fly back to Miami for work.

Two months later, he is dead, at age thirty-one. His book is published posthumously. I attend his funeral in Leesburg, Virginia. At his grave, I meet his grief-stricken parents. Standing by Kamil's grave, I can't help thinking about my mother, and some of my other great friends who died in their prime, but above all I think about Kamil, who never had the chance to live out his full potential.

• • •

In early 1995, I spend a few months staying with Madonna at Castillo del Lago. We wake up one morning to find that a small, silk, red-and-blue Persian rug, worth around $5,000, is missing. I check the house and find that a door has been jimmied open.

I've told Madonna so many times that she needs security, but she has always ignored me. This morning's theft of the rug, however, has proved me right.

"Madonna, we've had a break-in, and someone has stolen the Persian rug. At least that's all they took, and nothing else. You really do need security," I tell her firmly.

"No, we haven't had a break-in," she says. "It was a ghost that took it."

"Are you kidding me?"

"No, I'm serious." And she is. "I keep hearing weird sounds at night. This house is haunted."

I tell her she's crazy, that she needs security, but she keeps insisting that she doesn't. Her rationale is based partly on finances and partly on not wanting someone around her all the time. Unfortunately, it turns out that I was right.

On April 7, 1995, while I am in New York working on the apartment, Liz calls me and tells me that a stalker, an ex-burglar named Robert Dewey Hoskins, has been caught at Castillo del Lago. He is utterly obsessed with Madonna and, a few months before, hung around her gate, left her a letter saying, "I love you. You will be my wife for keeps," and threatened her with certain death if she refused to marry him. This freaks Madonna out so much that she finally hires a security guard.

This time around, Hoskins jumped a security wall and was

shot in the arm and pelvis by Madonna's newly hired security guard, Basil Stephens.

Fortunately, she wasn't at Castillo that day.

I call her immediately and ask her if she is okay.

She tells me she is, and I am vastly relieved.

I'm happy when she tells me that from now on she will have security 24-7.

THE CASE AGAINST Hoskins comes to court, and to Madonna's horror and mine the judge decrees that Hoskins can remain in court when Madonna gives evidence against him. Her attorney, Nicholas DeWitt, has done his best to have Hoskins expelled from the court while Madonna gives evidence because, in his words, "Mr. Hoskins really wants one thing in this case more than anything else. He wants to see the fear he has instilled in her."

I agree, but after Hoskins's attorney, John Myers, claims that Hoskins has a constitutional right to face Madonna in court, asserting, "He's entitled to be in the courtroom, just like in any other case," Madonna's proposal that she give her evidence on video is rejected out of hand.

The following day, she takes the witness stand against her stalker. I feel really bad for her. She looks justifiably tense and nervous, but is determined not to betray her fear to the loathsome Hoskins, and I am thankful that she succeeds.

"I feel sick to my stomach. I feel incredibly distressed that the man who threatened my life is sitting across from me and has somehow made his fantasies come true. I'm sitting in front of him and that's what he wants," she says, and wisely closes her eyes so she doesn't have to meet Hoskins's gaze.

In court, where Hoskins is charged with one count of stalking, three of making terrorist threats, and one of assault, Basil Stephens testifies that he has seen many people attempt to scale Castillo del Lago and come face-to-face with Madonna, but that Hoskins was different.

According to Basil Stephens, Hoskins was determined, fearless, and refused to leave the property. Evidence is put forward that Robert Hoskins had come to Castillo del Lago three times in two months, and that he twice scaled the walls and sprinted through the grounds.

Fearless in the extreme, according to Basil Stephens, Hoskins had said that if Stephens didn't give Madonna his note, he would kill him. Then Hoskins went further and issued his chilling threat: "Tell Madonna I'll either marry her or kill her. I'll slit her throat from ear to ear." The brave and resourceful Basil Stephens called the police and chased Hoskins off Castillo del Lago land, or so he thought.

But on May 29, Stephens was alone and on duty when Hoskins lunged at him and said he was going to kill him. "I drew my weapon and said if he didn't stop, I'd shoot. He lunged at me again and I fired. He didn't go down. He spun around and lunged at me again, and I fired again and he went down. I was upset. I thought I'd taken somebody's life."

Hoskins is convicted on five counts of stalking, assault, and making terrorist threats. I am dismayed, however, when he is only jailed for five years. Fortunately, in September, Madonna's involvement in *Evita* means that she is sent to London and is out of harm's way, for a while.

She spends two months in London, recording the *Evita* sound track, and calls me from there. Before she leaves, in person and over the telephone, and while she is in London, we have various long conversations about her relationship with Carlos.

I know that she wants their relationship to last forever and ever and ever and has cried on his shoulder, complaining that she feels that most people are out to rip her off and wants him to understand. Once I become aware of what she's told him, it is clear to me that she is trawling for sympathy. For the absolute truth is that despite the longevity of her career, few people have tried to rip Madonna off. Her concept of being ripped off is checking a balance sheet and seeing that one of her employees is receiving a high salary, even though she originally green-lighted it. No matter how much people deserve it, she gets mad that they are making too much money off her and characterizes them as "ripping" her off.

I know that she has conveyed to Carlos her desire that he pull his weight in the relationship and has insinuated that he should contribute to it financially.

I think she is wrong. Carlos has no money, and he cannot financially sustain a relationship with her. But she isn't ready to confront the reality of their situation because she misses him so much. In fact, reading through the lines of what she's said, she is patently insecure, feels she can't live without Carlos, and has begged him to never stop loving her.

UNTIL NOW, MADONNA and I have been extremely close, but with the advent of Carlos in her life, we are starting to drift apart. I am not that necessary to her anymore, except as a designer. Fortunately, I am so busy with my own life that I don't mind too much.

By now, I am doing business as C.G.C. Art + Design, and all the purchases I make on Madonna's behalf are paid through C.G.C. and then reimbursed by her, or through her official art adviser, Darlene Lutz.

One morning, I flick through the Sotheby's catalog and notice three nineteenth-century landscapes—nothing major, just decorative items costing a total of $65,000, but perfect for the Coconut Grove house.

I send the catalogs over to Madonna's apartment, with the paintings highlighted. She approves the purchase. Normally, for "small" purchases I would lay out the money myself on behalf of C.G.C., then when the items were delivered to her, Madonna would pay me back.

This time, though, I do have slight misgivings because recently, with her prior approval, I bought two antique French lamps, paid for them with C.G.C. funds, which were, of course, really mine, but when they were delivered to her, she informed me that she didn't like them after all. She flatly announced that I should just take them back to the store and get an immediate refund. After negotiating with the store, they did, indeed, take back the lamps and refund me the money, but the experience was dismaying.

Despite my misgivings, Madonna says she wants the landscapes and tells me to make an offer for them, so I go over to Sotheby's, bid $65,000 for them, and win. Then—with the bulk of my savings—I pay for them.

Invoice in hand, I take the paintings over to Madonna's apartment and present them to her.

"I don't want them," she says.

I assume she must be joking. "You're fucking kidding me, Madonna."

"I don't want them anymore and I'm not paying for them."

As she is well aware, Sotheby's policy is that if paintings bought from them in auction are returned, they will, within a year, re-auction them. If a subsequent sale is then made, they will retain half the proceeds. But for her own reasons, Madonna is obviously pretending that she doesn't know that.

"I can't take them back, Madonna, Sotheby's has a no-return

policy. They won't give me all my money back. If they do sell at auction, I'll only get half the money back—and I can't afford to lose the rest of it. You have to reimburse me for the landscapes."

"I don't care. I don't want them."

I feel as if I am going to throw up. "But, Madonna, I've spent my own money on them. I don't make the kind of money you make. I never have. I can't just drop sixty-five thousand dollars. That's all the money I have."

"I don't care."

"But you can't not care."

"Sell them to somebody else. If they are worth that much money, sell them to somebody. I don't care what you do. I don't want the paintings. Anyway, I have to go to a meeting."

She gets up and sweeps out of the room, leaving me standing there, clutching an invoice for $65,000, with three paintings, and feeling as if she has punched me hard in the stomach.

I sink back into the deep purple club chair I'd so lovingly selected for her living room, struggling with a combination of shock and sheer bafflement at what she is doing to me, what this means, and what she has become.

I reason that in her head, she must be telling herself that because I am her brother, I should cope with whatever hand she deals me. After all, I am not only her brother, but also her employee, even though we have nothing in writing. Still, I never dreamed that she would ever treat me with such a lack of caring, lack of respect.

Because I was her brother and because I was honest, no matter how famous she was, no matter how much money I was offered for my story, I never did interviews about her, never talked to people about her. I protected her, lied for her, fired people for her, was loyal to her, advised her on her career, supported her, apologized for her, and loved her.

Today, I suppose, is a milestone. The day on which I first experience the full force of my sister's dark side, her lack of concern for someone whom she purports to love.

Our father had instilled the value of loyalty and honor in all of us. But over the years, my sister's sense of loyalty, fairness—the ability to discern who is on her side, who is not, whom she can trust and whom she can't—has clearly been eroded by the adulation, the applause, the sense of entitlement.

IT TAKES DARLENE and me six months to resell the three landscapes. Six months during which I can't pay my rent, have to borrow from friends, have to struggle to survive. While my sister, the cause of my predicament, knows, yet does nothing. By the time I finally manage to sell the pictures and recoup my money, my feelings for her have undergone a radical shift.

NINE

Big sisters are the crab grass in the lawn of life.
Charles M. Schulz

I FIND NO excuse for Madonna's grossly unfair treatment of me. But when, in November 1995, she tells me that she is deeply unhappy with Carlos, I conclude that she might have been venting her unhappiness by treating me so unfairly.

Madonna feels mistreated in her relationship and says that she won't stand for being treated like a doormat or disrespected. She thinks Carlos behaves like a spoiled child. She is hurt and unhappy, and I know from her that she feels that she has never before given so much love to one person in her life. Despite that, she changes the locks on the New York apartment, which she and Carlos have been sharing, and has his things packed up and sent to him.

I realize that she regards Carlos—who, in happier times, called her by the endearment "baby chicken"—as far more than a stud she has cast in the Daddy Chair. That she really is in love with him and is fighting for their relationship to survive. An excuse for having left me in the lurch with the paintings? Perhaps. I give my sister the benefit of the doubt. So I forgive her. But I don't forget.

• • •

I'M IN MIAMI in November 1995 and celebrate my birthday there at the opening of Ingrid's new club, Liquid, where I meet the British supermodel Kate Moss, who soared to fame at the age of just fourteen when she became Calvin Klein's muse. Like most child stars catapulted to success far before their time, Kate is outwardly fragile and gives the impression that she might easily fall apart at the slightest provocation. Yet underneath her frail facade, she is extremely self-assured. I instantly click with her and her best friend, her fellow supermodel Naomi Campbell. The three of us become firm friends and, now and again, party together. Madonna hears that I'm hanging out with them and berates me for spending time with drug-user models.

That is not, of course, a fair description. Kate and Naomi are both stylish, elegant, smart, and fun. Kate has an apartment off Washington Square, where we often hang out. Naomi lives in a large TriBeCa loft with rolling racks of clothes people have given her from shoots. An open kitchen. A large living area and two bedrooms, with clothes covering every surface. She owns art books, but not a lot of art, with the exception of three paintings that I did for the Wessel and O'Connor exhibit, which I have give her.

One night David Blaine, the magician, is over at her apartment. He is young, unknown, and full of enthusiasm.

We are in the kitchen together talking. He asks if he can show me something.

I don't know what to expect. When he levitates himself off the floor a full five inches, I call Naomi. He does it again for her. We are both amazed. Soon he will be levitating for all the world to see.

Naomi tells me that one of her greatest ambitions is to become a singer. She plays me her record, which she has been working on with Quincy Jones. It isn't very good, but I hold my blunt Ciccone tongue and tell her it is great and that she should keep working on it. I am not being altogether insincere, because I respect her for attempting to express herself artistically and want to encourage her to persist.

I see an uncut version of the documentary about the trip she and Kate made to Africa. The entire film makes them both seem ridiculous. It features a scene on a plane in which a fellow passenger wants to snap a picture of Naomi, but she doesn't want her to, and a rather funny yet absurd fight ensues.

In South Africa, competition breaks out between Naomi and Kate over who is going to get the better present from a rich South African guy who is flirting with them both. He gives Naomi a really expensive jewel-encrusted egg, a Fabergé knockoff. And Kate gets really annoyed. In the end she also gets a gift from him that he says is expensive. She takes it back to the shop, where she finds out it isn't that expensive at all. So she goes to the guy and complains he didn't give her as expensive a gift as he did Naomi. (It could be the other way around.)

Neither Kate nor Naomi is happy with the movie because they both come out of it poorly. I commiserate with them, but have secretly spent many a night with friends laughing at one hilarious scene or another.

Kate is seeing Johnny Depp who is living in Bela Lugosi's former mansion above Sunset Boulevard. I visit them there, and when I walk in, the first thing I see is an electric chair. Johnny is in the library, and I am impressed by the breadth of his literary tastes, which range from *Moby-Dick* to an Einstein biography. I note that every single volume in Johnny's extensive library is well thumbed—no books-by-the-yard on display for decorative purposes or to impress for this most erudite of Hollywood stars. Johnny exudes smartness in spades.

We chat briefly about a movie he's working on, then he joins Liam and Noel Gallagher of Oasis in his dark-wood-paneled lounge, furnished with dark-brown-leather club chairs, a dark-wood bar, and boasting a view of West Hollywood. Johnny offers me a shot of bourbon. I refuse, then go up to the finished attic where Kate is hanging out with Naomi. The three of us lounge on blue velvet cushions, drink champagne, and party. After a while, I feel that I ought to go back downstairs and pay some attention to our host, but find Johnny and the Oasis boys swigging bourbon. The air is thick with the smell of pot. I spend the rest of the evening shuttling between the supermodels in the attic and the men downstairs in the living room.

In contrast, Johnny and Kate hardly hang out together at all. They don't kiss, don't hold hands, don't even touch, and it seems to me that—despite their stunningly sexual good looks—they are far more buddies than wild, unbridled lovers. The whole evening has a distinct whiff of high school about it: the boys downstairs smoking and drinking and the girls upstairs giggling and doing blow.

AROUND THE SAME time, I move from my duplex into a high-rise apartment building in Hollywood. One Friday night, Ingrid comes over with a few friends. During the evening, she pulls out a bottle containing some cocaine and asks for a mirror. I find a small framed one. Ingrid cuts three or four lines and offers me one. I am paranoid about doing drugs in public with anyone else. I never do lines, either, "because that's too much of a commitment for me," I say to her. I prefer doing small key bumps—putting an extremely small amount of cocaine on the end of a key and taking it that way. While I like the little pick-me-up coke provides me, I have always been determined not to lose control because of it—the way I did the first time I did it with Martin Burgoyne all those years ago. I've always maintained a very casual ralationship with cocaine—I like it, but don't need it. So I refuse Ingrid's offer of a line, but do a key bump with her instead.

Within days, Madonna writes me a concerned email insinuating that Ingrid has told her that I may have a drug or alcohol problem. Neither is true.

Madonna chides me in a rather maternal way: "I only want to say that I know you're unhappy and I'm here for you if you need support or a friend" and "it infuriates me that my favorite brother is treating himself so badly. You have so much talent and so much to offer." But she is also stern, telling me that if I want to live a self-destructive lifestyle, that I don't do it around or in her homes. The email ends on a nice note, though: "I love you dearly and I want you to take care of yourself."

I am mollified by her concern, but am furious at Ingrid. She has drug problems of her own, and has apparently accused me of being a drug addict. And my sister believes her. From this point on, nothing I can say or do will ever change Madonna's mind.

John Enos has become a co-owner of Atlantic Restaurant on the corner of Beverly and Sweetzer. He asks me to design the interior. I've never designed a restaurant before, but once again jump at the chance to try something new.

Then Madonna finds out and calls me. "You're not to hang out with John, Christopher."

"But he's one of the owners of the restaurant; I have to," I explain with as much patience as I can muster.

"I don't care. You have to stay away from him."

"Sorry, babe, I'm hanging out with John." And I do.

Meanwhile, I am painting more than ever. On weekends, I am the unofficial host at Atlantic Restaurant. I am starting to feel independent, to crawl out from under Madonna's shadow. Celebrities flock to the club, including Brad Pitt and Denzel Washington. One night, Denzel is at the restaurant and two drag queens walk in.

"What the hell is that shit!" he says.

"That shit is what makes the world go round and makes it interesting, so deal with it," I say indignantly.

He instantly apologizes.

In preparation for *Evita,* Madonna is taking regular voice lessons. She has always shunned formal training, but she's really enjoying them and the strength they bring out in her voice. She is nervous, though, about making the movie, and in the wake of all the bad ones she now recognizes she's made, she is determined to make a good one at last. I tell her this is the perfect part for her and that I know she will be wonderful. During filming, she tells me things are going relatively well, but that she never sees the dailies because she's afraid to. Not to mention that director Alan Parker is keeping her and her ego on a tight leash, which I secretly applaud.

Soon after, she discovers that she is pregnant by Carlos and she is expecting Lola, as she has chosen to call the baby who will be baptized Lourdes. Madonna decides that because she is now pregnant, Castillo del Lago is too cumbersome for her and might be hazardous for a new baby. So she buys a new house on Cockerham, in Los Feliz, and asks me to decorate it.

We meet at the house and together figure out what I am going to do with the interior. During the meeting, she raises the subject of my supposed drug addiction and tells me that she is worried my drug use will distract me from my work on the house. I feel a surge of anger that Ingrid's report of my drug use is coming between me and my sister. After all, our filial bond is difficult enough to sustain—what with the ripple effect of Madonna's fame and fortune and my own role in her professional life.

I take out my anger for Ingrid's meddling on Madonna. I tell her she's wrong about the drugs and that if she has any doubts about my professionalism, she ought to get another designer who might suit her better. She assures me she won't, and we decide to go ahead together on the house.

Although I get over my anger at Ingrid, Madonna's unfairness over the Sotheby's paintings still rankles. I may have forgiven her, but I haven't forgotten. I decide to be more self-protective this time around, as I am determined that she will never put me in the same position again. From now on I won't lay out any of my money for her. So I draw up our first decorating and designing contract. Just to soften it, I call it a "Letter of Agreement." It reads:

> *This is a letter of agreement between Madonna Ciccone (the Client) and C.G.C. Art + Design (the Designer).*
>
> *For interior design service to be rendered at* [her address], *Los Angeles, California.*
>
> *Fee for services rendered for phase one of the job as discussed in meeting on Thursday, July 11, 1996, at above location will be $50,000 (fifty thousand), one half of which is due upon the signing of this agreement. The other half is due one week after Madonna Ciccone occupies the premises. If this agreement is canceled by the "Client" prior to final payment the retainer is forfeit. If the agreement is canceled by the "Designer" the fee will be prorated per day from the date of the signing of this agreement to the 15th September and paid on that daily rate from the signing to the date of the cancellation, any outstanding monies will be returned.*
>
> *All items billed by C.G.C. Art + Design must be paid*

in full prior to purchase of said items. All sales through C.G.C. Art + Design are final. Any items purchased directly through the wholesaler or retailer of said items are not the responsibility of the "Designer."

C.G.C. Art + Design will oversee work but takes no responsibility for any work done by sub-contractors not billed through the "Designer."

C.G.C. Art + Design takes no responsibility for any items damaged or destroyed in shipment or en route from one residence to another.

C.G.C. Art + Design takes no responsibility for any delays due to inaccessibility of the premises.

C.G.C. Art + Design promise to make its best efforts to see that the job is complete on or about the 15th of September but makes no guarantee to do so by that date.

Signed,

I am not altogether sure how she will take me asking for a contract, so I fax it to her along with this cover letter:

Dear Madonna,

I realize that this is the first contract that you and I have ever signed between us and at first glance may appear one-sided and to the point, but it is fairly standard as far as design jobs go.

I also understand that you are concerned about my supposed lack of interest in the job. That could not be any further from the truth. I would like to do this job for you if that is what you want. I am well aware of your "condition" and all that that implies and it would bring me pleasure to be able to provide you with a space that will be comfortable for you and Lola. I believe I have proven my abilities to you in the past and would hope that that would give you some measure of relief.

I have no doubt that the house can be put in order in the time allotted, obviously I could not guarantee that but I will do my very best to achieve it.

I feel that I should also say that if it is your desire to approach other designers to do this job I will not be offended. That is surely up to you. We have achieved great things, you and I, both in private and public and I would never begrudge you the opportunity to try something new and different. I suppose I have seen too many people latched on so tightly to your star only to see them come crashing down when one feels the need for change. Obviously I am not made of stone and using another designer would give me some pause, but alas I am only human.

So read the agreement and let me know how you wish to proceed.

Yours ever, Christopher

I go out to run some errands and come home an hour later. The red light is flashing on my answering machine. I don't have caller ID, so I don't know ahead of time who has left the message. I push the button and Madonna's voice screams at me.

She is pissed off that I sent her a contract and calls me a fucking piece of shit, and tells me she made me what I am. She ends by telling me that she's not signing the contract and that I am not working for her anymore. Click.

I freak out, furious that just by asking for what any designer would has automatically unleashed this monster. I stare, livid and hurt, at my answering machine, the rage building in me.

I sit down at my desk, open my computer, and write a response in which I push every button I know Madonna has.

Madonna,

To even bother discussing whether or not you have done me favors in life or if I'm taking advantage of you is a waste of my time. I know what you have done for me and you know what I have done for you.

Further, I know that at no time nor in any way have I taken advantage of you. More often than not it was the other way around.

It has become very clear to me these days that it's your preference to have someone's nose up your ass rather than hearing the truth. That, I suppose, is the prerogative of an aging pop star. But it is not a path I will walk, the truth had always worked for us and I will take no other route.

Nor will I be spoken to or treated as you treat the sycophants around you. I am not Ingrid.

You may not address me in the manner that you did on my phone machine. No one does and no one will. Your questionable status as a star does not give you the right, nor will it ever.

I expect a full apology from you and an explanation of your rude behavior before I will speak to you again. And I want you to know that it saddens me to think of your child living in the world you seem to want to create around you.

It's amazing how the love you have for a person can turn to hate. For me it has not been easy, but if you persist in treating me like you treat others, that is where it will remain and then, one day, it will sadly turn into indifference.

Christopher

I know her vulnerabilities, and I hit on all of them. I am furious and I am not thinking, and I don't step back, I just do it as a gut reaction.

Soon after I send the fax, I hear through Darlene that Madonna is furious with me and thinks I am a complete and utter drug addict. This is her explanation as to why I wrote her such a vitriolic letter. I must be an addict. I must have been high when I wrote the letter. She can't imagine that I was angry when I wrote the letter or that she hurt me deeply.

I realize that these days she only hears what she wants to hear. Nothing gets through to her. But I have finally said some things to her that have been burning within me for years; the concept that I don't matter. Not treating me as a person, the lamps, the paintings, the fees, the fact that Danny didn't exist for her. Worst of all, I now understand, after all this time, that to my sister I am just as disposable as any other flunky who might get out of line.

She doesn't respond to the letter. A month passes and I start hearing from people around town that she is telling everyone that we are now estranged. I don't call her, but I begin to regret having written that letter.

As I ponder the professional repercussions, and my status in Hollywood, I know that I am fucked and have to somehow rectify the situation. Darlene compounds this when she tells me that I can carry on fighting with Madonna, but that having her as an enemy won't do me any good. Darlene suggests that I swallow my pride, apologize, admit to my hubris, and make the admission sound sincere.

In a replay of the angel-food-cake scenario, I am about to admit to everything of which I am innocent. I write a letter to Madonna in which I apologize profusely, although I don't mean a word of it.

I basically say, "You are right; I need to get control of myself. Drugs are a problem. I am going to take care of it. I am extremely sorry I wrote the fax and I hurt you. I have not been feeling like myself lately, please forgive me."

She believes me and is taken in by my apology. I now realize that she doesn't know me at all. Getting to know someone on a deep level just isn't her style. From her perspective, she is the only person in the universe, so why should she take the time to get to know anybody? *They* need to get to know her. Nonetheless, I do believe that she still loves me and that her love has depth.

She replies immediately. She draws a heart at the end of the letter. She says that she is relieved and happy to have received my fax and that our not speaking feels "strange, foreign, and extremely uncomfortable." Without exactly apologizing for the message she left, she lets me know that it's hard for her to trust people and often feels pulled in too many directions.

True to form, she tells me that she knows that my rage wasn't directed at her at all, but that I was angry at the burden of being her brother—then adds that although she sympathizes with me, she isn't going to apologize for that, since being her brother has also brought me great opportunity, which is undeniably true.

Half of the letter, however, is Madonna outlining her insecurities to me and explaining that they were partly the reason for her outburst against me. Reading it, I feel she is being sincere.

And if I am still feeling hurt and defensive about her, she fully disarms me by ending her letter with: "I will tell you once more how supremely talented I think you are and how much your happiness means to me. And of course how much I love you."

I LOVE HER, too, but that love is tested to the limit after I fax and ask her for a decision regarding designing Cockerham, and she faxes me straight back just a few lines without any explanation—"I've decided to use someone else."

I am hurt and annoyed, but most of my annoyance is directed at myself. I hate myself for having sent that fax. Then again, a small voice also tells me that perhaps I did it deliberately, perhaps on some level I feel too attached to my sister and really need to detach from her. At the same time, I can't blame her for cutting me out after the nasty things I said to her. And she did forgive me. Nevertheless, I'm still angry with her, but far more angry with myself.

October 14, 1996, Madonna's assistant Caresse calls and tells me that Madonna is about to give birth to Lola. I jump into my pre-owned black 560SEL Mercedes, which I've finally managed to buy, and drive to Good Samaritan Hospital. Outside the hospital, hundreds of press scream out my name.

Security checks my credentials from the list of five—Caresse, Melanie, Liz, Carlos, and me—who have clearance to visit her. I go up to her suite of rooms, 808, on the eighth floor—living room, bedroom, chintzy florals everywhere, and browns and pinks—hideous, and not Madonna's or my taste, not that it matters. I am happy she is about to have the child she's always wanted so much. I put aside my hurt and anger at the way in which our relationship has deteriorated so badly.

She is lying in bed in a white flannel nightgown. Her hair is washed and pulled back. She isn't wearing any makeup. She looks pale and wan.

"I love the decor," I tell her.

She throws me a weak smile.

She is in a break from labor.

She tells me that they may do a C-section.

"Is that what you want?" I ask.

"Well, they think it's best. They just want to make sure the baby is all right, so I think I'll agree."

I tell her to do whatever she thinks is best.

She doesn't seem afraid at all and says she is looking forward to giving birth. "I can't wait to get this thing out of me."

Then her mood changes. "I wish Mom were here."

"I wish she were as well," I say. "She would be so happy to see you give birth, and to know her grandchild."

Outside the suite, Carlos is pacing the hallways. Liz is there, too, and so are Caresse and Melanie. Around noon, they take Madonna away for the procedure. Melanie suggests I go home and wait for news there.

Just after four, Melanie calls and tells me that at 4:01 p.m. on October 14, 1996, Madonna gave birth to six-pound-nine-ounce Lourdes—"Lola"—by C-section and that mother and daughter are resting comfortably. I am simultaneously relieved and overjoyed.

The following day, I go to visit Madonna at home. I bring her gardenias, and a tricycle to give to Lola when she's old enough.

Arriving at the house, I feel strangely ambivalent. I am excited to be seeing my new niece, but I also feel weird about visiting Cockerham—the only one of Madonna's homes I have not designed—for the very first time. I loved creating and designing the look of my sister's homes in the past, but now I feel cast out in the cold.

The house is a Spanish, single-level Wallis Neff house. A brief glance at the interior and it's obvious that all Madonna has done is bring over the furniture we purchased for Castillo. It hurts me to see furnishings I'd purchased for her now redone and reorganized by someone else. For the first time ever, Madonna's home is foreign territory to me. But I am gratified to see that my painting of Eve is hanging in the living room and hope it indicates that, on some level, she still intends me to be part of her new life.

I go down the hall to Madonna's bedroom to see her and to meet Lola.

Madonna looks tired and places Lola in my arms.

"Lola, this is your uncle Christopher."

"Hi, Lola, you're very pretty," I say, terrified that I'm going to drop her.

I hand Lola back to Madonna and ask how she's doing.

"I'm exhausted; I feel like I've given birth to a watermelon."

Then she shows me the incision on her belly. I can't believe how small it is. No more that five or six inches. I am amazed at the thought of a baby fitting through such a tiny opening.

I can see my sister is really sleepy, so I leave quietly.

On the way home, I remember thinking how thrilled I am for her, how sweet Lola looks, but how her birth means that our relationship will change even more.

There is now a growing distance between Madonna and me. I don't feel as close to her as I did before. For the first time ever, I have no connection to her home and no longer have my own room there, either. She has always been more my family than anyone else, but I can sense that connection weakening immensely. I'm happy that she's starting her own family, just as she wanted; still, I mourn the loss of the old "us." And I miss Danny and think about him constantly. I feel bereft and sad.

THANKSGIVING 1996. MY parents fly out to see Lola for the first time. The entire family gathers at Madonna's house, including my older brothers. Melanie and I are in the kitchen, cooking. Madonna pops in every now and again to check that everything is all right. Although Melanie and I are doing the cooking, Madonna is still somewhat frantic.

I set the table. Madonna flies past me. I sense something odd about her tonight. I go into the kitchen and bring back a stick of butter on a butter dish. Madonna takes one look at it and blows up.

"What the fuck are you doing putting butter on the table, Christopher?" she yells.

I am completely thrown by the tone of her voice—the identical tone she used with me on my answering machine many months back.

"But, Madonna," I say patiently, "we are having bread. So we need butter on the table."

"But we have enough butter in the food. We don't need it on the table as well." She snatches the dish from the table.

I grab it back from her. "I want butter on my bread and so will everyone else."

"Well, I don't." She picks up the butter and stomps out of the room with it.

When she isn't looking, I put it back on the table. It dawns on me that she hasn't really forgiven me for my fax at all. Just as my apology was fake, so was her forgiveness. I thought I was handling her, but realize that, in actuality, she was—more than skillfully—handling me. In fact, we were handling each other. She is still mad at me, still angry, and our relationship has altered almost beyond recognition.

Nevertheless, after the butter incident, from that point on, Thanksgiving Day passes uneventfully. I visit Lola in her crib, which is in Madonna's bedroom—the most feminine bedroom I've ever known her to live in, pink and cream with silk curtains, pretty and soft. After dinner, Melanie and I spend a few moments in the kitchen, bitching about Madonna. Then we all go home.

Despite the tensions between us at Thanksgiving, Madonna still invites me over for Christmas Day, which also passes uneventfully.

Madonna spends the rest of 1996 promoting *Evita* wherever and whenever possible. I believe that the movie deserves to do well, and that she should be honored for her performance, but audiences are not flocking to see it. She invites me to be her date on March 24, 1997, at the Oscars at the Shrine Auditorium. She has already won the Golden Globe for Best Actress in a Motion Picture, Musical or Comedy, for *Evita*, and I'm disappointed that she's not up for the Best Actress Academy Award.

At the ceremony she performs "You Must Love Me," written by Tim Rice and Andrew Lloyd Webber, which she sang in *Evita*. It wins Best Original Song, and this reflects on her well, and I am delighted.

WHEN *Madonna: The Girlie Show—Live Down Under* is released on DVD, I am temporarily pulled back into pleasant memories of our work together. But I am now playing hard, doing drugs a couple of times a week, and Madonna is hearing about it. She calls me and says, "I am hearing awful things about you. Are you addicted to cocaine?"

I don't think that I am, and I tell her so.

She hangs up, unconvinced.

TEN

Big Sister is watching you.

Adapted from *1984* by George Orwell

IN MAY 1997 I direct Dolly Parton's "Peace Train," my seventh music video. We meet and she is friendly. She's dressed in a tight dress, but her arms are covered, as they will be whenever I see her. She tells me she doesn't want a bunch of dancers behind her. I ask her what kind of dance she plans to do herself.

"I'm a mover, not a dancer. And I'm a bit top-heavy . . ." she says.

Before the shoot, she asks that we send a car to the airport to pick up her wig lady, and a second one to pick up her wigs.

Some of the video is shot with her placed on a dolly in front of a wall. As I don't want the wall to be much higher than Dolly, I call her manager, Sandy Gallen, and ask how tall she is. He says he will get back to me.

After a few hours, he calls: "Dolly is five foot nine in hair and heels."

She's probably five three without. On the day of the shoot, I arrive at 5 a.m. The wig lady arrives at six in one car, as do the wigs in another. Dolly arrives at seven, completely made up, in a wig and outfit. She disappears into her trailer for two hours, while the makeup man does her makeup. He leaves, then the wig lady goes in and does her hair.

Dolly never wears the same dress twice in public. She has three dresses made for the shoot, all in a similar cut: long sleeves, tight cleavage, arms covered.

On the set, she is casual, easy to work with, cracks a few dirty jokes, and says, "I'm not all boobs; I'm partly brain, too."

She finds it difficult to move around, though, because her shoes are so high and her wig so carefully balanced. She ends up doing a little wiggle that I christen the Dolly Chug, and she is amused.

We break for lunch and she sits between me and my producer, Michelle Abbott. Dolly is rail thin, with a tiny, tiny waist, but orders fried chicken and collard greens. Michelle asks her how she can eat that kind of food and stay so slim.

"Well, aah always leave a little on ma plate for the angels," she says.

In part of the video, we use doves supplied by a dove wrangler. Dolly is supposed to hold one of the doves, then let it fly away, but the doves refuse to fly. So every time the wrangler puts a dove into Dolly's hands, instead of flying away, it flops to the ground again. He puts it in her hand again, she throws it up in the air, and it flops to the ground.

"I'm sticking my finger up its ass, but I think it likes it," Dolly jokes.

She's great to work with, we have fun, and everything goes really well. The next morning, she leaves me a phone message: "Hi, Chris, I just want to tell you that I had a good time last night." I am so amazed by that. The first time in all the videos I've shot that an artist has done that.

Not long afterward, I suggest to Dolly that she and Madonna record an album together, each one recording five of the other's hits. Dolly tells me she thinks it's a great idea, but Madonna just says, "I'll think about it," which really means no. She and Carlos have now split for good, and I am not surprised.

I ADD ANOTHER string to my bow; I've become a screenwriter. Before I started, I read a basic book on the rules of screenwriting, then just began to write. I know I could take screenwriting classes, but I don't want to. As usual, plunging headfirst into a new endeavor without any training for it challenges my creativity.

My screenplay, "Nothing North," is inspired by a documentary I see about a female bullfighter named Christina. At first, though, I write it as a short story set in Seville, Spain. I send it to Madonna.

She calls me and says, "This is a really beautiful story. Have you ever been to Seville?"

I tell her I haven't.

"Well, I have, and you described it perfectly. What are you going to do with the story?"

I explain that I am going to adapt it into a screenplay.

She tells me to go for it, then offers me space at her Maverick Records offices in West Hollywood, and I am grateful.

I write for four months, and when the script is finished, send it to Madonna asking whether she would like to help finance it. She says she wouldn't. Naturally, I am disappointed. Her clout as executive producer could easily have gotten the movie financed, but she simply doesn't want to get involved. I find her refusal both disappointing and confusing. But once my disappointment has subsided, I come to the inescapable realization that—because I so wanted my sister to like my script—I had mistakenly jumped to the conclusion that her sisterly enthusiasm and encouragement meant that she wanted to produce it as well.

In May 1997, Naomi, Kate, and Johnny Depp—whose movie *The Brave* is showing at the Cannes Film Festival—rent a house in Cannes. Naomi invites me to join them and generously offers to pay my fare. So I fly to France, and by the time I get to Cannes, the Gallagher brothers (Oasis) and Marc Jacobs join me at the house. After a day or two—with the exception of Johnny, who only smokes pot—we are all well into the party scene and have a great time.

Later, on May 11, I meet Demi Moore at the opening party for Planet Hollywood, and we immediately hit it off. Iggy Pop sings, and during his song he accidentally spits on Kate. I duck. Kate is swigging champagne straight out of the bottle and doesn't even notice.

All of us—Kate, Naomi, Demi, Harvey Weinstein, and Johnny Depp—go back to Demi's room at the Hotel du Cap. Naomi dances around the room in a perfect imitation of Tina Turner, while Johnny and Harvey have a serious conversation concerning why Harvey doesn't want to distribute Johnny's film. "Because it's bad," Harvey tells him in the end.

Later that night, Demi invites me to go to Paris with her in the morning. I tell her that all my stuff is at Naomi and Kate's. She sends someone to pack up my stuff and bring it to the hotel. I am duly impressed.

We stay up all night. Everyone is having a blast. At around four in the morning, for some strange reason, I decide to take a bath. I turn on the water, then promptly forget about it. The next thing I turn, Demi's Louis Vuitton luggage is floating around the room. I feel foolish, but she laughs it off. The hotel staff promptly set about cleaning up the room. In the morning, we fly by private jet to Paris and hang out there together.

From then on, Demi and I get closer and closer. On June 5, 1997, I am her date at the Gucci evening for AIDS Project L.A. From that time on, we hang out together at least once a week. I like her enormously, but am slightly put off by her heavy-handed spiritual sensibility. She carries around a deck of cards that look like tarot, but aren't, lays them out for me, telling me that they will predict my future, but I'm not that interested. I'm focused on the present.

In the past, Demi has had drug and alcohol problems. She's been sober for years, but still exhibits obsessive habits. She lives on coffee, Red Bull, and dried green apples. One night, we go to dinner at Benvenuto on Santa Monica. She brings with her two cans of Red Bull. She orders pasta, which she doesn't eat, drinks Red Bull and coffee, and smokes Marlboros in rapid succession.

Some nights, she picks me up with some of her girlfriends and we all go to this Latin drag-queen club on La Brea, where Demi gets onstage and dances with a group of drag queens. She and I also make great dance partners. At Christmas she sends me a black-and-white card featuring a little boy in a suit and bow tie dancing with a Kewpie doll. In it, Demi writes, "Someone to dance with when I'm not around." By now, she and I are very close. Sometimes a little too close for my comfort.

"Are you sure you are really gay, Christopher?" she would ask me over and over. "I mean, couldn't you turn straight for me?"

Later on, when I meet Farrah Fawcett and start hanging out with her as well, she also repeatedly poses the identical questions to me.

I don't know how serious either of them is, but I do have some experience with women who have the hots for me. Ever since my college days, I have been pursued by women set on luring me into their beds. Of course, few of them have succeeded.

Thanks to Demi, though, the media are about to start posing interesting questions about my sexual preference.

One Saturday night, when I am hosting an evening at Atlantic, Demi and three or four of her girlfriends show up. As always, at around eleven, we clear the center of the restaurant, a DJ starts spinning music, and all of us—along with the restaurant patrons—spend the rest of the night dancing. All great fun.

On this evening, at around 3 a.m., Demi—a girl who no longer drinks, but clearly still relishes having fun—persuades me to get up and dance on the black granite bar with her.

Within moments, I'm up there and we're dancing wildly. Demi pulls off my shirt, gets behind me, and starts grinding into me.

Normally at this time of the night we would have had the restaurant doors bolted shut, and the blinds would have been pulled down tight, so that anyone passing by would have assumed that the restaurant was closed. But by some strange Murphy's Law, although I didn't realize it at the time, that night one of the blinds is left open enough for some enterprising paparazzo to point his lens through the crack and snatch a photograph of our revels.

THE FOLLOWING MONDAY, I am walking through Los Angeles airport, about to catch a flight to New York, and out of the corner of my eye catch sight of what looks like a picture of me on the cover of the *National Enquirer*. I walk up to the rack and discover that I am also on the cover of the *Star*.

Both covers feature fuzzy shots of Demi and a shirtless me

dancing together on the bar at Atlantic. Inside one tabloid is a spread and the eye-catching headline "It's Three A.M. No Bruce, No Bra, No Problem." The second carries the cover line "Demi's Big Night Out with Madonna's Brother."

I am a little troubled that both articles might give Demi pause and cause her to think that I set the whole thing up to get publicity for Atlantic, which I definitely did not. I was afraid she wouldn't believe me and would then lose trust in me. But I am innocent, and thankfully Demi believes me.

Apart from that, I enjoy all the unexpected attention. I am on the cover of the *Enquirer* and the *Star*, both in the same week. For just a few days, I feel as if I am a star and I like it. I am, after all, my sister's brother.

ON JULY 15, 1997, in front of his mansion on Ocean Drive, South Beach, Gianni Versace is shot at close range by crazed killer Andrew Cunanan. Madonna and I are both deeply shocked by his senseless murder. Just a few weeks later, we are both shaken by the death of Princess Diana in Paris. We think back to how we were also chased through Paris by the paparazzi and realize that, but for the grace of God . . .

ON SEPTEMBER 8, 1997, Madonna and I attend the Gianni Versace memorial service at the Metropolitan Museum of Art. Madonna and Gianni have always had a business relationship, have never been great friends, but out of respect to his memory, Madonna and I attend the memorial service anyway.

We gather in the museum's Temple of Dendur, which is decorated with magnificent white flowers. Madonna reads a poem she's written to commemorate Gianni; Elton John and Whitney Houston sing. Many of the supermodels—Stephanie Seymour, Christy

Turlington, Helena Christensen, Cindy Crawford, Naomi Campbell, and Amber Valletta—are there. So are Donna Karan, Calvin Klein, Tom Ford, Ralph Lauren, and Marc Jacobs.

Donatella, making her first public statement since Gianni's murder, gives a speech commemorating him and touching on the profound influence he had on her and her brother Santo. "By the time he was calling Santo and myself to be part of his dream, we were already part of it. He let me do many things that made our mother pale. . . . I laugh when I remember the adventures that came with being his little sister. . . . Each time Gianni would ask me to do what back then seemed like these impossible things, I'd tell him I couldn't do it, he'd tell me I could, and I did. He was always the most exciting person I knew; he was always my best friend."

Her speech, which brings tears to my eyes, is close to what I might have said about Madonna, with the exception of the last line: "In spite of his giant personality, it was impossible to feel overshadowed by him, because his special art was to shine the light on others." The speech is extremely moving, and I am very sad for Donatella.

Afterward, she invites us back to the mansion off Fifth Avenue. Like the Miami Versace mansion, the five-story Manhattan Versace mansion is all done in heavy neoclassical style, lots of gilt, marble, black-marble floors, and Picassos on many of the walls—hard to relax in, extremely formal.

Madonna and I join a circle of guests in the small garden, sitting on clear plastic folding chairs, all arranged in a circle. Madonna sits on my right, and a woman who looks like a bag lady sits on my left. Madonna whispers to me that the bag lady is Lisa Marie Presley. I am incredulous, but on second glance realize that she is, indeed, Lisa Marie.

Then Pavarotti makes his entrance and, although we all know exactly who he is, goes around introducing himself.

"Hello, I'm Pavarotti. Hello, I'm Pavarotti," he announces to each and every one of us.

Courtney Love is also there, but Madonna avoids talking to her because she thinks Courtney is crazy. Courtney and I have a moment's conversation in which she says, "I see Madonna and me as Joan Crawford and Bette Davis, but I can't work out who is who."

I smile and shrug.

At around ten thirty, Madonna, who always goes to bed at eleven on the dot, leaves, but I stay.

By this time, Donatella has changed from her black outfit into white jeans and a white shirt. Her face isn't tear-stained, but she looks pensive. She sits down next to me briefly, then excuses herself and disappears.

I go upstairs to the bathroom.

When I pass one of the guest bedrooms, I see Courtney—dressed in a beige silk minidress with spaghetti straps, her hair as messy as ever—sitting on the bed, looking sad.

She is all by herself, so I sit with her and we start talking. Then she pulls out a packet of coke, which may well have been half an ounce.

"I've got this," she says, "but I've never done it before. Would you like to do some?"

I fight to stop myself from bursting out laughing. "You've never done it before?"

"No, I've never done it before."

"Would you like me to show you?"

Courtney nods, so I go through the pantomime of showing her how to cut lines, which I suspect we both know she knows only too well, but I play along.

We start to party together.

Then Donatella beckons from her sitting room across the hall—furnished with black leather sofas, with a white mink rug on the floor—and we join her. I break my rule about not doing lines and we all do them. It's patently obvious that the drugs are a continuing symptom of her anguish at the loss of Gianni.

Every time Courtney does a line, she proclaims, "Okay, that's my second time. That's my third time. That's my fourth time."

In the end, I say, "Courtney, just stop counting."

Meanwhile, Donatella keeps saying, "Chreestopher, Chreestopher, play 'Candle in the Wind' for me."

So I put on the CD, and the moment it ends, Donatella asks me to play it again.

"Chreestopher, Chreestopher, play it for me one more time, one more time for me, Chreestopher."

I do. Over and over.

All the while, Courtney is still counting. "This is my fiftieth time. This is my fifty-first time."

Then the doorbell rings and it's Ed Norton, whom Courtney is seeing at the time.

She says, "Christopher, go tell him I'm sleeping."

I refuse. Then I decide that the time has come for me to escape this surreal scenario and get back to reality, so I leave.

On October 14, 1997, Demi invites me to escort her to the premiere of *G.I. Jane*. I am slightly nervous that the memory of the photographs of our wild dance at Atlantic on the cover of the *Star* and the *Enquirer* might still rankle with her estranged husband, Bruce Willis, who will be attending the premiere that night.

As I don't want there to be any lingering misconceptions about my relationship with Demi, or about my sexuality, when I am introduced to Bruce, I say, "I want you to know that I'm not having an affair with your wife, and I'm a fag."

He says, "Don't worry about it."

Just before Demi meets Ashton for the first time, I am in Manhattan and so are she and Bruce. She invites me over to her apartment at the San Remo. When I tell her I am flying to L.A. the next day, she says that she and Bruce are flying to Idaho the next morning. She is stopping there with the children, but he is flying on to L.A. Would I like a ride? I would and accept the offer.

Their private jet is comfortable, with a sofa, a dining room, a banquette full of candy and mags, a galley, and a big bathroom, and all can smoke whenever they want, which suits me fine.

I suggested to Madonna that she should get her own plane, just so she could fly whenever she wants to. But she says, "That's too expensive. I'm not spending my money on a plane. And I don't have to! I'll use the Warner company jet." She does, and we travel on it together quite often.

Demi and I talk during the flight, then play cards, but Bruce and I have little to say to each other. We land in Sun Valley. Demi and Bruce have split up and live in separate houses there. She drives to her house alone. While the plane refuels, Bruce and I drive over to his house in his Suburban to get something he needs to take to L.A. He points out the little theater he's restored and all the property he owns there. He seems like a good guy, but a sense of unhappiness surrounds him, a sadness that he and Demi have split up. We stop at his house. I remain in the car and realize that his home is across the street from hers.

During the short flight to L.A., awkward silences occur between us. We smoke cigarettes and read magazines, but the short flight feels like five days to me. When we land, Bruce's Bentley is awaiting him. I have a car pick me up and we go our separate ways.

I see Bruce and Demi again when they bring their daughter up to a music school in Traverse City, Michigan, while I was there visiting my family. They call and ask if they can come over and I show them around the vineyard. There, Bruce meets one of the blondes who works in the tasting room and starts flirting with her. Demi is wandering around somewhere else, and I tell him to stop flirting with the staff.

Three weeks later he calls me. "Remember that blond girl I was talking to? Well, I'd like to go on a date with her. Will you call her up and ask her?"

"Sure, no problem," I say in amusement.

So I call my father, ask for the girl's name, and call her.

"Listen," I tell her, "this is going to sound rather strange, but Bruce Willis would like to go on a date with you. His daughter is at school in Traverse City so he is coming up here a lot. Do you feel like going on a date with him?"

She says she doesn't because she has a boyfriend.

I tell her to dump him, but she just laughs at me.

I give Bruce the news.

"Too bad," he says.

I don't feel that bad for him, though. After all, he's Bruce Willis and has a thousand romantic options.

A year later, he calls me again and asks about her, if she's still with her boyfriend, if she'll go out with him.

She is and she won't.

And then again a year after that.

The blonde is still with her boyfriend, so Bruce strikes out.

• • •

I AM STILL painting. In Miami, over lunch with Ingrid, I meet a fourteen-year-old Colombian schoolboy named Esteban Cortazar, whose parents are artists. He tells me that when he grows up, he wants to become a fashion designer. I sense a fire burning in him—an intensity that reminds me of the young Madonna. Following my instinct, I invite him to dinner that night with her and Bruce Weber.

Once I study Esteban's fashion design book, I discover that my hunch about him was right—he is an original talent. So I tell him that I believe that he has a bright and brilliant future ahead of him and that I want to make a documentary about him that I will film over at least ten years. After his parents consent to the project, I set up a dinner for ten of the people closest to Esteban and interview them about him on camera. Over the next decade, each year I will do the same thing, as well as film him during important moments in his life.

At the time of this writing, Esteban has just been appointed the head of women's wear for the house of Ungaro. I almost burst out with pride in him and am also delighted that my faith in Esteban has been eminently justified.

THANKSGIVING 1997 AND Madonna says I can invite a few friends down to the Coconut Grove house, which she doesn't visit much anymore now that she has Lola. Naomi, Kate, and Demi come down; so does Barry Diller. I realize that I am getting far too caught up in the celebrity thing. It's fun, but I am also quite lonely.

At the start of 1998, Madonna calls and tells me she is planning to go on tour and asks me to come over to Cockerham and talk possibilities with her. I am thrilled at the prospect of touring again. I bring my ideas book, in which, through the years since *Girlie,*

I've been collecting photos, art, anything that I think might be inspiring.

Madonna and I have an in-depth conversation about the tour. I suggest that onstage, she have a big tree with leaves that change color, symbolizing the change in seasons—and that her songs parallel those changes. She likes the idea. She keeps the file containing my tree concept. I am excited, and—once more craving the heady euphoria of collaborating creatively with my sister and the adrenaline rush of being on tour with her—can't wait for rehearsals to start. A few weeks later, she calls and tells me she has decided to postpone the tour, and I am bitterly disappointed.

However, I don't voice my disappointment to her. And I am happy when, on July 1, 1998, she invites me to see the Spice Girls concert at Madison Square Garden with her and Lola.

We arrive at the last minute. When the crowds see Madonna, they start shouting and screaming. Madonna and I sit on either side of Lola and are invited backstage to meet the girls forty-five minutes into the show, during intermission.

We go into Madonna's old dressing room, and it looks just like a girls' dorm room. Clothes are everywhere. The girls are sitting on the sofa, eating hot dogs.

Madonna can't believe her eyes. "What are you guys doing? How can you eat a hot dog and onions in the middle of the show, and then go out and sing?"

They tell us that it doesn't bother them, and when Madonna and I go back to our seats, it seems that the hot dogs don't have any impact whatsoever on their singing or dancing.

"They can't really dance; they can't really sing. And who the hell eats hot dogs between sets!" she says, shaking her head in disbelief.

For Lola's sake, we endure another fifteen minutes of the show, then split.

Madonna and I see *Cabaret* on Broadway, starring Alan Cumming and Natasha Richardson. The production is set up with the audience seated café style in front of the stage, affording us the illusion that we are participating in the show. Madonna loves it, even though she isn't big on Broadway musicals.

By now I have written a second screenplay, "Fashion Victims," based on a Cunanan-style serial killer, who sets about murdering all the world's great fashion designers. I show it to Madonna. She tells me I am going to get in trouble over the script, as it is a daring but funny take on the fashion industry. I go ahead anyway and try to interest producers in it, but no dice.

DONATELLA VERSACE AND I are now extremely good friends. Only a year has passed since the death of Gianni, and she is extremely delicate. She was his sister, his muse, but was never intended to run an empire.

Nonetheless, in July 1998 she launches her first collection and invites me to Paris to see the show. She is still wounded by the loss of her brother, and I can see the sadness in her eyes. She tells me how frightened she is about doing the show on her own. I know that everyone is waiting for her to fail, and I sympathize with her.

I suggest that I make a documentary about her, starting in Calabria, where she was born, through her brother's death, and ending with her first solo show. She loves the idea. She arranges a ticket for me and a room at the Meurice. I arrive there at seven on a Sunday morning, take a nap, and call Donatella, who tells me to come over to the Ritz and bring my camera. Liv Tyler, Billy Zane, and Catherine Zeta-Jones are all staying there as well.

I say hello to Donatella, then sit in a corner and film the models. Suddenly, I notice that none of the clothes have been completed. I can't understand how Donatella can put on a show in five days. Then she walks me into the Ritz ballroom, where fifty Italian women, all with sewing machines, are primed to make the collection. In a second ballroom, the fitting models are waiting around, with cloth draped around them.

The following three days, I go over to the Ritz and shoot. Every half hour, someone brings food down for Donatella to eat, but she refuses to touch it. Every couple of hours, she grabs me, pulls me up to her suite, and we do blow together. This goes on 24-7 for three days, during which I get about two hours of sleep a day.

The show models arrive on Thursday. On Friday, an hour before the show, Kate walks in, comes right up to me, and says, "Christopher, I need some coke and a glass of champagne."

I say, "Kate, are you crazy? You just got out of rehab and you are not getting it from me."

The day after the show, Donatella and I are supposed to fly to London together, but when I get back to the Ritz, I find out that she is sick. Her assistants tell me she is staying in Paris and that I should go ahead to London without her.

I check on her, thank her for arranging for me to come to Paris, and wish her well.

Just as I am about to leave, someone pulls me back into the room and hands me a film canister full of cocaine.

"Take this, we need to get it out of the room," he tells me.

I tell him that I can't take it with me because I'm about to get on a plane.

He forces it into my hand and says I should do whatever I want with it, but just get rid of it.

I take it back to the Meurice and stare at it regretfully, trying to work out some way of keeping it because the cocaine I had with Donatella is the best I've ever had in my entire life. I sigh and flush ten grams of the finest blow in the stratosphere right into the French sewer. It's just as well. This week, I've done way too much and I've started to like it more than I want to.

I take the train back to London, then fly to L.A. There, I view the footage, and it's fascinating. A few days later, Donatella writes and tells me that the family doesn't want her to do the documentary after all. I am disappointed, but understand. I still have other options: directing videos, painting, designing furniture, working on Madonna's new tour. Although I don't dwell on it, I am acutely aware that most people look at me and see Madonna.

A prime example: I meet a tall, thin, blond, lively young man at a party in L.A. We talk a lot and I ask him if he wants to go on a dinner date with me that Friday. He tells me he does. I pick him up, and we go to Benvenuto on Santa Monica. Afterward, we have drinks at the Abbey, then he invites me back to his apartment in West L.A.

When we arrive, we go straight into his bedroom. The lights are out, and the room is only illuminated by a small candle. We start making out on the bed, then, all of a sudden, he clicks on the light switch. There, above his bed, a life-size picture of my sister, half-naked, draped only in a sheet. For a second, I stop breathing. Then I look around the room. Pictures of my sister all over every inch of the wall, and on every surface. Talk about a buzz kill.

I immediately throw my clothes on and run out. The experience freaks me out completely. Later, however, we become very good friends, simply because I now know exactly where he is coming from. He's a Madonna fan, not some weird stalker, and I feel that I can trust him.

• • •

On December 9, 1998, Donatella hosts the Fire and Ice Ball at Universal Studios in Hollywood and asks me to design and create for it a Diva Room for her at 360, the penthouse restaurant with panoramic views of L.A. So I devise a French-courtesan boudoir look: pink heavy brocade drapes, pink flowers, candles everywhere, a massive chandelier, and a baroque baby carriage full of Cristal Champagne.

On the night of the event, Goldie Hawn arrives dressed in a halter dress, looking great. I dance with her, and she seems a bit tipsy. Ben Affleck and Gwyneth Paltrow arrive. Madonna introduces me to Gwyneth. It's love at first sight.

But before we get to know each other, I meet Jack Nicholson, who is at the party along with Dennis Hopper. Jack, Dennis, Donatella, and I go into the Diva Room. Donatella pulls out some cocaine and hands me a key.

Jack takes one look at me dipping the key into the bag of cocaine and says, "I'll try that. I've never done it like that before."

I think, *Bullshit*. Famous people like Courtney and Jack never want to admit anything about their drug use. I make Jack a bump. He does it and so do all of us. Afterward, we have some inconsequential coke chat, then Jack leaves. I never see him again. But I've just done a key bump with Jack Nicholson!

On February 24, 1999, Madonna and *Ray of Light* are nominated for six Grammy Awards: Album of the Year, Record of the Year, Best Pop Album, Best Dance Recording, Best Recording Package, and Best Short Form Music Video. Although Madonna won a Grammy in 1992 for Best Long Form Music Video for *Madonna: Blond Ambition Tour Live*, none of her albums or songs has ever won a Grammy—it's about fucking time and I am rooting for her. She asks me to design and direct her for the opening number.

By now I have a new boyfriend, let's call him Mike. We have been dating for three months and he is artistic and charming. He tells me he isn't a Madonna fan, though I haven't introduced him to her yet.

On Grammy night, Madonna is in her trailer at the back of the Shrine Auditorium. I check the stage and make sure that the cameraman knows he mustn't shoot her closer than midshot, as she refuses to allow close-ups. I run through shots with the director, just to be on the safe side.

I go back to see Madonna in the trailer, and I take Mike with me. She's in a rush. I introduce Mike to her. She says, "Great to meet you," and he says, "Likewise."

As we leave, he turns to me and says, "She looks old. Is that really her hair?"

I am stunned, but am far too busy to say anything. I've already invited him to the after party at Le Deux and haven't got enough time to disinvite him. As an afterthought, I tell him that as I am going to be busy at the party, he should invite a friend. He does.

I am thrilled when Madonna wins four Grammys, including Best Dance Recording and Best Pop Album. As she accepts the award, she has tears in her eyes.

"I've been in the music business sixteen years and this is my first Grammy—well, actually I've won four tonight. It was worth the wait," she says.

Technically, she had won once before for the *Blond Ambition* tour video seven years earlier, but winning awards for the *Ray of Light* album and single made it feel like the real thing.

I tell her that she does really deserve it, and she glows.

When we arrive at the after party at Le Deux, I meet up with Gloria Estefan and Lenny Kravitz in the garden. Madonna stays inside, and out of the corner of my eye, I see that she's dancing wildly, blissed-out to have won.

After an hour or so, I'm outside in the garden when I hear her yelling my name. I run inside the restaurant and see her crouching on the floor, picking wax off her arms. Wax is all over her hair as well. I can also tell that she's had a few lemon drops too many.

Ingrid and Liz are standing over her.

"Someone dumped a candle on me," Madonna says.

Liz whispers that Madonna's had two lemon drops.

She and Ingrid take her into the bathroom and help her get the wax off.

A trail of women follow her. Two stand guard outside the door. I can hear a lot of chattering in the bathroom. I grow impatient and peek in.

Madonna is standing at the basin trying to remove the wax from her hair. Everyone around her is yelling helpful hints at her.

I push my way through to the sink and help her. Then I tell her that I think it's time for her to go home.

Ingrid and I, and Chris Paciello (Ingrid's then business partner) walk Madonna to the restaurant door.

As we are about to get her into the car, Mike springs out of the shadows, pulls out his camera, and says, "I want a picture of Madonna."

"Over my dead body," I say, and grab the camera.

He runs over to Madonna, puts his arm around her neck, and says, "I want to kiss you good-bye."

We pull him off Madonna and then throw him out. Exit artistic boyfriend, never to be seen again.

MADONNA NOW HAS a $6.5 million contract with Max Factor to promote several new cosmetic products and appear in commercials throughout Europe and Japan. I see the commercial and note her geisha look, remembering the evening we spent together at the geisha house, and applaud her for remembering and using the image.

On March 21, 1999, I go with Madonna to the Academy Awards. Afterward, as we walk into the *Vanity Fair* party at Morton's, a fifteen-piece salsa band is playing. The party is jammed. Fatboy Slim is deejaying. Warren, Barry Diller, Ricky Martin, David Geffen, and all of Hollywood are here. But only a solitary couple is on the dance floor. The band strikes up a great salsa number.

I ask Madonna if she wants to dance.

"Let's go," she says.

I offer her my hand.

We go onto the dance floor together.

Within moments, everyone stands back and watches us on the dance floor. We fit together perfectly. She responds to my slightest touch, and I to hers. This truly is dancing with the stars. We are completely in step. We are so in tune that night—my sister and I—genetically so similar, trained by the same teacher, ideal dance partners.

Cameras film our dance, and it's displayed around the entire restaurant and outside in the street. The music stops, we end on a perfect dip, everyone at the party applauds. A precious memory, and though I don't realize it at the time, my last dance ever with my sister.

Madonna is still hearing about my partying—which I generally just do on a Friday or a Saturday night, and not more—and she continues to disapprove. She is not altogether wrong. After partying so hard in France, I am finally forced to confront the fact that

I am clearly capable of sliding down the slippery slope far too fast, and make the decision to cut back once and for all.

Nonetheless, presumably as a result of her suspicions that I am partying too much, Madonna opts to have a London decorator, Irishman David Collins—who designed for Victoria's Secret, as well as many celebrated London restaurants—update the New York apartment instead of me. When I see the results, it is as if someone sticks a knife into my gut and twists it. He has taken my timeless classic design for the New York apartment and made it déclassé.

He has changed the living room lighting, installed a chandelier that is far too big for the room, replaced the furniture I bought with oversize pillows that don't suit the apartment. He has painted both the walls and ceiling of the media room a bright kelly green and, in my opinion, has destroyed the feel of the place completely. I am relieved that he hasn't touched the blue bedroom I had custom-made for Madonna. But it hurts that she hasn't hired me. I tell myself not to be angry with her. It is after all her home, and she can change whatever she wants. I suppress my anguish.

I realize that the main reason she hasn't hired me is because she believes that I have a drug problem. Drugs have never impacted my work. Although Madonna has taken Ecstasy and smoked pot in the past, she won't tolerate anyone who does drugs on a regular basis, in particular, cocaine. There is no middle ground for her and although I just dabble—and like most recreational drug users, don't let my use impinge on my professionalism—Madonna views drug-taking in black-and-white: either you do drugs or you don't.

Perhaps because of my feeling of alienation from Madonna, I hang out more with Gwyneth Paltrow. In a way, without perhaps realizing it at the time, ever since Madonna's role in my life lessened, and our relationship started to downward spiral, I have established a Daddy Chair of my own—except that, in my case, it's called the Sister Chair. Kate, Naomi, and Demi have all been candidates, but I feel that Gwyneth fits my Sister Chair better than any of them. She isn't seeing anyone at the moment, so we spend time commiserating. She is more real than any of the other actresses I've met. Besides, she never mentions Madonna to me at all, a stellar qualification for my Sister Chair.

Around this time, I design a line of furniture for Bernhardt Design, a furniture manufacturer, which includes a scroll-armed sofa, a Vanitas table, and an armchair I've named "Leda."

The line is launched at the end of September 1999, at a party thrown at the Oriont, the newly opened restaurant on Fourteenth Street, which I spent six months designing. The restaurant is inspired by my vision of a Shanghai bordello, complete with black tile floors, deep-olive velvet banquettes, and chairs covered in a blood-red silk that I unearthed in New York's Chinatown.

The restaurant gets rave reviews for food and design. But just a month later, an electrical fire starts on the third floor and the restaurant burns to the ground, leaving me unpaid and incredibly unhappy.

Fortunately, my furniture is well received. In July 2001, rather than spend thousands of dollars on a high-priced designer, President Clinton personally selects my Prague furniture line for his Harlem office. I am extremely pleased.

In March 1999, Madonna asks me to work on a new addition to the Coconut Grove house, and I fly down to Miami and spend some time there working on it.

Madonna comes down for my birthday on Thanksgiving. Naomi and Kate decide to throw a birthday party for me at the Delano.

Madonna takes some coaxing to agree to go.

"I don't like those model girls," she says, "and I don't like that you are hanging out with them."

"Look, Madonna, they're very good to me. I trust them. They are just girls having a good time."

"Yes, but I don't want to have it with them."

"Well, then, come or don't come," I say, exasperated. "But it's my birthday, and I really wish you would."

She finally agrees to go, and we drive to the Delano in separate cars.

At the Delano's Blue Door restaurant, of which Madonna is part owner, a big table has been set up.

Kate and Naomi have done the place cards. Madonna, dressed in black Dolce & Gabbana, is at one end of the table with Ingrid. I am at the other end with Kate on one side and Naomi on the other.

I am seated with the hostesses and enjoy this rare occasion of being in the same room as my sister and not being eclipsed by her. I can see her looking down her nose at Kate and Naomi and whispering to Ingrid about them. Kate gives me this funny pack of dirty girlie cards from the fifties. Even from far down the table, I can feel Madonna's disapproval, but I don't care. I'm enjoying myself.

The cake is served. The girls toast me. Madonna joins the toast. Then the girls start getting raucous. Madonna makes a face, then she and Ingrid get up abruptly and leave.

Kate, Naomi, and I all go dancing after dinner. I arrive back at the house at five and set off the alarm by accident. Madonna is livid and accuses me of doing drugs. She isn't wrong. I am not painting much and am just hanging out, kind of lost, playing with supermodels. My mood is growing darker and darker.

Madonna, in contrast, is very much involved with Lola and

immersed in the Kabbalah movement, and has a new man in her life, ten years her junior: British director Guy Ritchie.

Trudie and Sting introduce him to Madonna when they both attend a lunch party at their home in Wiltshire. Like Sean, Guy comes from a middle-class family, with links to the Scottish military dating back to the twelfth century. I later find out that Guy has been named after two forebears who served in the Seaforth Highlanders, a romantic-sounding Scottish regiment. His great-grandfather Sir William Ritchie was a gunner major general in the Indian army, and his grandfather Major Stewart Ritchie was posthumously awarded the Military Cross after he was killed in the escape from Dunkirk during World War II. Guy's father, John, was also in the Seaforths, and Guy's stepfather, Sir Michael Leighton, is an English aristocrat. All in all, young Mr. Ritchie seems to have a lot of history behind him, and a great many illustrious forebears casting a heavy shadow over him.

It seems to me that he has a great deal to live up to. Consequently, in a way, I can understand why—instead of focusing his filmmaking talents on immortalizing his patently distinguished family history—he employs them on making what some term a "homophobic" movie about London gangsters, *Lock, Stock and Two Smoking Barrels.* I am eager to meet this Brit who appears to have captivated my sister so much.

ELEVEN

The Wedding Guest sat on a stone:
He cannot choose but hear.

Samuel Taylor Coleridge,
The Rime of the Ancient Mariner

December 31, 1999, Donatella has a New Year's Eve party at Casa Casuarina, her Miami mansion, where I first meet Guy Ritchie. He is friendly to me, and I remember thinking that he looked boyish and seemed like a nice guy. He is conventionally dressed in a white shirt and dark-blue trousers and jacket, and I warm to him. He is personable and respectful and seems as if he might be fun to hang out with. Nonetheless, I tell myself that I doubt he'll outlast Madonna's usual two-year relationship cycle.

I go into the garden with my good friend Dan Sehres. We find Donatella sitting at a corner table, glamorous in a silver dress. She looks beautiful, but seems depressed—no doubt thinking of Gianni and happier times at the mansion. She chain-smokes, lighting cigarette after cigarette with her glittery pink diamanté-covered lighter. Next to her, her own special packs of Marlboro, exclusively designed and manufactured for her at the Milan Versace atelier—

with the words SMOKING KILLS eradicated and replaced by her initials, inscribed in Gothic script.

We have cocktails with her at the table, along with Madonna, Guy Ritchie, Rupert Everett, and Gwyneth, who is currently in a flirtation with Guy Oseary, now running Maverick Records for Madonna, and sits close to him.

Just before midnight, Ingrid rushes out into the courtyard.

"J.Lo is here," she announces, "and we're not talking to her."

I flash back to a recent newspaper article and remember that Gwyneth and Madonna are feuding with J.Lo because J.Lo was quoted by a journalist as saying that Madonna couldn't sing and Gwyneth couldn't act. Most unwise.

Everyone, with the exception of Donatella and me, gives J.Lo the cold shoulder.

At midnight sharp, we are all momentarily distracted from the dramatic J.Lo-related tension when we all gather round the TV screen and watch the New Year's Eve celebrations all over the world. The pope gives his blessing, then they cut to fireworks. It looks as if the pope has blown up. We all dissolve into hysterics, then, of course, look up warily toward the heavens, just in case.

I dance with Donatella on the acrylic dance floor that covers the sunken, gilt-inlay swimming pool. Then someone, I don't recall whom, comes over to me and whispers into my ear that a bunch of us are going to do half a tab of ecstasy.

Around two in the morning, we all move on to the VIP Room of the Bar Room, Ingrid's new club. The VIP is a dark room, small—about fifty by fifty—with large glass windows overlooking the main dance floor.

We all drink Veuve Clicquot, and I can tell everyone is feeling good.

Madonna, Gwyneth, Ingrid, the two Guys, and I are all sitting in a booth.

Gwyneth gives me a playful, lascivious look.

I jump up and pull her onto the dance floor.

It's now around four in the morning. Madonna, who is definitely feeling no pain, is dancing on the table. Gwyneth joins her, and they dance together. In the middle of the dance, Madonna grabs Gwyneth, and kisses her full on the mouth.

It is that sort of a night.

My friend Dan has brought a nineteen-year-old boy to the party with him. The boy is always handling his crotch. And as a result, I call him Scratchy. Madonna, in a knee-length pink chiffon Versace dress, is on the dance floor, dancing with a group of people. We all look good together, and we know it. Suddenly Scratchy squeezes up to Madonna. He edges between us, puts his arms around her, and they dance a slow dance close together.

Within an instant, Guy Ritchie strides across the dance floor. He kicks Scratchy in the leg to get his attention and drags him away from Madonna. Then he swings his fist at him. I push Guy back and yank Scratchy out of the room.

THE MOMENT PASSES. The dancing begins again.

I'm on the dance floor, dancing with Gwyneth again.

Suddenly I sense someone coming up behind me.

Guy grabs me from behind and starts bouncing me up and down like a rag doll.

"Put me down!" I say.

I extract myself from his iron grip.

I shove him up against the wall, push into him, and grind my hips right into him.

"If you want to dance with me, this is how we dance here," I say grimly.

He flushes and pushes me off.

I walk away. I don't give Guy another thought. Rupert, however, is watching us intently, and apparently does. Later, in his autobiography, he comments, "Guy and Chris were from different planets, and in a way the one's success relied on the other not being there." At that stage, though, I don't focus on Guy's actions because I'm distracted by a commotion on the dance floor: two people are openly doing drugs. Security grabs them both and throws them out.

We all keep on dancing.

The evening fades away.

Somehow, and I can't remember how, I get home.

The next day, Madonna throws a barbecue in the garden, but most of us are so hungover that we just chill out, lounge by the pool, and speak softly.

We only come alive when Lola starts screaming that Mo, Rupert's puppy, is drowning. We dive into the pool and rescue him, whereupon he collapses, and we are terrified. Fortunately, though, after being ministered to by Elsa, the New Age priestess, he recovers.

The afternoon ends, and everyone leaves. Throughout the day, Guy and I haven't said a word to each other. I decide that he is a bit of an oaf, particularly on the dance floor, a drawback with regard to Madonna, as she likes her lovers to dance well.

Above all, it has always been of paramount importance to Madonna that the man in her life be able to deal with the gay men in her life. I can't imagine that Guy will be around for long.

I am wrong, of course. Perhaps I was too close to my sister, too caught up in the drama of that New Year's Eve, to read the writing on the wall. I have no intimation whatsoever that the advent of Guy in Madonna's life is the death knell for my relationship with her.

THE DECADE ENDS with *The Guinness Book of World Records* listing Madonna as the most successful female solo artist, citing her as having sold 120 million albums worldwide. The *Blond Ambition* tour is named the Greatest Concert of the 1990s by *Rolling Stone. Entertainment Weekly* lists Madonna as the fifth Top Entertainer of the Half-Century (1950–2000). She is anointed Artist of the Millennium by MTV Asia.

Madonna's latest movie, *The Next Best Thing*, which she makes with Rupert Everett, opens on February 29, 2000. She invites me to the premiere. I go with Billie Myers, a good friend and favorite singer of mine. Madonna is sitting two rows in front of me. The movie is awful. I pretend that I have to go to the bathroom and hope no one notices that I don't come back.

Instead, I stand in the hallway and listen, but at least don't have to watch. Afterward, I tell Madonna that she was great and the movie is funny, but this isn't true. I am glad that I am not alone with her because if we had a proper conversation about the movie, I know she would realize that I am lying. She has no idea whatsoever how bad she is in the movie but I realize that nothing good would come of speaking my mind so I decide not to. The movie has already premiered, and there is nothing that can be done anymore to improve it or my sister's performance in it. Commenting on it negatively to her would be both pointless and destructive and I refuse to go there.

THAT SAME MONTH, four months after I finished the latest addition to Coconut Grove, Madonna decides to sell the house. The end of an era. She also still hasn't paid me my final installment for work on the addition.

She is now living in London, where she starts the year by filming her "American Pie" video. In America, *The Immaculate Collection* is certified as having sold 9 million units, and on March 20, 2000, Madonna announces that she is pregnant with Guy's child. I am still not convinced that Guy is in her life to stay, reasoning that she had Lola with Carlos, but still didn't stay with him.

On August 11, 2000, Madonna and Guy's son, Rocco, is born at Cedars-Sinai Medical Center, in Los Angeles. I am in Miami working and so am not there for his birth.

Madonna clearly doesn't intend to stay in California, though, as she is now permanently based in London. There, she meets Prince Charles at a charity dinner at his home in Gloucestershire and, later in the year, gives her first UK concert in seven years, at Brixton Academy, which is seen by 9 million viewers throughout the world and is the biggest live webcast ever, breaking Sir Paul McCartney's 1999 online record of 3 million.

She will become so much a part of life in her new country, England—the country she and I once disliked so much during our first trip there together, all those years ago—that she is even asked to present the prestigious Turner Prize at the Tate Britain Gallery. Doing so, she demonstrates that she hasn't quite lost her American-style Madonna ability to shock: "At a time when political correctness is valued over honesty, I would like to say, right on, motherfucker, everyone is a winner!"

Her comments so scandalize the British television-viewing public that Channel 4 is compelled to issue an apology for them.

Along the way, she breaks the news to me that she and Guy are getting married. I tell her I am glad for her. I am, because I realize that she is vulnerable and needs him. Apart from the fact that Guy must remind her of Sean, she is getting older and needs a father for her children. She casts such a big shadow, and most men just aren't prepared to subjugate themselves to her. I guess that Guy isn't either, but at least he is prepared to marry her.

By October 2000, my finances are in shambles. I have been working on Central, a new restaurant on Sunset Plaza, for most of the year and haven't been paid. I have no choice but to downsize. I give up my apartment in Hollywood and rent a three-bedroom house in Los Angeles proper, renting out the other two rooms. Madonna continues to stall my payment for Coconut Grove. I protest, and we argue.

On October 9, 2000, she sends me a letter saying that she is putting her "indignation aside"—referring to our payment dispute—and inviting me to her wedding. In a backhanded compliment, she says that she is inviting "my close friends and family members that are not insane." She adds, "We will be married by a vicar in the Church of England because Catholics are a pain and GR doesn't want to convert and besides I'm a divorcée."

I am not keen to attend the wedding, as I really can't afford it. Moreover, I no longer have any affinity for Guy. So I call to make my apologies.

Madonna isn't around, but her assistant Caresse calls me back: "Madonna told me to tell you if you want to be paid the final payment for Coconut Grove, you have to use the money to buy a ticket to her wedding."

A knot forms in my stomach. "You are joking, right? Because if you aren't, then she is blackmailing me." I hang up.

Caresse calls back. "We are going to take the money Madonna owes you, buy you a ticket to Scotland, and send you the money that is left over."

I ask again if she's kidding, and she tells me she isn't. This is how Madonna wants to proceed.

I spend a few days mulling over the situation. I feel I don't know this person who is attempting to blackmail me into attending her wedding. However, I am consoled that my sister and I can't be on such bad terms as she really does seem to want me at her wedding. So I capitulate.

Caresse gives me the rundown of the wedding plans. I will fly to London a week before the wedding, be fitted for a tuxedo, and the following morning fly to Inverness, a forty-five-minute drive from Skibo Castle, in Dornoch, on the shores of Dornoch Firth in the Scottish Highlands. On December 21, Rocco will be christened, and the wedding will take place on December 22.

Later, I discover that before the wedding, the staff are forced to sign a four-page confidentiality agreement, that none of the guests is allowed mobile phones, and that we are all banned from leaving the castle during the five-day wedding celebrations. Moreover, seventy security guards will be on hand to ensure that no press infiltrate Skibo, and no guest escapes either. Colditz Castle, here I come!

A business-class British Airways ticket is messengered to me from Madonna's office. When I check the price, I discover that only a few hundred dollars of my final fee remain.

Once in London, I follow Caresse's instructions and go to Moss Bros on Regent Street to rent my tuxedo. They hand me this gray cutaway that all the male guests are supposed to wear. It's pure polyester, and when I slide the jacket on, it burns my fingers. The shop assistant presents me with the rental bill. "Put it on Guy's bill," I say, and walk out.

That night, I go out to dinner with friends. We party, and I end up going to bed at five in the morning. Consequently, I miss my flight to Inverness. At the airport, a BA official takes pity on me and arranges for me to fly to Edinburgh, and from there to Inverness. I am not particularly happy, but I am still curious about Scotland and am interested to discover what it's like.

A car meets me at the airport. After about an hour's drive, we arrive at Dornach, drive up a sweeping beech-tree-lined drive, and Skibo Castle looms in front of me cloaked in mist, big: beautiful, mysterious, and set on seventy-five hundred acres of prime Highlands land. A flag featuring the Union Jack on one side and the Stars and Stripes on the other—a tradition stemming from Andrew Carnegie, who restored the castle in the nineteenth century—flies from one of the turrets.

My first sight of the Skibo main hall is straight out of any Hollywood movie featuring an ancient Scottish castle. A crackling log fire burns brightly, the walls are Edwardian oak-paneled, some with stuffed animal heads displayed on them. A sweeping oak staircase leads to a landing with a stained-glass bow window, where Madonna's wedding ceremony will take place.

I expect Errol Flynn to swagger down the magnificent staircase at any moment and start fencing with me. My fantasies are punctured, however, when at the reception desk I am asked to hand over my credit card for incidentals. I tell the receptionist that I didn't bring my credit card with me. The result is that all my charges will be billed to Madonna and Guy. My white lie is, of course, motivated by my reaction to Madonna having blackmailed me into attending her wedding. I don't want to feel that way, but I just can't forget her bullying, overbearing behavior toward me.

I follow Skibo's kilted "greeter" to my accommodations, assuming they will be baronial and splendid, given the grand entrance hall. We walk up two flights, three flights. We walk up four flights, five flights. We walk up six. Along the way, we pass various suites, all magnificent, all with four-poster beds and furnished with antiques.

My room is on the top floor in a turret attic. I go through a little door, into a small hallway, then into a room about six by six, with a claw-footed Victorian bathtub in the middle and a toilet against the wall. That leads to another doorway, another low-ceilinged room, and there is my bed.

The phone rings and I am informed that dinner will be at eight. Moreover, it is black-tie. Madonna never warned me that there would be black-tie events. I've only brought one suit with me—Prada—so it looks like I'll be wearing the same suit every night.

I go down six flights of stairs. I pass a library and a billiards room. I take a walk outside, see the small gym and serene spa, and the historic Edwardian indoor swimming pool. Skibo is imposing yet beautiful, and I think to myself that I can deal with this for a week.

A pretty girl rides by on a horse. She introduces herself to me as Stella. The penny drops. Stella McCartney. Madonna's maid of honor. As far as I know, she and Madonna have only just met, yet Madonna has chosen her—not Ingrid or Gwyneth—to be her maid of honor. Stella designs and makes a free $30,000 dress specially for Madonna. Still, Ingrid can't be happy.

Stella explains the drill to me. Every morning, the men will go shooting, and the women will have a themed luncheon. She knows, because Madonna has told her.

"So I either have to go to lunch with the women or go shooting?" I ask Stella.

She tells me that no men are allowed at the lunches.

Shooting is out of the question for me.

I dress for dinner, then go into the library. Guy's friends are in there. I don't know any of them, but one or two look familiar so I guess I've seen them in some film or another. They are relatively friendly, and they all clearly have a history with one another.

We have cocktails and I try to make small talk. I ask how the shooting went and they tell me that they have shot three hundred birds.

I ask them if they are kidding.

They tell me they aren't. They are going to get hung up, where they are meant to rot. I flash back to the goat heads I saw hanging in a primitive Moroccan village all those years ago. Guy and his friends may be civilized Englishmen, not North African peasants, but their pursuits are similar.

"So are we having them for dinner?" I ask.

They all laugh and tell me that we aren't.

I GO TO dinner. Madonna walks in, says, "Welcome to Scotland," and gives me a hug. Guy shakes my hand.

Trudie and Sting arrive. I met him when he played the Pacific Amphitheatre in 1993 and like him.

Melanie and her husband, Joe, walk in, and I'm glad to see them.

The large dining table is set for ten. Madonna has a seating chart, and on this first evening she's put me next to Melanie and Joe, and I'm glad. Scottish food is served. For a while, I pick at it halfheartedly. Then I ask for some chicken.

Tonight, and every night afterward, the guests toast the bridal couple. Tonight, one of Guy's friends makes the toast, which culminates in a crack with the subtext "Wouldn't it be funny if Guy were gay?"

I don't laugh. It wouldn't be funny.

After dinner, I decide to read up on Skibo's history. I learn that the castle stands on the site of an original Viking edifice. Through the years reduced to ruin, Skibo was reborn in 1898, when it was bought by Scottish-born philanthropist Andrew Carnegie, who immigrated to America at age twelve and as an adult accumulated a $10 billion fortune by manufacturing steel. Having made a fortune beyond his wildest dreams, Carnegie returned to Scotland, determined to buy the castle of his dreams, and spent $2 million restoring and decorating Skibo.

Since then, King Edward VII, Edward Elgar, Lloyd George, Helen Keller, Rudyard Kipling, and the Rockefellers have all stayed at Skibo. Moreover, Paderewski even played the vast organ in the Great Hall. I relish Skibo's illustrious history, but still feel lonely there.

In the morning, I am awoken by a bagpiper playing under my window—apparently, a Skibo tradition dating back to Carnegie.

When I go down to breakfast, where all manner of Scottish delicacies are on offer, I discover that I am condemned to spend the day on my own. The guys are scheduled to go shooting, the women to spend the day behind closed doors taking part in various female pursuits. Madonna doesn't suggest any alternatives for me. Generally, a prospective bride isn't responsible for entertaining her guests, but I can't help wondering about the point of inviting someone to a wedding in the middle of nowhere, then leaving him to his own devices.

So I work out and then read. I'm curious, though, about what's going on in the girls' room. It's all very hush-hush. After a while, Stella comes out and says, "I'm tired of the girls, I'm going to ride my horse."

In the evening, I check the seating chart and discover I am sitting between Trudie and Sting. At first, they talk about the castle and the weather.

Then Trudie leans in to me and says, "Christopher, do I have BO?"

"Huh?"

"Do I have BO? Do I smell?"

"Not that I can tell," I say, perplexed.

"Are you into that sort of thing?" Before I can think of an answer, she chips in, "Mightn't you be?"

"Isn't the smoked salmon delicious?" I say.

GUY'S PRIDE IN his own heterosexuality swells noticeably when he's in the presence of a gay man like me. And during this wedding week, when there are nightly after-dinner toasts made by his male friends—many of which are aimed at underscoring his overt masculinity—he is in his element. I, however, am far from amused when many of the speeches trumpeting Guy's heterosexuality include the word *poofter,* a derogatory British expression for "gay."

Ignoring all the other guests—Sting, Trudie, Stella McCartney, my sister Melanie and her husband, Joe—Madonna, who is at the head of the table, stands up and issues the instruction, "Christopher, tonight it's your turn to give the toast."

I lean down the baronial table and, with great emphasis, reply, "Madonna, you really don't want me to do that."

It's a statement, not a question.

Madonna looks back at me blankly.

"I think you should ask someone else," I volunteer helpfully.

"No, Christopher, it's *your* turn!" she bark in a tone identical to the one she always used as a kid when she and my siblings all played Monopoly together; if she didn't get Park Place, she invariably stamped her feet and said, "But it's *mine*!"

In those days, in the face of her strong will, I always capitulated and rescinded my purchase of Park Place.

Nothing seems to have changed.

I stand up.

My fellow guests fall silent out of respect; the brother of the bride is about to make a speech.

I raise my glass, "I'd like to toast this happy moment that comes only *twice* in a person's lifetime." Then, without skipping a beat, I go on, "And if anybody wants to fuck Guy, he'll be in my room later."

Everyone erupts in peals of laughter. Everyone, of course, except Madonna, who keeps saying, "What did he mean? What did he mean?" and Guy, who I suspect knows exactly what I mean, says nothing.

Afterward, he avoids looking at me. Soon after, I go to my room. I'm walking along the corridor, thinking that at least I got my dagger in when Trudie comes up behind me.

"That was hysterical," she says. "Your sister didn't get it, but I've been listening to all those homophobic jokes, and if you weren't pissed off, I'd be worried about you. I just want you to know that we were aware of how you must be feeling."

At that moment, I fall in love with Trudie, and she knows it.

The next day, my parents arrive, along with Paula. Initially, Madonna didn't invite her. Paula tells me that she called Madonna and said she really wanted to be at her wedding, and Madonna said that as long as Paula paid for her own plane ticket and incidentals she could come. I am really pissed off at Madonna for treating Paula so badly. She is working as a graphic artist and only earns a modest salary. Yet Madonna still expects her to pay her own plane fare to this far-flung place.

My mood improves when Rupert, Alek, Gwyneth, and Donatella arrive. We take a golf-cart ride, and I tell them about the homophobic toasts and how awful everything has been. They laugh and console me. Gwyneth says, "Poor Christopher, we'll look after you." We spend the rest of the day together.

The christening is in the evening. A long line of Range Rovers pull up in front of the castle, ready to take us to Dornoch Cathedral. A press pack of five hundred photographers and even more journalists is waiting for us outside the castle gate. We drive past them, but they follow us all the way to Dornoch.

More than a thousand fans are gathered outside the small, 776-year-old cathedral, famous for its beautiful stained-glass windows. Inside, the cathedral is lit with candles and garlanded with ivy and flowers.

I sit with Gwyneth and Rupert and only see Rocco—swaddled in his white-and-gold, $45,000 Versace christening outfit, a gift from Donatella—from a distance. I learn afterward that a journalist has been hiding in the massive pipe organ for three days. By the time someone discovers him, he has passed out cold.

Guy Oseary has been awarded the distinction of being Rocco's godfather. I try not to mind and, instead, focus on Sting's moving rendition of "Ave Maria." After around thirty minutes, the service is over. We are driven back to the house, with the press following close behind.

Dinner is served, toasts are given. I experience a sudden urge to smoke, but know I can't, as Madonna has banned smoking.

Gwyneth and I leave at the same time. On the way up to my room, we stop at her suite, which is massive and beautiful. It occurs to me that I—who sometimes signed my letters to Madonna "Your humble servant" just to annoy her—have been relegated to what must be one of the smallest rooms in the castle, perhaps even the servants' quarters. A joke? Or just my sister's way of keeping me in my place.

THE NEXT EVENING, the evening of the wedding, I put on my rented tux, but in a moment of rebellion akin to Madonna's cutting holes in her ballet clothes all those years ago, I pair it with my own Vivienne Westwood waistcoat.

Just before 6:30 p.m., we all gather in the Great Hall, now lit by candles, and take our seats at the foot of the staircase, the balustrades of which are garlanded in ivy and white orchids. It is beautiful.

I am sitting in an aisle seat, five rows from the front. The strains of the hymn "Highland Cathedral," played by a lone bagpiper, fill the foyer. He is replaced by a pianist, Katia Labèque, who plays as Lola, in a long, ivory, high-necked dress, descends the staircase to the landing above us, scattering red rose petals in front of her.

Lola is sweet, winsome, and adorable. I feel sad that all week she has either been with her nanny or her nurse, or sequestered in the locked room with Madonna and the other girls, as I would have liked the opportunity to get to know her better.

Then Madonna, beautiful in a fitted ivory silk dress, enters on our father's arm. In his tuxedo, our father looks handsome, distinguished, and every bit the aristocrat. For a second, I wonder what his father, Gaetano—who arrived in America with just his $300 dowry, all those years ago—would think of his son now. Not to mention his granddaughter.

On the landing in front of the stained-glass bay window, Madonna joins Guy, who is wearing a green Shetland-tweed jacket, green tie, green and diamond antique cuff links, which, I later learn, are a gift from Madonna, white cotton shirt, and a kilt that someone explains to me is in the plaid of the Mackintosh clan. Rocco, snuggling in his nanny's arms, is dressed in a kilt made from identical fabric.

Guy and Madonna exchange diamond wedding rings. Then, in front of a female pastor, they speak the vows they've written themselves. I wish I could hear them, but the ceremony is so far from where we are all sitting that although we can hear Katia play "Nessun Dorma," and Bach's "Toccata and Fugue," none of us can make out a single word of the vows. Déjà vu—Sean and Madonna's wedding all over again. Although perhaps Sean isn't looking like such a bad choice of brother-in-law anymore.

After fifteen minutes the ceremony ends. The wedding party descends the staircase and we all congratulate them. We sip champagne, then Madonna and Guy go up to their rooms to change. After a short while, Madonna emerges in a Gaultier dress, and Guy in a blue suit.

AT EIGHT, WE all come back to the Great Hall, where a bagpiper pipes us into dinner. Tonight there is no long table, but rather seven round tables. Madonna and Gwyneth and Guy are at the front table, along with Sting and Trudie and Donatella. My parents are at a side table with Joe and Paula and Melanie.

Perhaps as a direct result of my toast, I have been allocated a seat at the back of the room, sitting with my back to the bride's table. I'm not surprised because, after all, I've been a bad boy. Alek Keshishian is sitting at my right and spends most of the dinner—salmon and mussels, Scottish beef, roast potatoes, cabbage, and the Scottish national dish, haggis—bitching that he isn't sitting with Madonna, which irritates me to no end.

The best man, nightclub owner Piers Adam, stands up to give his toast. Behind him, a screen features images of Guy as a baby,

Guy as a schoolboy, and even Guy in a dress. One picture shows Guy as a child, lying across a black dog, with his hand near the dog's penis. Piers Adams points at it. "You see, Guy was a poofter early on," he chortles, really pleased with himself.

I restrain myself from getting up and throwing a plate at him.

I glance at my sister, hoping to see a look of outrage on her face, but there is none. And I am sad that Madonna, whose early success was built on her legions of gay fans, can listen to these antigay comments without protesting. I feel even sadder that she is now married to a man who seems so insecure in his masculinity that he thrives on homophobia, and his friends know it.

I leave the dinner, go upstairs, and fall asleep. I wake up at around two in the morning and go downstairs to get something to eat. I hear music coming from the castle's cellars and take a look. A big party is going on, and everyone is dancing. Among them, Madonna's maid from America. While a very nice gesture that she paid her maid's way, it is almost beyond my comprehension that Madonna categorically refused to pay for our sister Paula to fly to Scotland as well. In the morning, we all pile into the bus taking us to the airport and we fly back to London. I breathe a sigh of relief. I've served my time at Skibo and it's over.

Madonna, at least, enjoyed her wedding. She later said, "It was a truly magical experience. It was very personal and very intimate." And she makes a conciliatory gesture toward me, suggesting that I stay at her Holland Park home on Christmas Eve, then on Christmas Day join her and Guy at Sting and Trudie's fifty-two-acre Wiltshire estate, where the newlyweds are spending their honeymoon.

Once I get there, the honeymooners naturally keep to themselves, and I hang out with Trudie and Sting. After the disappointment of the wedding, it's nice to be with friends, however new.

At dusk, Sting and I walk around the property together. He and Trudie keep sheep and they run everywhere. There is also a little lake with an island in the middle, with a large tree growing on it. Sting tells me a story about a girl who died out there. According to him, at certain times of the year you can still see her ghost, dressed in a white gown, sitting on a chair, gazing out over the lake. The property is unmodernized, beautiful, and for that evening I feel as if I have gone back in time.

But even the serene surroundings and the kindness Sting and Trudie both show me don't eradicate the unhappy memories of my week in Scotland. And when I arrive back home in America again, open my mail, and find an invitation to join Skibo's exclusive private members' club, I don't, for one second, consider accepting it.

TWELVE

Everything you do affects the future.
Kabbalah wisdom

I BEGIN 2001 feeling positive and happy. But in March, I make the chilling discovery that Madonna is going on the road again on her forty-eight-city *Drowned World* tour, but isn't hiring me to direct it. Perhaps as retaliation for my wedding toast and the disdain I have demonstrated for her new husband, she has hired another director, Jamie King, instead. I get the news from Caresse. I email Madonna about it and her reply is that she feels that—because of my drug taking—I have become unreliable. I immediately write back telling her in no uncertain terms that my drug use is recreational and that I have never allowed it to interfere with my work.

Although she doesn't retract her accusation and clearly still believes all the rumors about me, a few weeks later she writes inviting me to sit in on one of the rehearsals. In the same letter, she tells me that she, Guy, and the children are now eating a macrobiotic diet—no meat, chicken, bread, sugar, dairy, or alcohol—prepared by a

French macrobiotic cook. She also invites me to come to a Kabbalah class.

Although I am slightly intrigued by Kabbalah, I decline. But I do accept Madonna's invitation to attend the *Drowned World* rehearsal. In an irony that feels decidedly bitter to me, rehearsals are being held at Sony Studios in Culver City, where—just eight years before—we rehearsed *The Girlie Show.*

When I arrive at the stage door, the first thing I see is Jamie King's brand-new black Mercedes. Only recently, he was driving a late American model. I can only surmise that Madonna is paying him a fortune to direct *Drowned World,* certainly much more than she paid me, and this rankles with me.

I go inside and watch the "Ray of Light" segment, in which Madonna sings three songs. She is wearing a kimono with fifty-foot-long arms. Despite her commitment to Kabbalah, the overall vibe is angry, violent, and not fun to watch.

I don't want to sound unsupportive, so I say a few constructive things. Then, referring to a scene in which she is supposed to be momentarily submissive, I suggest to Jamie that she look down first, as it will then make more of a dramatic impact if after that she looks up.

He snaps, "We want to do it our way."

I don't react.

Later, I mention my suggestion to Madonna. She gives no response. But later on, when I go to the dress rehearsal, I see that she has followed my suggestion.

NOW THAT MADONNA and Guy are married, she puts the Los Feliz home on the market, sells Coconut Grove, and makes an offer on a new house on Roxbury Drive in Beverly Hills, which belongs to Diane Keaton.

At the moment I am still designing the new L.A. restaurant Central—still unpaid—and I am broke. So I ask Madonna if I can design the house for her.

Caresse has recently told me that Madonna was shocked when she received David Collins's bill. Until then, she had no idea what kind of fees designers routinely charge. Now, however, she understands how low my fee really is. She's ready for me to work for her again. As she knows my situation, she haggles over my rate. I have no choice but to settle for a low rate, and she agrees to hire me.

She pays $6.5 million for the house, which was designed by architect Wallace Neff. Before the sale closes, we go to look at the house together. It's north of Sunset, an odd Spanish Mediterranean house with no wall around it and no gate. The yard is full of big agave plants and cacti, with huge six-inch spikes growing out of them, and lavender is everywhere.

Diane still hasn't moved out of the house, but isn't there today. Her children's toys are by the pool, all lined up in perfect order according to size.

Madonna and I exchange glances.

"Why are they lined up like that? And how can the kids play in the yard without stabbing themselves on the cacti?" she says.

The first thing I do is get rid of the cacti. The backyard is dug up, and underneath the lavender we discover a great many rats and immediately have them exterminated.

Before I start work on the interior, Madonna takes me aside and says, "You know, Christopher, I've got kids now and a husband, and you are going to have to design the house for the kids and to deal with my husband as well."

I tell her it won't be a big deal, but I am wrong.

In theory, decorating Roxbury should be easy. The only construction required is changing the bathroom upstairs so it suits Madonna, building a closet for Guy, and enlarging the pool. The rest of the job really only involves moving furniture from Castillo del Lago into the new house.

However, Guy's closet turns out to be a massive enterprise, particularly as it involves my dealing with Guy directly.

We meet at the house and he tells me what he wants.

"Nothing mincey, mate. Nothing twee," he says.

I stop myself from knocking his front teeth in.

He tells me that the closet must be six feet long and five feet wide, with hanging space just so, drawers of only one kind, and—most important of all—a glass case for his cuff links and watches. The case, he says, must be lined in red velvet, with lights, so he can see his cuff links and watches displayed there.

It has to be made out of dark wood; the grain must match and run from left to right.

Through it all, he addresses me as "Chris," even though he knows I prefer Christopher. He is lordly, not in the least bit friendly—as if I am just another employee and not his brother-in-law.

Madonna, too, treats me as if I am nothing other than a serf paid to decorate her home. In the past, I researched fabric and furniture for her, narrowed the choice down to three samples of fabric, or three types of chairs, and brought her the samples and the photographs so she could pick which she wanted.

Now, though, she says three samples are not enough. She instructs me to bring her at least ten samples, photographs of at least ten types of chairs, and so on. And when I do, she says, she will then confer with Guy regarding the right choice.

Up till now, I have designed eight of her homes and she has

always trusted me implicitly. Not anymore. I show her five samples of paint color and suggest the appropriate one for the house, but she ignores me and asks to see more.

If she does agree on a color, the following morning she will come back to the house and tell me, "Guy doesn't like that color, so we have to pick another one."

I sense that her obstinacy stems from a deep desire to please Guy, and that he is secretly working to edge me out of every aspect of her life.

When it comes to selecting the wood for his closet, he is hands-on. I show him twelve samples and he tells me that they all look "twee." He uses the word over and over, and I get the message: I am gay and he doesn't want the house to reflect my sexuality, which is hardly likely.

Perhaps to safeguard the entire interior of the house from becoming contaminated by my homosexuality, he has his assistant decorate his office, at the back of the yard. A large picture of the queen is hung on the gray wall above his desk, along with an enormous white leather sofa and filing cabinets.

Meanwhile, Madonna and I argue over fabrics and textures. We argue over the slightest little detail—a doorknob, a light switch. We've never argued over such details before, and I feel as if I am falling into a strange, dark hole. I am angry and bitter.

Finally, this seemingly never-ending job is at last completed, and I go over to the house to meet Madonna and together assess the finished interior.

When I arrive, she is alone, but Guy is to come home and pick her up. We then stand in the driveway, talking about the house for a few hours. She is facing me and I am facing the front gate.

The gate opens. Guy drives up in Madonna's black Mercedes.

She doesn't turn around. Guy drives in my direction and when he is about a foot away, he veers the car away, just missing my foot.

I neither flinch nor move from my position in the driveway.

He stops the car, rolls down the window, and says, "Are you trying to prove a point?"

I say, "No, but I think you must be."

He rolls up the window and drives into the garage.

Madonna turns to me. "What just happened?"

I say, "I don't want to talk about it," and leave.

In April 2001, the London *Sunday Times* names Madonna and Guy Ritchie as number six on their list of Britain's richest people, citing their joint fortune as $260 million. When the *Drowned World* tour tickets go on sale at London's Earls Court, sixteen thousand are sold out in fifteen minutes, and eighty thousand tickets for five extra dates are sold out in only six hours. In the United States, one hundred thousand tickets for the show will be sold out in just a few hours.

The *Drowned World* tour will become *Billboard*'s number one Top Ten Concert Grosses, for five concerts at Madison Square Garden with sold-out crowds of 79,401 and gross sales of $9,297,105. When *Madonna Live! Drowned World Tour* is broadcast live on HBO from the Palace of Auburn Hills, it is seen by 5.7 million viewers and is the network's third-highest-rated prime-time concert special since 1997.

Microsoft announces that it has licensed "Ray of Light" for $15 million as the official theme song in their advertising campaign for Microsoft Windows XP.

The Immaculate Collection is certified as having sold 10 million copies and will become the all-time bestselling greatest-hits album ever made by a female artist.

The *Drowned World* tour grosses $74 million.

Madonna is named Britain's highest-earning woman with an annual income of £30 million—$43.8 million.

My work on the Roxbury house is now completed. I wait for my last payment, which is around $10,000. I can really use the money, so when it doesn't arrive, I call Caresse and ask where it is.

She stalls.

Within moments, she calls back again. "Okay, Madonna will pay you the final payment just as long as you agree to go to Kabbalah. The next meeting is at my house on Wednesday."

I tell her I'll think about it and hang up.

That same afternoon, Caresse messengers over *The Power of Kabbalah—Technology for the Soul* by Yehuda Berg, which is an official publication of the Kabbalah Centre International. On the cover, there is a quote from Madonna: "No hocus-pocus here. Nothing to do with religious dogma. The ideas in this book are earth-shattering and yet so simple."

I read the book and learn about Kabbalah, a power that has been around for the past two thousand years, which has influenced the world's leading scientific, philosophical, and spiritual minds throughout history. A mix of Judaism, Buddhism, Catholicism, and a bit of old-fashioned common sense thrown in for good measure, Kabbalah immediately interests me. As I study the book, I begin to think about spiritual issues I've long stopped pondering, and I am curious. I also realize that I've bought into the L.A. scene far too much and for far too long. Besides, I know that my connection with my sister has weakened and feel that attending Kabbalah may strengthen it once more.

The following Wednesday, I attend a meeting at Caresse's

house on Sunset Plaza. A two-story colonial brick house, nicely landscaped, on an expensive street. She's only Madonna's assistant. I can hardly pay my rent. I push all bitterness aside and join the meeting.

Inside are Madonna, her real estate broker, her masseuse, her costume designer, her choreographer, two assistants, her acupuncturist, and her two dancers. Clearly, she's involved everybody in her life with Kabbalah. The edict that you have to belong in order to work for her hasn't yet been formalized, but I suspect it will soon be. I also know that since Kabbalah has become so integral to her existence, she sees less of people who aren't involved in it.

We all sit down in a big circle. This meeting—and all that follow—has a particular topic, which Eitan, our teacher, teaches, then we all discuss it. The meeting lasts a couple of hours. Caresse serves crackers and other snacks.

Most of the time, I attend meetings at Demi's, Caresse's, or Madonna's, and on some Friday nights I go to the L.A. Kabbalah Center for Shabbat. There, I am not surprised to find that Madonna and Guy are treated like the uncrowned king and queen of Kabbalah. One of the basic premises of Kabbalah is that no individual is entitled to anything more than he or she has earned, yet every time I attend Shabbat at the center, Madonna and Guy sit on either side of the Bergs, who founded the modern Kabbalah movement.

"I've been coming here for fifteen years, and I've never gotten to sit next to the Bergs," I hear one woman complaining.

Kabbalah teaches the antithesis of envy, yet I can feel the envy rippling through the center, particularly when Guy, dressed in white robes, is regularly given the honor of carrying the Torah up to the altar.

Madonna has given millions of dollars to Kabbalah, and the movement is looming increasingly larger in her life and that of Guy.

I attend a twenty-four-hour Kabbalah session with them and Madonna's assistant Caresse in Anaheim. This is the first big Kabbalah event I've ever attended. Held in a hotel conference hall, the session starts at 7:30 p.m. All the men are instructed to wear white. Madonna and Guy are seated at the top table on the dais, but sit on opposite sides of the table to conform with the rest of the male and female attendees, who, according to tradition, sit on opposite sides of the hall. As the night proceeds, there are readings from the Torah. I follow as best as I can, but have no idea what is really going on. Even in that environment, for much of the night all eyes are on Madonna, and she is still the star of the show.

The press may report that Guy isn't as involved in Kabbalah as Madonna, but that isn't true. In fact, Guy's world and his conversations nowadays revolve around Kabbalah. According to Melanie, who still sees Madonna and Guy regularly, they often come over for dinner, but will only talk about Kabbalah. If the conversation strays to any other topic, they lose interest.

As for Madonna, I believe that Kabbalah has given form to her nebulous world, and I think it has given her a purpose. Because she is treated differently from all the other acolytes, she feels that her existence has been validated. After all, she has an entire spiritual movement backing up her decisions. She now believes she has God on her side. Armed with that belief, she often seems to use Kabbalah as a weapon.

However, during my involvement with the L.A. branch of Kabbalah, I discover that Madonna isn't the only star to do so. One of the lessons Demi and I attend centers around the topic of asking for help and teaches that one shouldn't be afraid to ask for it. I take that to mean that if you are lost on the highway, ask for directions, or if you are in pain, seek help.

The following morning, Demi, who is staying at the Peninsula, calls me and says, "Wasn't that a great lesson last night!"

"Really interesting," I say.

"I'm just about to make *Charlie's Angels II* here and I've decided to rent another house because I'm bringing my daughters out as well."

"Cool."

"Well, Christopher, I need help in decorating the new house. Will you help me?"

"Of course I will."

The next morning, we meet and talk about the house, but Demi doesn't mention a word about my fee. But I've committed to doing the job, so I feel I have to follow through.

Inside, though, I'm annoyed.

Perhaps it was just an oversight by Demi, and I certainly could have raised the issue myself, but instead I end up feeling as if Demi has taken the Kabbalah lesson on asking for help a little too literally. It's as if a producer asked her to help him by starring in his movie for free. Using Kabbalah in this way is not in my view what the movement teaches. So I go to IKEA, pick all the furniture for the house, the children's furniture, everything from top to bottom—all unassembled—and have the bill sent to Demi.

I feel sorry for her assistant, who is left to deal with assembling a truckload of furniture. But in the end, I don't think Demi gets the message or the joke. She is just as friendly as ever and probably assumes that IKEA is my designer of choice.

Demi isn't the only actress with whom I've become friends. I meet Farrah Fawcett at superagent Ed Limato's Friday-night Oscar party, which he throws each year for all that year's Academy Award nominees and their friends. We instantly connect and spend most of the evening talking exclusively to each other. I walk her to her car when we leave.

Some months later, Farrah invites me to her cluttered apartment in a high-rise on Wilshire Boulevard. She paints and sculpts and tells me she wants me to look at her work. I flash back to Lauren, but Farrah's paintings—abstract—are for the most part quite good. We do shots of tequila together, I play her Mary J. Blige, and she tells me her dream is to have her own art show. Eventually, that dream comes true. She has an art show at the L.A. County Museum of Art. I attend and am pleased that she has achieved her long-standing ambition.

I AM INVITED to the 2002 Academy Awards, but have been allocated just one ticket to the *Vanity Fair* after party. Farrah's assistant calls and says Farrah would like to go with me. I call *Vanity Fair* and they say I can bring her.

On the night, I drive my car—now a used black Cadillac Escalade with 50,000 miles on it—over to her apartment. When I walk in, she's in the bathroom. I wait half an hour for her. Then I yell through the door that we have to go because they won't allow anyone into the party after midnight.

Farrah opens the bathroom door. She is wearing a simple black silk knee-length dress with spaghetti straps. She looks great. I notice that she has powder all over her dress from leaning against the sink while doing her makeup. I brush it off for her. Then she checks her makeup in the mirror and gets powder all over herself again. I brush it off. Then she does it again. I brush it off. Then she does it again. I brush it off, then drag her away from the mirror and we leave at last.

We pull up outside Morton's, where there is a long press line. I ask Farrah if she wants to walk the line alone. She says no and asks me to walk with her.

The first reporter to stop us is from the E! network, who asks Farrah how she's doing.

"Hey, you got my name wrong last time you did an item on me. You didn't spell it right," she says.

She goes on like that for the next fifteen minutes, while the E! reporter just stands there, stunned. I gently pull Farrah away, and we continue down the line together.

Finally, we make it into the party. The first person we run into is Ryan O'Neal. She is visibly unnerved, but tells me she is going to talk to him. I go off and dance with Helen Hunt.

When I come back, Farrah is sitting with Ryan.

She tells me that they are going to Harvey Weinstein's party, but that if I want to go, I can follow. I tell her that I am not on the list and don't want to be turned away, so she should go without me. She thinks for a few moments, then decides to go with me after all.

We end up at a party at my friend Andy Will's house, which is full of gay men who all fall in love with her on the spot, and she is thrilled.

In August 2002, Madonna invites me to her birthday party at Roxbury. The invitation to the fifty select guests is from "Mrs. Ritchie." It strikes me that when she was married to Sean, she never called herself Mrs. Penn. She now bears practically the most famous name in the universe and has never before relinquished it, yet now she has—just to make Guy feel better about himself. A kind and loving gesture, perhaps, but I also feel that she is acting a part.

The invitation states that the dress code is kimonos only. Anyone not wearing one will not be admitted to the party. I have a really nice red cotton kimono with white writing all over it, which I bought in Tokyo during *The Girlie Show*, so I wear that.

At the house, all the pathways are lined with lit votive candles and the garden looks really pretty.

Gwyneth and I start chatting.

All of a sudden she screams, "Christopher, you're on fire."

I look down. Flames are curling up my kimono. I rip it off, pour water over it. Gwyneth and I step on it and stamp the fire out.

I am wearing black trousers and a black shirt underneath. I stay at the party dressed like that.

Madonna walks by. I show her my burned kimono, which now has a hole in it as big as a beach ball.

She shrugs. "Put that back on. No one is allowed to stay at the party if they aren't wearing a kimono."

Don't ask me if I am okay, don't ask me if I am burned, just stick to your fucking rules.

I ignore her and go back to dancing with Gwyneth.

Despite my insubordination at the party, Madonna invites me to attend the dress rehearsal of *Drowned World.* With mixed feelings, I go along to Sony Studios at Culver City. When I arrive, the stage is dark. The lights go up, and there, center stage, is my tree. My concept. Only it looks like something out of Caligula, dark, ominous, and unfriendly. Just like the show.

Watching, I am sad. It hurts me to see Madonna performing at half her potential. She seems to be in a very dark place, and that is reflected in the show. I don't tell her, though, because I know how much her tours mean to her, and I want to be supportive.

Driving home alone after the dress rehearsal, I feel like crying. I know that I could have done so much better with the show, and I know how much better Madonna can be when she is properly directed. And I wish fervently that our relationship hadn't downward-spiraled so much.

My sister and I rarely share feelings when we are alone together, but we do so from time to time through letters. In early 2002, our correspondence affords me a glimpse into the issues in her marriage and how they deeply affect her. My sister tells me that she relies heavily on Kabbalah, and sees her counselor frequently.

Her love for Guy shines through her sentiments. Despite all the acrimony between us, I realize that she is committed to him. I wish the marriage well. I send her a positive letter, in which I take Guy's part and try to help her understand his vulnerability. I tell her that he is living in this incredible world with her, has an ego of his own and an idea of what he is, and that she may have shattered the illusion, but he is clearly now trying to find his way. I suppose, to some extent, I am writing about myself as well.

She responds immediately, telling me that London can be lonely at times, but that she is hopeful she will find her way. I hope she will. No matter how much I dislike Guy, he's her husband and I want her to be happy with him.

Still, I worry about Madonna. Guy is ten years her junior, and she's given him latitude to pursue his own interests. But they are very different people, with different approaches to things, and I wonder whether they will be able to bridge the divide. I suspect that Kabbalah will help them through any rough times. And I only hope that the openness of her communications with me signals a new phase in our relationship and that we will one day be close again.

In May 2002, she invites me to London to see her opening in the play *Up for Grabs.* I fly over to London with my good friend David Cooley, stay at Home House, and on May 23 attend the first night with Rupert and Gwyneth. The play is confusing, with Madonna playing a commercial art dealer who makes out with a woman. At one point, she holds up a black dildo, and the entire scenario eludes me completely.

Guy is in the audience, but we don't talk. The next day, Madonna invites me to lunch at her house in Marylebone. She has obviously weathered the crisis in her marriage, and I am relieved.

The restored Georgian terrace home, not far from Hyde Park, has a dramatic staircase, five reception rooms, a large library, eight bedrooms, fifteen-foot ceilings, and a huge twenty-eight-square-foot drawing room. But I am far from happy with the way David Collins has decorated the house. Her office, though, is similar to my work in the New York apartment.

We go out for a walk. Suddenly she says, "Guy told me about this pub; let's take a look."

"But you don't drink beer, Madonna."

"I do now."

We go to the pub, and she orders a pint of bitters. I watch her face as she drinks it. She is pretending to like the beer, but by the look on her face, I can tell she doesn't.

"My husband is a beer drinker, and I want to experience what he experiences," she says in explanation.

I realize that it isn't just Kabbalah that has saved Madonna and Guy's marriage. Madonna is striving hard to please him and probably always will.

• • •

Back in L.A., I continue working on my designs for Central Restaurant on Sunset Plaza. My fee trickles in slowly, but I have a stake in the restaurant and am forced to wait for it to open before getting paid. Madonna invests $45,000 in the restaurant, which is nice of her and indicative of hope for our relationship.

In June *Forbes* puts Madonna fourth on its list of the highest-paid entertainers of 2002, citing her income as $43 million. Soon after, she begins filming a small part as a fencing instructor in *Die Another Day,* the next James Bond movie, for which she records the theme song, "Die Another Day."

I see the movie and smile at the irony that as a teenager I studied fencing and one of my dreams was to emulate Errol Flynn in that arena. Trust Madonna, as always, to get there ahead of me!

Aside from working on the long, drawn-out, and currently unprofitable Central job, I am also now writing for *Interview, Instinct, Icon,* and *Genre* magazines and—with *Swept Away* about to be released—get an interview with Madonna for the magazines. I'd like to think that she is letting me interview her because she wants to help me, but promoting *Swept Away* is no doubt her primary motivation.

I go to Madonna's Roxbury house for the interview. There, for the first time since her birth, I manage to spend a few quiet moments with my niece Lola. I put her on the tricycle I gave her when she was born and push her around the garden. She laughs and is obviously having a good time. She is learning French and Spanish, and we exchange some words in both languages. The moment is a happy one.

In many ways, Lola reminds me of Madonna: big eyes, watching everything going on around her, taking it all in. She is now exactly the same age as Madonna was when she, and all of us Ciccone children, lost our mother. I watch her and wish our mother could be alive to see her grandchild. I feel momentarily sad for Lola as well. But other than not ever knowing her maternal grandmother, the world is hers.

After I interview Madonna, she and I and Lola have lunch. Madonna, who, I think, is probably being stricter just to impress me, makes Lola sit at the counter and eat her lunch there. She gives her pasta with tomato sauce.

"I don't want to eat it," Lola declares, throwing down her cutlery.

Madonna tells her she has to.

"But I don't want to."

Madonna starts pleading.

Lola doesn't back down.

Madonna tries negotiating with her. "Look, Lola, if you eat your lunch, I'll let you wear your special new outfit tonight."

Lola's eyes light up. Then she shakes her head.

In the end, Madonna agrees to let Lola wear her special outfit as long as Lola eats half her food.

Lola beams. She has manipulated Madonna and won.

Even though this scene plays out in kitchens everywhere—a mother trying to convince her daughter to eat—I was fascinated by the dynamics between Madonna and Lola. Lola's powers of persuasion over her mother were interesting to me. She had managed to handle Madonna in a way that I—and perhaps to one else in Madonna's life—can do.

ON OCTOBER 8, 2002, *Swept Away*, a remake of Lina Wertmuller's 1975 movie, directed by Guy and starring Madonna, opens in Los

Angeles. I love her in the dream sequence, but as with most of her past cinematic output, I am embarrassed by the rest of the film. The movie was slaughtered by critics and won five Golden Raspberry Awards. After the *Shanghai Surprise* debacle, I think Madonna should have known better than to work with her husband. But just as Sean made *Shanghai Surprise* as a gift of love for her, I am sure she followed his example and made *Swept Away* as a gift of love for Guy.

THIRTEEN

Remember that everything in your life is there for one reason and one reason only: to offer you the opportunity to transform.

Yehuda Berg, *The Power of Kabbalah*

At the end of 2002, the London *Mail on Sunday* names Madonna Britain's second-highest-earning woman and cites her income that year at $56 million. "Die Another Day" becomes her thirty-fifth Top 10 hit, and she becomes second in career Top 10 singles behind Elvis, who had thirty-eight. She has now also surpassed Aretha Franklin to become the female solo artist with the most Top 40 singles in music history. On January 13, 2003, she wins the Michael Jackson International Artist of the Year Award at the Shrine Auditorium. Later in the year, Madonna signs a $10 million contract with Gap to star in TV commercials and print ads for its fall campaign.

I am nearing the end of working on Central, but so far have made little money from the project. I am forced to further pare down my already Spartan existence by selling some of the small number of antiques that still remain from my New York years.

• • •

MADONNA GETS IN touch and tells me she is selling Roxbury and has bought a new house on Sunset Boulevard. At her suggestion, I go to see the house, a bizarre reproduction of a French château, with a large swimming pool, a tennis court, and an indoor theater.

I hate it on sight, but when she asks me to design and decorate it in three months flat, I agree. If I hadn't needed the cash so badly, I would have turned her down because the time frame she has allotted me for the job is so short. After I agree to do the house, the emails fly back and forth between us regarding the design. Madonna senses my feelings about it, and an argument blows up between us, which rages in our emails.

On May 19, 2003, I write back to her, "M . . . Once again you have read anger into my letter to you where there is none. . . . I am fully aware of the fact that you've helped me out in the past and it has both contributed to my creative development and financial and now spiritual, since you introduced me to Kabbalah . . . I did ask you to come and see my new work ages ago . . . but as to my . . . photos, they are not just random shots of ass . . . they are an extension of my creative need as an artist and frankly they are quite good as photos and I intend on showing them in a gallery here in L.A. . . .

"I see no need to belittle my art simply because you don't understand it or have not seen it . . . you of all people . . . it is true, I have not attended various family functions and video showings because I had other more important things to take care of. . . . I am making time for Kabbalah because what little I have learned has made a difference in my life already . . . and will continue with it for that reason . . . not because I want to please you. . . . As to the stories that you hear . . . again, you of all people should know better than to believe that sort of shit. . . . I have never been thrown out of a club even . . . and for the most part am quite congenial when in public. . . .

"However there are times when out, that my reactions to certain people friends and strangers has been rather pointed . . . but consider this . . . after 15 years of being prodded and prodded with question after question about you and what you are doing and your movies and records by people who have no interest in me whatsoever . . . for years and years everywhere I go . . . I am bound to react in a less than friendly way from time to time. . . . However, for the most part I take this in stride as best I can . . . you see it can give a person the feeling that they don't exist except as a vague outline of you . . . and I suppose my avoidance of events and things with you may well be an extension of that frustration. . . .

"This of course is not your fault and I've learned to live with it as best I can . . . and will continue to . . . but please understand . . . it is not an easy task to have people look at me but only see you . . . do you understand this . . . Anyway . . . I am not a drunk or a drug addict and have for a long time been doing my damndest to crawl out from under the rather large shadow you cast . . . the problem is that you have given me a great many opportunities to be creative and work with you. . . . Now that period seems to have ended I am trying to find my way . . . stumbling sometime, yes . . . making the wrong decision sometime, yes . . . but doing my best always. . . . Take care of yourself . . . all my love . . . Christopher."

Our relationship begins to normalize once more. Then I send her another email asking her to film an acceptance speech for the Gay Film Festival, and on June 19, 2003, she replies, opening with the blunt sentiment "I do not want to film an acceptance speech for the Gay Film Festival but thanks for asking. I get requests all the time for things like this and I always turn them down."

I flash back to our life in downtown Manhattan, to Martin Burgoyne and to Christopher Flynn, who both died of AIDS and to whom Madonna owes so much, and I think of her gay fan base. I also think of the good times we both shared with her gay dancers, dancing with them at Catch One, Club Louis, along with the drag queens, all of whom adored her. And I can't believe how alienated my sister has become from the gay world and the fans who made her what she is now.

She no longer seems to have any sense that she owes the gay world much of her career and that the debt will never be paid, because clearly she thinks it has now been. Or perhaps she has simply erased that element in her past from her memory altogether.

WHEN I ASK for help in mounting a Las Vegas production of *The Girlie Show*, in which she would only have to participate by allowing me to open the show with a hologram of herself, she writes to me dismissively: "I really have no interest in participating in the show other than giving them my name and my concept and my songs. . . . If and when I come to perform in Vegas again it will be because they pay me zillions of dollars up front."

Subject closed. I feel as if she has told me to go play in traffic.

Then she switches to the subject of the house and proposes paying me $45,000 for designing and decorating it over three months. My fee, she tells me, will be paid as follows: $10,000 just to get started, $5,000 at the end of the first month, $15,000 at the end of the second. Another $15,000 at the end of the third month, and another $5,000 if the job takes longer than projected.

This fee is identical to the one she paid me for designing and decorating the second version of her New York apartment many years before. Next to what other designers get, the fee is insultingly low, but there is more: "This is contingent on you making yourself totally available to me and devoting the majority of your time to this project."

She is fully aware that I am working on Central, but is demanding my services 24-7.

I have no choice but to acquiesce to all her terms. I am broke and no one is beating down my door to employ me. I am my own worst salesman and have never used an attorney to negotiate the fees or contracts for my designing jobs. Then I talk to a friend of mine, another designer, who is shocked at my paltry fee. He tells me I am getting paid a quarter of what another decorator/designer would charge for the same job.

He explains that on every job, all designers/decorators bill clients 30 percent above the retail price of furniture and all other aspects of an interior. He suggests that I do the same thing, then at least I will at last be properly recompensed for my work. I decide not only to do just that, but also to hire him to work with me on the job, as the restaurant continues to take much of my time.

I start work on the house. Fortunately, it has exactly the masculine feel that Guy requires, so I don't have to do much radical work on it. All I have to do for him is change the fittings on his dark green marble bathroom from brass to chrome. Luckily, he decrees that his closet should be a replica of his at Roxbury. One less trauma. When Madonna tells me he won't be attending any of our meetings, I am relieved that I won't have to deal with him. I tell myself that this job is destined to go really smoothly.

However, the first time I am involved in work on Central and I can't attend a meeting with Madonna and send my designer friend instead, she goes ballistic.

She calls me screaming, "I fucking told you that if you took this job, you have to be around twenty-four/seven."

I start to disagree.

"I don't care," she says. "Just get over here."

I do.

Over the entire three months it takes to complete the house, Madonna is difficult at every turn. My sister, who used to implicitly trust my design judgment, now doesn't trust me at all, and I am both mystified and frustrated. I can't fathom why she doesn't realize that my talent has not diminished but may well have matured. She demands that I supply her with design boards, complete with paint and fabric samples, and, however many I give her, she insists on seeing more. And when I have to go to the fabric store and to the furniture store, she tells me she is coming with me. This is a first, and I am not amused.

Generally, when those types of stores are dealing with a decorator/designer, bringing the client to the store is frowned upon. Only this time, of course, the client is Madonna.

We arrive at the fabric store, and everyone from the manager to the assistants all swoon, "It's Madonna! It's Madonna!"

I cringe and try to do my job. But I know it's going to be a long afternoon.

I show her fabric, but I know she isn't listening to me. My anger is mounting.

I show her something else. She tells me she doesn't like it, but won't give me a reason.

I try to remain patient, to explain to her why a particular color fits a particular room. And that we aren't just decorating one corner but the entire house, and that everything has to mesh.

But she insists on seeing the house in fragments, not as a unit.

She argues with me at every turn.

This light switch shouldn't be here.

This electrical outlet shouldn't be there.

Suddenly she is a decorator and a designer and knows better about everything. We are continually at odds with each other.

I think back to the days when she had so much faith in my taste that she gave an interview to *Architectural Digest* declaring, "We call Christopher the pope because everything has to get his seal of approval. Who could I have more in common with than someone I grew up with? We like the same things, from music to what we eat."

Now, though, my sister has morphed from being my best and most appreciative audience to an amnesiac, carping stranger fixated on undermining me whenever possible. On August 26, 2003, she dashes off an imperious memo with a curt list of items about which she wants updates. Have I ordered fabric for a living room bench? Have I purchased a wood frame for screening the powder room? Should a curtain rod in her bedroom be cut down for another room? Have I purchased a small area rug to be placed in the hallway? There is more—including her demand that I send her photographs of the various curtain rails I intend to use in her yoga room and in what she describes as "GR's office."

I respond as politely as I can. I realize that her obsessive need to control every aspect of my work on the house has partly been prompted by her belief that as I am still working on Central, I am not devoting my entire time to her.

Her refusal to listen to or even attempt to understand my design ideas for the house frustrates me even more. The best element in the house is a two-story sunroom constructed entirely of floor-to-ceiling glass windows. I conceive of turning it into a botanical music room, furnishing it with white-painted metal furniture, hanging plants from the rafters, so that being in the room would feel like being in the middle of a garden, with sunlight flooding in—the perfect setting in which to make music.

I try explaining the concept to Madonna.

"I don't get it," she says.

"Try picturing it."

"I still don't get it. Can't you draw it for me?"

"But I've described it to you in detail."

"I wanna see it before you do it."

I give a big sigh.

She glares at me. "You want to keep this job?"

I nod miserably.

"Then don't give me attitude," she says.

SHE ALSO INSISTS on hanging a weird, larger-than-life, eight-by-twelve-foot photograph of her—in the style of Helmut Newton, but taken by Steven Klein—in the hallway.

I think it sad that poor Rocco and Lola have to wake up each morning and come face-to-face with this huge picture of their mother dressed in a blatant S&M outfit, lying on a bed with dead animals all around her. The creepiest thing I've ever seen. This is a Madonna I don't know anymore.

SOON AFTER, MADONNA leaves for New York. It's now the middle of summer, and L.A. is in the throes of a heat wave.

One afternoon, I call Caresse and ask if some friends and I can use Madonna's pool. Madonna sends word that we can.

So four of us hang out by the pool, drink beer, and sunbathe.

We don't set foot in the house and, at sunset, go home.

Later that night, Madonna calls me, fuming.

She says that a security guard has reported that we spent the afternoon taking drugs and having an orgy.

Nothing is further from the truth.

But the die is cast.

By now, Madonna has convinced herself that I am a major drug addict and smoke crack daily, whereas I have never once contemplated even trying it.

She suggests that I have weekly individual sessions at the Kabbalah Center with our teacher, Rabbi Eitan Yardeni.

I agree, as I am increasingly interested in Kabbalah.

I see him once a week for a few months and each time give a $50 donation to the center. I grow to view the sessions as therapy, enjoy them, and trust Eitan with my innermost thoughts.

By now, the Kabbalah meetings are held in either Madonna's, Demi's, Lucy Liu's, or Caresse's house.

When the meeting is at Madonna's house, she serves vegetarian appetizers. Demi Moore serves the best food of all—shrimp and other delicacies.

Each meeting begins with Eitan lecturing from the perspective of Kabbalah on the topic of the day, such as "Finding Your Soul Mate," "Making Money," "Speaking Ill of Other People." Afterward, we all discuss the topic. As the meetings rotate between houses, I notice that the person at whose house the meeting is held that week gets to monopolize the conversation, to hog the limelight from everyone else.

Around that time, Demi calls me: "Something really strange happened last night. Your sister invited Ashton and me over to her house for Sunday dinner. We got all dressed up, but when we arrived at the house, your sister and Guy were in workout clothes.

"We all sat down for dinner, had the main course, then your sister stood up.

" 'Guy and I are going to see a movie. But you and Ashton are welcome to stay for dessert,' she said.

"Ashton and I exchanged glances, then we went home."

Another example of the way in which my sister seems to have lost touch with other people.

In September 2003, Madonna publishes her first children's book, the forty-eight-page *English Roses.* It is released in one hundred countries and thirty languages, but I am not impressed. Her experience with children, other than her own, is minimal, as is her understanding of people except on a business or practical level. Moreover, the plots of this and all her subsequent children's books are written more for adults and are not particularly child-friendly.

Meanwhile, our conflict over the house escalates when she sends me a vitriolic fax on September 23, 2003, in which she accuses me of not having approached the job with "gusto, enthusiasm, urgency and gratitude" and claims that "you hate the fact that you have to work for me. There is no sense of urgency or gratitude and frankly I'm fed up with all of it." She ends by saying, "This is not a healthy relationship and when you have gotten rid of your issues with me over the fact that I am what or who I am then perhaps we can work together again."

The message is clear: for my sister, our working relationship is over.

I write straight back to her.

"m . . . I have no idea what you're talking about. I have given you all the information that is possible to give . . . I am at the house every day . . . and doing everything that you ask . . . I spoke to angela this morning. . . . your reaction is bizarre to say the least. . . . obviously you're frustrated with other things and looking for an outlet. . . . fine . . . fire me. . . . I will consider this my last day of work for you. I am fully aware of the concept of "Bread of Shame" and believe me, I worked and have always worked for every penny you have paid me, and generally it was pennies. . . . rob and I have worked our asses off to get this job done in the time frame you requested . . . but that doesn't seem to matter . . . You really need to assess how you react to things and consider taking the calm, intelligent and peaceful approach to the house and life. . . . Your overeaction to things is only going [to] make every thing seem unbearable. . . . you really need to take another look at Kabbalah and [its] teachings m and start practicing it yourself instead of using it as a weapon on others. . . . take care . . . peace . . . oh and . . . let me know if you want rob to continue in my place. . . . of course you realize you will have to pay him to continue. . . . i still love you, crazy as you are. . . . c"

The following morning, at just after 6 a.m., she fires off another fax to me in which she ends our working relationship. Along the way, she admits, "Perhaps I expect too much because of history, water under the bridge and the fact that you are my brother. Who knows but it's not good chemistry." She ends, "I am calm and I love you too."

I am still angry, but I am also sad.

I spend all morning mulling my reply, then write, "funny how it all comes down to money . . . hmm . . . and just for the record . . . I am the last person in your world who has always had your back . . . and despite the fact that u live in a fantasy world . . . I will always have your back. . . . I love u too much and too deeply to ever let that go. . . . peace . . . c."

I SUSPECT THAT although Guy has never been to the house while I was working there, he was somewhere in the background, pulling my sister's strings. Or perhaps he told her she should exercise more control over what I'm doing. Either way, she has made my life a misery during the entire Sunset job.

FINALLY, THE HOUSE is completed according to schedule.

However, I don't receive the final payment of $15,000, so I call Caresse.

"Madonna wants me to tell you that she doesn't feel you did enough to warrant the final payment. So she isn't going to pay it," she says.

For a moment, I digest the latest blow my sister has dished out.

"You tell Madonna if she wants to see any of the rest of the furniture I bought for her and she's waiting for, she had better pay me my final payment."

Caresse gulps and hangs up. Within a few hours, my final check is messengered over to me, and I arrange for Madonna to get the rest of her furniture.

BY NOW, MADONNA and I are hardly on speaking terms. But we are not completely estranged. Then, at the end of October 2003, in a quirk of fate, she inexplicably decides to return one of the light fixtures I've purchased for her for Sunset. Caresse takes it back to the shop, whereupon she learns that I have charged a percentage above the cost of the item—the standard markup every designer takes.

On October 24, Madonna calls me and says that she can't believe I've done this to her, calling me a thief and a liar, and the most untrustworthy person she's ever met, accusing me of betraying her after she has put all her love and loyalty into my work. One of the accusations that hurts the most is when she yells, "I've made you what you are. You wouldn't be anything without me."

I do my best to defend myself. She hits back with a fax in which she hurls further accusations at me, ending, "Please never contact me again."

It is as if my sister has taken a knife, stuck it into my stomach, and twisted it twenty-five times. Or ripped my heart out and carved it into a thousand pieces.

I've spent the last twenty years helping make her a star, supporting her, protecting her, without much financial reward. And now this.

I stare at the computer screen for what seems like hours, reading the poisonous words over and over, enraged.

In frustration, I smash my fist on my desk.

I break a bone in my hand and, for weeks after, have to wear a cast, but the physical pain is negligible next to the psychological pain my sister has just inflicted on me. Every bit of anger I've ever felt at her, every disappointment she's ever caused me, every iota of pride I've swallowed on her behalf, every bitter rejection, comes to the surface.

I sit down and reply to her email.

"you have never in the entire time I have worked for you since 1985 paid me even close to what i was worth. . . . I gave up my fucking life to help make you the evil queen you are today. . . . 15 years listening to your bitching, egotistical rantings, mediocre talent, and a lack of taste that would stun the ages . . . every ounce of talent you have, you have sucked dry from me and the people around you . . . i certainly never worked for you for the money. . . . now you accuse me of lying and cheating you. . . . you've got some fucking nerve. . . . as usual . . . you have lost all sense of reality. . . . i guess I always thought that one day you'd see my worth and behave accordingly . . . but you never did. . . . a little fucking respect was all I ever wanted from you and you couldn't even manage that."

I end the email with "Don't forget to remove me from your will." Then I press SEND.

As I do, the weight of the world falls off my shoulders. All of a sudden, I am free of Madonna. I don't have to protect her anymore. I don't have to worry about how my public behavior will reflect on her. I can be myself at last. Christopher, not Madonna's brother.

Then I am overcome by a deep sadness. The woman I loved above all others, the woman who I thought was incredibly creative and loving has surrounded herself with sycophants who do nothing but agree with her and who I feel have poisoned her against me. The Madonna I once knew is lost to me forever. And I am sorry for her, and us.

SHE DOESN'T REPLY to my email. When I email Demi to ask where the next Wednesday Kabbalah class is being held, she replies that she isn't sure. After that, silence. I email her again. Silence. The message comes over loud and clear: I have shared my thoughts and hopes with my fellow members of the Kabbalah class, but because of my rift with my sister, I am no longer welcome.

Despite having been excluded from Kabbalah classes, I continue to practice Kabbalah's tenets and precepts all on my own. Kabbalah has taught and continues to teach me a great deal about the manner in which I exist in this world and the consequences of my actions, and is invaluable to me.

Kabbalah has now become as integral a part of my existence as my Catholicism. My view of the world has changed and become more positive, and my reactions to other people have become more cerebral and serene. Through Kabbalah, my once negative and somewhat dark reactions to other people have become far more positive.

However, I do acknowledge that—given my human shortcomings, my human frailties—my study of Kabbalah is ongoing, but necessary if I am to curb those elements within my nature that have often proved to be my undoing.

My commitment to Kabbalah is, and will always remain, so profound that I now have one of the seventy-one names of God—the one which, in Kabbalah, represents the precept that "everything you do affects the future"—tattooed on my left forearm, never to be removed.

I also volunteer to get involved with the Spirituality for Kids program, which is run by Eitan's wife, Sarah.

I develop a ten-week program in which children ages eight to twelve are presented with disposable Kodak cameras. Each one of them is given a word. Then they spend a week illustrating that word through photographs.

I enjoy working with the children. The project eventually evolves into a book. I have no part in it, but am glad to have been involved at the early stages of the program.

TWO WEEKS AFTER I emailed Madonna, VH1 calls me and asks if I would like to appear in a show on design. I am delighted and say that I would. A week passes. I receive a second call from the same producer asking if I've spoken to Madonna recently. I tell him I haven't.

"She doesn't want this show to happen, so could you call her?" he says.

"No," I say, "if she doesn't want the show to happen, it probably shouldn't."

And it doesn't.

• • •

The word is out and my stock in Hollywood plummets accordingly. Wherever I go, I am haunted by my sister—by her voice and her image. She is on the radio, in the ring of a telephone, on the TV, and I can't escape her. I talk to a friend, and he asks about Madonna. I go to a bar, one of her songs comes on, the entire room turns to look at me, and my stomach turns over.

Central Restaurant opens. The *Los Angeles Times* calls it "one of the most beautiful rooms in the country." But after just three months, it closes. I have spent three years working on Central, as I have a share in the restaurant and believed that I would be recompensed when it was a success. Now, of course, I won't be. All the investors in the restaurant, including Madonna, lose their money.

I still have my two lodgers, but my car is repossessed because I can no longer afford the payments. To add injury to insult, while I'm out with friends one night, I tear a ligament in my knee. I have surgery on it and am forced to spend the next four months recovering.

This enforced period of rest does not help my financial situation at all, nor does the surgeon's $10,000 bill, which—as my partners in Central failed to pay my insurance premium—I am compelled to settle myself.

My consolation is my art. And on June 26, 2004, at the opening of Gay Pride Week, the Booty Collection (twenty-five color Polaroids, blown up to eleven by fourteen, of my friends' backsides) is shown in San Francisco at the Phantom SF Gallery, to great fanfare. Alan Cumming, Armistead Maupin, and Graham Norton all attend and are extremely complimentary about my work.

I continue with my paintings and photography, and on August 15, 2004, the Mumford Gallery in Provincetown, Massachusetts, also shows the Booty Collection. It's well received, but my sister makes it clear she doesn't approve of it and doesn't consider it art. The subtext is that she assumes that the photographs are the product of a couple of drug binges. Totally untrue.

MEANWHILE, MADONNA LAUNCHES her *Re-invention Tour.* I don't go to see it, but afterward view the DVD: *I'm Going to Tell You a Secret.* The show opens with "Vogue," distant and cold, which sets the note for the rest of the show. Throughout, she attempts to force-feed the audience. The show is confrontational, unsubtle, angry. I am amused, though, that in the documentary she features scenes from our father's vineyard and says that she grew up there. Not so; she merely visited a few times. The scenes featuring Lola and Rocco both touch and sadden me. I am sad, as I have seen so little of them. I am touched at how much Lola reminds me of Madonna. And I miss not knowing her or Rocco.

I AM VIRTUALLY destitute, save for the largesse of a few friends, especially my long-term friends Daniel Hoff and Eugenio Lopez, as well as Dan Sehres, who is kind enough to let me stay with him for the duration. His kindness and hospitality will continue for the next two years.

One night, however, back in L.A., as fate would have it, I am invited to a dinner party where I meet Andrea Greenberg, the head of marketing for Fortune International Properties. She offers me a job designing the lobby of their Miami headquarters. The job is projected to last six months, and intensely relieved at getting out of L.A., I relocate to Miami temporarily and begin work.

After I've been in Miami for only a few days, a friend invites me to dinner at China Grill, where I see Ingrid. My impression is that Guy may have attempted to edge her out of Madonna's life, but he hasn't completely succeeded. The moment we meet again, she tells me that she knows Madonna and I aren't talking.

"You should definitely email her right away," Ingrid says, giving me one of her intense looks.

"I don't have anything to say to her. I won't speak to her until she treats me with the respect I've earned and deserve."

Ingrid looks shocked. The thought of not speaking to Madonna is clearly anathema to her.

"Anyway, I'm out of her life now. And I'm doing fine," I say.

There is more, and if, by the time I get home, I've forgotten much of it, an email from Madonna is in my inbox, reiterating every word I've just uttered to Ingrid and refreshing my memory.

I haven't spent time with Ingrid for so long that I've forgotten that one of her geniuses is seducing me into having a conversation about Madonna, getting me to spill my guts, letting my guard down. Whereupon she reports back to Madonna. I promise myself never to let my guard down again with Ingrid.

It takes me a while before I decide to open Madonna's email. She never puts a subject, so I have no warning whether an email will be friendly or not. This email is neutral. She insists that she does treat me with respect, but she doesn't say she was wrong or apologize for the hateful things she said in her email. I answer her in polite terms.

Toward the end of my job with Fortune, I am offered the chance to be the interior design director for the Calypso at Caribbean on Thirty-seventh and Collins, a luxury condominium development, a new and an existing building by architect Kobi Karp.

Along the way, a friend sends me an article about Madonna, featuring her move to the twelve-hundred-acre Ashcombe House in the English countryside—and depicting her in her latest incarnation: English country lady. A lifetime's distance away from Madonna the modern dancer, Madonna the punk pop star, and all the other guises my kaleidoscopic sister has assumed in the past. I look at the pictures of Madonna in her manor house, think of my new life in Miami, and am sad at how far apart we now are, how far from each other we have traveled.

I AM DOING well in Miami and L.A., carving out a life as an artist, interior decorator, and designer on my own merits, not on the back of my sister's name. On my birthday, in November 2005, I make sure to invite Ingrid to my party, just so she will see for herself that I'm thriving and report accordingly to Madonna.

At a friend's house, I meet the co-coordinator of the White Party, given each year to benefit AIDS research. He asks me if I know someone who might like to host a benefit dinner at the Versace mansion. I suggest supermodel and *America's Next Top Model* judge Janice Dickinson, whom I had met at Central. He loves the idea. I open negotiations. Initially, Janice demands five first-class tickets and luxury suites for herself and countless members of her entourage. At which point, my experience in handling divas kicks in. Janice ends up toning down her requirements and flies down to Miami to host the dinner. I am grateful to her for her participation.

WHILE I AM working on the Caribbean, I design and manufacture a line of T-shirts that I name Basura Boy. *Basura,* Spanish, loosely translates to "trash." The T-shirts each feature a symbol from either Kabbalah or Buddhism. The slogan of the company is "Spirituality Is Our Business."

In June 2006, I film two episodes of the Bravo show *Top Chef,* advising on restaurant designs. With the producer's consent, I give full rein to my acid tongue and observe of one chef's culinary creation, "If this is a vegetable medley, I'm a monkey."

When the show is aired a year later, the reviews of my appearance are extreme and veer between love and hate, but even the negative ones don't sour me on the experience of making the show. I loved it.

I am also now managing a young singer named Julien. He's a little David Bowie, a little Freddie Mercury, but fresh and original. Most of all, though, he reminds me of the young Madonna. He has her passion and drive. I sense his potential and feel I can help his career. He agrees to let me manage him, and we make a nine-track demo to send out to record companies. He also has his first gig at the Roxy in L.A., then another one at Crimson in Hollywood. He receives great reviews and I am optimistic about his future.

In May 2006, Madonna's assistant calls and invites me to the May 21 L.A. opening of her *Confessions* show—a sixty-city tour that will go on to make $260 million. I haven't seen or spoken to her in two years. I'm sitting in the front row.

The show is lighthearted, and for the first time since *The Girlie Show,* Madonna looks as if she is enjoying herself.

Watching, I am overcome with a sense of nostalgia. I remember the past, when things were great between us. I miss the sister I knew so well, the closeness, the respect, the being part of something that was so great. Suddenly, I yearn to turn back the clock, to be on the road with her again, part of the show, part of her life.

After the show, I go backstage to the greenroom to see Madonna. As I walk in, a man with a full beard taps me on the shoulder. I assume he's a rabbi.

In a polite but distant voice, I say, "Hi."

"It's Guy, dummy."

I didn't recognize him at all. I stand in the entrance of the greenroom and wait to see Madonna. In a white T-shirt and jeans, light makeup, her hair pulled back, she is perched on the edge of a chair. She knows the show has gone well and looks relaxed.

A line of people wait to shake her hand.

Our eyes meet.

She smiles at me.

I bypass the line.

We hug.

I tell her the show was great.

She thanks me for coming.

"You look good. You look happy," she says.

I tell her she does, too, and I mean it.

We have reconnected at last, and I am glad.

IN JUNE, I go to my father's seventy-fifth birthday in Traverse City. Joan throws a big party for him in a large barn on the property that holds five hundred. Madonna doesn't come. I'm pleased because otherwise the party would have been about her, not him.

During the day, my father comes up to me and asks what's going on with me and Madonna. I tell him we've had a disagreement and she's hurt me badly, but we're working on getting over it at last.

"I wish you would sort it out; it's making me unhappy," he says.

I don't want to make my father unhappy. I love and respect him far too much. And I am glad to tell him that I feel that Madonna and I have almost sorted out all our differences and that I believe that there is hope for us again, at last.

WHEN *CONFESSIONS* OPENS in Miami on July 22, I ask for tickets so I can see the show again.

The atmosphere inside the arena is electric, if steamy, as Madonna, contrary to all the rules, has prevailed on the management to kill the air-conditioning.

I sit next to Gloria and Emilio on my left, and Dan Sehres on my right.

As Madonna is lowered onstage in the disco ball, I flash back for a moment to the disco ball at the Rubaiyat and feel nostalgic for that night, that time, and our shared past together. At that moment, Madonna looks directly at me and gives me a little nod and I smile at her.

I notice that Ingrid hasn't got a good seat and keeps craning her neck for a view of Madonna. Ingrid is wearing the slightly hangdog look she has when she feels she's been dissed. She keeps attempting to catch Madonna's eye, but Madonna ignores her.

I am wrapped up in the show and really enjoying it when—all of a sudden—Madonna announces, "This song is for my brother, who is in the audience," and sings "Paradise," which she has cowritten.

Although the lyrics don't contain a particular message, I am utterly stunned she has dedicated the song to me. As far as I know, she has only twice dedicated songs to someone: once to my father, and once to Martin Burgoyne. She has paid me a compliment and I'm happy.

AFTER THE SHOW, I am invited to the party in the Raleigh's upstairs room. Madonna is in black, Ricky Martin stands on one side of her, and Mickey Rourke on the other. Ingrid hovers behind her.

I say hello to Madonna.

We have a repeat of our Los Angeles conversation.

After a while, I take a look at the dancers in the room. All of them are straight. None of them is dancing.

I go up to Madonna and say, "You don't have any gay dancers!"

She thinks for a second, slightly puzzled. "You're right, we don't. Isn't that weird?"

The question is rhetorical.

The party is dull. I think back to all the after-show parties Madonna and I have had in the past, when everyone was dancing and having fun and the atmosphere was joyful.

This party is joyless and dull.

After an hour, I leave.

IN OCTOBER 2006, Madonna and Guy fly to Lilongwe, the capital of Malawi, one of the world's poorest countries, with a population of 12 million, including an estimated 1 million orphans, many of them children whose parents have died of AIDS. As Madonna has put it, "I didn't choose Malawi. It chose me."

From Malawi's capital, they travel to the Home of Hope orphanage, thirty miles away, where they will meet twelve children—one of whom they are considering for adoption. They take one look at thirteen-month-old David Banda and the choice is made. It is not difficult. He is adorable, intelligent, and healthy. And I am surprised at the tidal wave of world media outrage that hits her and Guy after they make their decision.

I respect that Madonna is trying to help a young child from an impoverished third-world country. But the cynic in me reads about the publicists and camera crews who traveled with her and Guy on their first visit to the orphanage and—remembering *Truth or Dare*—can't help thinking, *Madonna is competing with Angelina Jolie. So she isn't going to stop with one child, she is going to help an entire country, and she wants the world to know about it.*

I'd like to think her motives are entirely altruistic, but am slightly disturbed that she couldn't adopt David quietly, without all the concomitant press attention, and a documentary crew to record it.

Yet whatever her motivations, she has also helped form the charity Raising Malawi and has pledged more than $3 million to help Malawi's orphans. She also does all she can to make the world aware that while Malawi may be a beautiful country, it has also been severely blighted by AIDS, famine, and war.

All in all, I respect her giving heart and know that whatever she contributes, the attention her involvement in Malawi brings can only help those less fortunate than herself.

BY THE TIME my birthday comes around in 2006, I am settled and feeling happier, traveling between L.A. and Miami, and assume that all my bitterness over Madonna has dissipated. I have a dinner at Karu & Y, then go to a party at the Sagamore, thrown for me by Ingrid.

She is running Saturday nights there, so she is primarily giving the party to get press. She tells me that I can invite twenty people, and that she will provide three tables and serve free vodka.

When I arrive, fifteen strangers are sitting at my tables. I ask Ingrid who they are. She brushes aside my question and tells me that when my friends arrive, she will make room for them. I tell her that this will make my friends uncomfortable. Then I take a look at the vodka she's provided: just two bottles for twenty people, and a cheap brand at that.

Suddenly, something in me snaps. I may be projecting Madonna onto Ingrid, but I just freak out. I storm out of the restaurant and my friends follow.

By morning, I have calmed down; I realize that I have overreacted. Although I have now created a life for myself based on my own talents and not Madonna's, I am still bitter at her. Kabbalah has not helped exorcise my demons, nor have I really forgiven her.

I turn on my computer and find two emails—one from Madonna and one from Ingrid. Ingrid is indignant, telling me that she did me a favor and how dare I walk out on her. It goes on, accusing me of having an exaggerated sense of entitlement. To some degree, she is right. I did feel entitled—because I was aware that my presence meant that the Sagamore would get press that night—but I was wrong to explode at her and to walk out. I write back immediately and apologize.

Then I read Madonna's email. She gives a blow-by-blow account of my behavior that evening, as described to her by Ingrid, and most of it is true. She doesn't berate me, though. The tone is relatively soft. The purpose of the email is to let me know that she still believes I am a drug addict and an alcoholic and that I need help. She suggests that I go to an outpatient rehab center and offers to pay for it.

I think about what she has written, then take a long, hard look at myself. I don't think I am an alcoholic or a drug addict, but I do know that—due, in part, to my relationship with Madonna—I've got some serious issues to deal with. I agree to go to Transitions Recovery Program in North Miami Beach, and Madonna pays the cost in advance for a consultation with a psychiatrist there.

There, blood is taken from me, and I spend hours with the psychiatrist, outlining my entire relationship with my sister. I explain to him that I don't know if rehab will benefit me, as I am not prepared to air my issues with Madonna in front of a group. He asks me to come back to the center when the results are in.

Four days later, we have another meeting, in which he tells me that neither the blood tests nor our conversation indicates either alcoholism or drug addiction. He recommends I have long-term one-on-one therapy and names a good therapist in Miami. With my consent, he emails a copy of his recommendations to Madonna.

Madonna rattles off an instant email in response, telling the doctor that he doesn't know what he is talking about. The doctor reads to me: "My brother belongs in rehab and that's that."

"Your sister has control issues," he tells me.

Ingrid has apparently also called the psychiatrist, expressing surprise that he had not told me to go into rehab.

He repeats his recommendations based on the tests and his lengthy consultation with me about my situation.

I get an email from Madonna telling me that she has received the doctor's assessment, that she disagrees totally with him, but is glad I am seeking help for my problems and will pay for a number of my sessions. Despite her control issues, I realize that she is being generous and kind in attempting to help me.

In January 2007, I start seeing my therapist twice a week. On the proviso that she receive progress reports, Madonna agrees to pay for a fixed number of sessions at $150 a time. With my consent, the therapist agrees to send her a weekly report on my progress in therapy, approved by me and without revealing the content of our sessions, as I want to find a way back to forming a real relationship with Madonna again.

My therapist writes to Madonna, reiterating the doctor's feelings regarding rehab.

Madonna apparently emails her back saying that she doesn't know what she's talking about, that she has no clue and can't be a good therapist. She tells my therapist that I am manipulating her.

My therapist reacts by telling me that she is glad to be getting such a good idea of my sister. She says that Madonna is not going to go away and I need to learn how to deal with her, and that she will help me. For the first time in my life, I have someone to whom I can talk openly and honestly. She validates my reality for me. I look forward to our sessions and feel that I am making progress. I am confronting my demons, acknowledging my strengths and weaknesses, and mustering the courage to explore them in this book.

In the early summer of 2007, as I am still looking for additional work as a designer, I write a letter to Madonna, asking her for a letter of recommendation for my résumé and design book. She writes back and says she can't, in good conscience, give me a recommendation until I have been in rehab.

I write back, telling her that my therapist says I don't need rehab, and that I have chosen to become a healthy person on my own terms, not Madonna's. I try to explain to her that rehab is a place to detox. It isn't a fix, which is why people who visit rehab without simultaneously having long-term therapy tend to end up returning over and over. Madonna's response makes it clear to me that she doesn't or won't understand. I let go of the need to have her understand and move on emotionally.

In late June, I go to Traverse City and spend two weeks with my father. I help him in the vineyard, and for the first time ever we talk to each other as if we are friends. It's been a long time coming.

At the same time, I am worried about him. He is seventy-six now, yet he gets up at six in the morning and works twelve hours straight doing exhausting manual labor. He has created several different varieties of wine and has won many medals for them. Madonna did help him financially to buy the vineyard, but I feel that he needs more help in promoting it.

He is about to auction a magnum of his dolcetto wine at a wine fair in Saratoga Springs, New York. I call the publisher of *Instinct* magazine and suggest that I write a story about the vineyard, and the auction. My concept—which is designed to help my father, the wine, and Madonna's charity—is that my father donate part of the proceeds of the auction to her Malawian charity. I email her requesting that she give me some quotes. She responds, but she says she's done plenty for Dad, and that perhaps she could provide a single quote.

Instead of erupting in a rage, as I would have in the past, I write back and ask her to write a couple of paragraphs about her charity, and we could run it unedited.

She tells me to go to her website.

I take the path of least resistance and email back, "Okay, I will."

The kitchen of my father's home in Traverse City, Michigan, 7 p.m., September 3, 2007

MELANIE AND I are in the midst of cooking Labor Day dinner for the family when she tells me that Madonna sent her a round-trip ticket to London as a birthday present, so Melanie can come and celebrate Madonna's birthday with her and her family.

Melanie tells me that she flew to England and stayed with Madonna at Ashcombe House. On the eve of her birthday, Madonna screened *I Am Because We Are,* her documentary on Malawi. President Clinton, Archbishop Desmond Tutu, and Professor Jeffrey Sachs all took part in the documentary, which includes the harrowing stories of many of the children left in Malawi, orphaned and alone.

According to Melanie, the documentary also features female circumcision, abject poverty, and is extremely bloody.

The following day, in celebration of her birthday, Madonna threw a party at Ashcombe. Gypsies and horses were flown in from Europe, knights in full armor strolled around the property, and every kind of luxurious food was served.

Melanie says that she found it difficult to understand the dichotomy between Madonna's work in Malawi and the opulent excess of her party.

I explain that no matter how altruistic Madonna may be in her Malawi work, it still generates publicity for her and burnishes her public image. Although I don't want to diminish the good she is doing in Malawi, at times the entire enterprise feels slightly self-serving.

According to Melanie, Kabbalah is the focal point of Madonna's and Guy's lives. While Melanie was at Ashcombe, the atmosphere between Madonna and Guy was very tense and a Kabbalah rabbi would come down from London and mediate between them. This does not surprise me.

I believe that Kabbalah is helping keep Guy and Madonna together. No matter how much I dislike him, how much I hold him responsible for the rift between me and my sister, I wish him and their marriage well.

Sadly, I've never met my nephew David; I hardly know Rocco, and I know Lola only a little. But I sincerely hope that some day, I will be able to forge my own relationship with them. I want them to know that, as their uncle, I will always be there for them—because *that,* when all is said and done, is the nature of family.

EPILOGUE

Time ripens all things; no man is born wise.

Miguel de Cervantes

MADONNA HAS NOW been world famous for a quarter of a century and is probably the most celebrated woman on the planet. She has sold an estimated 200 million albums worldwide and has been listed in *Guinness World Records* as the female singer with the highest annual earnings. Her latest album, *Hard Candy,* debuted at number one around the globe and has sold more than a million copies during the first month on sale, and her world tour, *Sweet and Sticky,* launches on August 23, 2008. She is now a global icon, a legend, and her importance to popular culture can never be overstated.

But when it all began for her, *Billboard*'s editor predicted, "Madonna will be out of business in six months." Madonna, in a moment of triumph, once admitted, "People underestimated me, didn't they?" Like me, she has the longest memory of anyone I know. She hasn't forgotten how little faith many people once had in her, and I'm proud never to have been one of them.

This year my sister will be fifty years old. I hope and believe that she still has many more years of performing ahead of her, and that I'll be there, right to the end, applauding her. And I believe that Guy will be there, too. Despite the fact that recent reports have claimed that Madonna and Guy's marriage is in serious trouble—which, of course, has met with several official denials from her camp—I know Guy and Madonna love each other, and that, apart from anything else, they have been passionately committed to working on their relationship with the guidance of Kabbalah.

LAST SUMMER, MY father and I unpacked boxes from my past that he'd been storing for me for more than fifteen years. I stood there staring at the contents—letters from Danny, bills, invoices, postcards, photographs, memories of another life—and I was momentarily paralyzed.

Then my father, the man who made me and Madonna exactly what and who we are, sensing my emotions, said, "Why don't we have a bonfire and burn everything?"

So we did. We took fifteen boxes filled with twenty years of my life and stood there, together, and watched the flames consume my past.

I turned and looked at my father and said, "You know, Dad, so many times in my life, I've felt like a loser."

And he said, "Christopher, you're not a loser. And I'm very proud of you."

His words made me happy, but I wished I could hear my mother say them to me as well.

THE PAST TWENTY-FIVE years have been a great adventure and a learning process for me. Through it all, I've often kicked against the fact that my name, my reputation, and my entire identity are inextricably linked to Madonna's. Now, though, with the passing of time, through therapy and the writing of this book, I have come to terms with the truth that I can never escape that reality.

Nor can I turn back the clock. If I could, I would not have written my sister those hurtful words. Even though I don't think it was her intention, she did hurt me, and I hurt her in retaliation.

Yet my lifetime with Madonna has yielded many lessons for me. The prosaic lesson that if you do business with a family member, no matter how close you are—always get a contract.

I don't know whether Madonna has learned anything from our years together, but if she has, I hope it is Kabbalah's lesson that she is not the center of the universe, and that every action, every decision she makes affects not only her but the people around her.

Yet if my sister's actions have ever affected me negatively, I know now that I also bear some of that burden and accept that I am responsible for the choices I have made.

Even though our contact is minimal these days, any bitterness I had once felt for my sister has long since evaporated. I look back on our life together with affection. I consider it a privilege to have been able to share her success with her.

I don't hold any grudges against her, nor do I bear her any ill will. I love her very much and will always be grateful for everything we shared. My sister has done so much for me, and all I have to do is look at her loving birthday cards—so emotional in expressing sentiments she could never have articulated to me in person—and I know how much she loves me.

I cherish all the memories of the good times I've had with my sister, the personal ones, the intimate ones, the professional ones. Looking back on our years of working together, of being together, it seems as if—after the dysfunctional nature of our childhood—we created a little world for each other, and I loved it. It was sure, protected, intensely creative, and I felt safe there. It wasn't a touchy-feely, intimate world, because Madonna isn't like that, nor am I. But in retrospect, it was my utopia, the place where, more than anywhere else, I could take refuge, where Madonna and I—two children forever yearning for their lost mother—could love and be loved as best we could.

In my heart, my mind, and my soul, Madonna and I remain inseparable in spirit. We are forever linked together by blood and the incredible adventure that is our lives.

ACKNOWLEDGMENTS

Many people have taken part in the telling of this story. I particularly want to express my sincere gratitude to my agent, Fredrica Friedman, for her expertise and enthusiastic support; my brilliant editor, Tricia Boczkowski; my superlative publisher, Jennifer Bergstrom. Thanks, as well, to the other folks at Simon & Schuster for keeping it legal and cutting edge, especially my art director, Michael Nagin. I also want to thank my coauthor, Wendy Leigh, who always had my back and without whom this would not have been possible.